Other books by Duane Acker:

Two at a Time: Reflections and Revelations of a Kansas State University Presidency and the Years That Followed. 2010, iUniverse

Can State Universities be Managed? A Primer for Presidents and Management Teams. 2006, American Council on Education Series on Higher Education.

Animal Science and Industry. First edition, 1963; seventh edition with co-authors, 2005, Prentice Hall.

Back to Troublesome Creek: By Way of DC and a Dozen Foreign Countries, forthcoming

FROM TROUBLESOME CREEK

A Farm Boy's Encounters on the Way to a University Presidency

Duane Acker

iUniverse, Inc.
Bloomington

From Troublesome Creek
A Farm Boy's Encounters on the Way to a University Presidency

Copyright © 2013 by Duane Acker.

All rights reserved. No part of this book may be used or reproduced by any means, graphic, electronic, or mechanical, including photocopying, recording, taping or by any information storage retrieval system without the written permission of the publisher except in the case of brief quotations embodied in critical articles and reviews.

iUniverse books may be ordered through booksellers or by contacting:

iUniverse
1663 Liberty Drive
Bloomington, IN 47403
www.iuniverse.com
1-800-Authors (1-800-288-4677)

Because of the dynamic nature of the Internet, any web addresses or links contained in this book may have changed since publication and may no longer be valid. The views expressed in this work are solely those of the author and do not necessarily reflect the views of the publisher, and the publisher hereby disclaims any responsibility for them.

Any people depicted in stock imagery provided by Thinkstock are models, and such images are being used for illustrative purposes only.
Certain stock imagery © Thinkstock.

ISBN: 978-1-4759-9355-4 (sc)
ISBN: 978-1-4759-9356-1 (hc)
ISBN: 978-1-4759-9357-8 (ebk)

Library of Congress Control Number: 2013910205

Printed in the United States of America

iUniverse rev. date: 06/13/2013

Aerial photo on the front cover from Iowa State University Geographic Information Systems Support and Research Facility (2013). 1950s Historic Aerial Photos—USDA (black and white) of Atlantic, Iowa area. Retrieved February 4, 2013, from Iowa State University Geographic Map Server.

The author and his future wife, Shirley, at a FarmHouse Fraternity formal dance, likely during his junior year at Iowa State.

Table of Contents

ACKNOWLEDGEMENTS

This book and its content would not be, but for the inspiration and support that my parents, teachers, college advisers, fraternity brothers, faculty colleagues, industry clientele, governors, legislators, and, especially, my bosses provided during the years it covers. They showed interest, encouraged me to try things, and helped build my skills and my confidence.

For this book, Ronald Ostrus, Garald Harris, and Betty Armstrong Boeck gave me needed information on the history of the Wiota School and its district. Margaret Emmert Slepsky gave me historic information on an Atlantic bank, and Clair, Leland, and Joan Acker and Lois Acker Weppler provided confirming information related to the Depression years. For the Roots section, I am especially thankful for details on the Noyer family that Loretta Noyer Jewell had gathered.

Ray Underwood provided later historic information on the Walnut Grove company and Barry Dunn, now dean at South Dakota State University, confirmed recent developments in the college I once headed. For accuracy and spelling of names in photo captions, I received help from Bradley Kuennen of Iowa State University Archives, former South Dakota State colleagues Richard Wahlstrom and Charles Cecil, and Brookings resident Millie Juel.

It would be impossible to identify all who provided the photos that came years ago into my files, but I do thank Joanne Rasmussen Magazino for providing several family photos and Roger Christensen, who provided a needed photo of my student advising years at Iowa State. Greg Henderson, editor of *Drovers Cattle Network*; Andrew Loder of Cargill, Incorporated; and Kevin Kane of Iowa State University's College of Design granted me permission to reproduce certain images sorely needed for illustration. Roger Underwood led me to the right person for one of those permissions, and Todd and Jena Waters retrieved and forwarded needed materials as I completed the work.

Freelance editor Michael Ream gave me valuable advice on manuscript content and structure, on what needed to be deleted or refined, and on ways to make the work more readable. Paula Wiebel of the *Our Iowa* staff gave me helpful suggestions for handling some of the items I wanted to highlight, and iUniverse provided helpful review and editorial assistance in the final stages.

In both this and previous writing, our daughters Diane Acker Nygaard and LuAnn Acker Deter provided much encouragement and helpful feedback. The inspiration and support mentioned in the first paragraph applies especially to my wife, Shirley, and I also thank her for her review and suggestions on the manuscript, especially the significance of the many life lessons scattered among the stories.

AUTHOR'S NOTES

As others reviewed the manuscript, they were struck by three things: the many life lessons to which I was exposed in my encounters, my evident satisfactions from work, and the degree to which my described encounters parallel those of people in other sectors and professions.

Lessons came from many actors and in many situations, a few from the study of my ancestral lines, and many simply from the circumstances of the encounter. There were lessons for growing up, lessons for parenting and teaching, lessons for handling failures or disappointments, and lessons for leadership and managing people. Most are lessons of universal value. Here are just a few of the lessons, with key phrases from the text:

Give your children your time: "Although lodge was important in Dad's life, after his term as master it would take a backseat to the school and our activities, PTA, class plays, and sports."

See that single or disabled people are included: "I yet recall Del's words as we left the farm and headed up the snow-covered road: 'This afternoon and evening with your family makes life worth living.'"

Avoid ultimatums: "When someone says to you, 'Do this or else!' they'd better be prepared for 'or else.'"

Impatience increases risk: "Impatient, I shifted from reverse to third and pulled open the throttle. In seconds, my front wheels pushed into the loose dirt, and my right wheel was off the ground. No time to clutch; it was rolling!"

When you need help, someone is willing to provide it: "It was clear he did not need an interruption, but I told him my problem. Clarence did not hesitate. He just dropped his tools and said, 'Let's go.'"

Before changing careers, find out if that other career will provide what you want: "If I wanted to be in the feed business, and, especially, be part of a company management team, I need not look further. However, throughout the day, I had a steady, deep-down feeling of discomfort, *What am I doing here?*

Always look at the data: "As the data were presented and discussed, the finger-pointing and defensiveness disappeared, and we moved to interpreting and discussing the data's significance. . . . The low pheasant count was just part of a normal cycle."

The satisfactions of productive work appeared early and regardless of my age, whether at seven, thirteen, or thirty-two. My satisfactions were no different from the satisfactions earned by a seven-year-old boy who folds laundry for his mother, a thirteen-year-old girl who carries a paper route, or a thirty-two-year-old who helps build a highway bridge. Satisfactions instill motivation to do more, to be productive, to contribute, and, of course, to earn more satisfactions. A tragedy in much of today's society is that too many are not given an opportunity early in life for the satisfactions of productive work.

Reviewers of both this material and my other books that relate management encounters mention the parallels in their own occupations or disciplines. A young instructor in biology or chemistry may encounter the same colleague resistance to new concepts or technologies for a course he or she is assigned that I encountered in teaching sections of a freshman animal husbandry course. The manager of a retail store may encounter senior colleague resistance to using social media for product promotion. An upper-level manager in a major equipment company cited personnel problems that paralleled the personnel problems I faced, and even a local minister told me how some of the lessons to which I was exposed apply to his task in leading both staff and a congregation.

For a few of the encounters described, especially those with students, names or circumstances have been changed where necessary to avoid any risk of embarrassment.

INTRODUCTION

"You won!" Mother yelled as she ran from the house. It was a Saturday morning, and I was under a nearby elm tree tightening a hydraulic hose connection on a two-row cultivator that I had just mounted onto our twelve-year-old Farmall F-20. I had won an Alice Graham scholarship, $500 per year for four years.

Wow! College—what I had considered out of my realm a few months earlier was going to happen.

Most unbelievable to me was that this had resulted from an eight-hour written examination a week earlier, in which I had competed with more than a dozen of the county's top students, many valedictorians from the county's larger schools, and several with a year of college under their belt. I was only number two in the graduating class at Wiota, the smallest school in the county. (Two scholarships would be granted, and the other winner was the number one in our Wiota class, my cousin.)

Here is my story—my roots and early life near the banks of Troublesome Creek, Benton Township, Cass County, Iowa, seventeen years before that Saturday morning and the twenty-seven years that followed, to the threshold of a university presidency. It is mostly a story of encounters and experiences that I remember well.

It is also a story of ancestral circumstance, such as the German tradition that caused the random sample of Acker DNA that resides in me to be born in western Iowa instead of a few miles west of the Philadelphia port, where the first in my line of Ackers disembarked, or that my random sample of Jones DNA was not born at or near Talycoed Farm in Wales.

It is also a story of what goes on in universities, how faculty may see their jobs, and how they relate to each other and to their students. In the case of agriculture or other more applied disciplines, it is a story of how faculty and deans relate to their statewide clientele and to their ever-changing industries.

Included are a few stories of connections, such as between the kids I hauled on the school bus I drove as a high school senior and the man who would hire me as a dean at South Dakota State, or how a comment by a local veterinarian for whom I held pigs for vaccination led me to FarmHouse fraternity and its lifelong impact.

The most important of my encounters is that cute and happy blonde I had found ten months earlier at the county fair, and the life and family she brought about. So many doors opened for the two of us after Mother yelled that Saturday morning, "You won!"

Chapter I

The Early Years

It was late afternoon in 1934, and I was three. I had been watching Mother's helper, Mrs. Derry, darning socks by the kitchen window. This was before the invention of more durable synthetic fibers. A widow whose only money source was her monthly thirty dollars of county old-age assistance, Mrs. Derry needed the work.

It suddenly turned dark, and Mrs. Derry turned on the lights to see her work. We heard distant rolling thunder and saw flashes of lightning. Mother rushed from window to window, visibly worried.

I do not recall if there was a damaging windstorm with pelting rain or more Kansas dust caught in the downpour (this was Dust Bowl time). Perhaps it was only a light spring shower, but it was the apprehension that fixed the event in my mind.

Another early memory: From that kitchen window or our fenced dooryard, I would watch Dad or his "hired man" on the tractor, a gray Farmall Regular, pulling a wagon to or from the feedlot. If only I were big enough to drive it! The Regular's rear steel wheels seemed huge and had wide, pointed lugs for traction. What caught my attention was a contraption on each rear wheel that scraped off the feedlot mud as the wheel turned, essential after the spring thaw.

A more exciting memory: Dad wheeling up the drive on a new, bright-red Farmall F-20, successor to that gray Regular. It was 1936. McCormick Deering had introduced this new line of rubber-tired tractors in 1932 but had not changed the color. When Dad was ready to trade, McCormick Deering had announced the F-20's color would shift to red, but the tractor on the dealer's floor was gray. He bought the tractor on the condition it be repainted red. Red was and still is my favorite color.

It was that same year that Dad rented cropland on the other side of the creek from a retired neighbor, Andy Thiel. From that I carry two visions, exciting because this was a new family venture more than a mile away. The first is Thiel sitting in a small shed, shelling the end kernels off selected ears of corn. Dad told me Thiel had chosen the larger ears, thinking the larger seeds from larger ears would yield a larger crop.

Thiel was either not aware or had not yet accepted college research that corn yield was not related to size of the seed or size of the ear from which it came. Yields could be increased, though, by using hybrids, seeds from a cross between two parent lines, each selected and self-mated several generations to fix desirable traits. Though Dad did not explain all that to me, I knew he planned to purchase some hybrid seed and that he would need to convince Thiel of its merits; in a crop-share lease, the landlord provided half the seed.

My second vision is following Dad and a "CCC field man" (the new Commodity Credit Corporation) as they measured the width of a field to be planted with corn near the Thiel farmstead. The field man carried a ring of wire stakes and a chain. He planted a stake just inside the gate and, while Dad held the chain's end at that stake, the man extended the chain and planted another stake, and that process continued across the field.

As we returned from the far end, he pulled and counted the stakes and then calculated the distance. From that and the field's length, he calculated the acreage. It was all part of the Depression's New Deal farm program of Franklin Roosevelt and Henry Wallace, with some crop price protection or subsidy from the CCC.

The 1930s

The first half of the 1930s was not an easy time in rural America. There had been a farm depression in the early twenties, and then good times, exploding land values, and optimism. But the 1929 stock market crash and other events took the wind out of the sails for most families. The Dow Jones Industrial Average, above 300 in early 1929, had dropped to 80 or below by 1932. Mortgage holders foreclosed on farms, and small-town businesses and banks failed. A loaf of bread cost eight cents, a gallon of gas ten cents, and a new car about five hundred dollars.

My father once told about needing to sell some corn in early 1929 so he could pay off a bank note. His father-in-law offered to loan him the money to pay the note and suggested Dad hold the corn for a higher price. Within days, the corn price had dropped by half.

My dad's younger brother was married in Omaha on December 10, 1932. His wife once told me that when they returned later that day to buy groceries at Atlantic's Nord's store, their check was no good. Two of Atlantic's three banks had closed; her savings were in one, his in the other. Though one of the banks would eventually reopen and the newlyweds retrieved enough money to buy a bedroom set, that day they had only the little cash in their pockets.

Then it would turn dry across the corn belt and the plains. My parents, as Dad described, "dried out in '34, hailed out in '35, and dried out again in '36." That they would maintain their optimism and good spirits and see to it that my sister and I would have a reasonably comfortable and secure early life deserves our respect. We were oblivious to the economic severity of the time.

In later years I would spend an evening among farm retirees in the Brookings, South Dakota, area, listening to their reminiscences of the early 1930s, when they were raising families and trying to make ends meet. They primarily recalled the happy times: "Sure we were poor, and our mortgage payments were overdue, but we were all in the same boat. We could gather with our neighbors, play cards, and still enjoy life. We got along."

Friday the Thirteenth

It was Friday, March 13, 1931, in our modest farm home overlooking Troublesome Creek, seven miles northeast of Atlantic. My mother, attended by Dr. Agnes Wilder, had been lifted onto the dining room table and was experiencing a very difficult birth.

It was likely cold; March in Iowa is that. Odds are there were several inches of snow on the ground, but that was not recorded. At least the road was not blocked with drifts, or Dr. Wilder and her driver/houseman would not have made it.

Dr. Wilder had practiced with her physician father and continued after his death in a solo practice in their Atlantic home. A cage full of monkeys on her enclosed porch, which I would watch from her waiting/living room, made my later visits to Dr. Wilder with my mother not only tolerable but fun.

My birth must have been difficult; it apparently took days for my head, misshapen by forceps, to return to some normalcy. In later years, when I misbehaved, Mother would tell me my birth had been painful enough that she hardly deserved such behavior. It must have been rough!

The farmhouse where I was born, the photo likely taken about four years later, 1935. Note the open porches, later enclosed, the attached "cob house" for storing cobs and cut wood for fuel, and just beyond, the front of a cave where potatoes and apples were stored for the winter. The power pole carried the lines that brought electricity from an Atlantic generating plant farther downstream on the banks of Troublesome Creek.

Mother, Ruth Fay Kimball Acker, was the youngest of six Kimball children and had lived in this farm home until, while she was still in her teens, her father retired from farming and she and her parents moved to Atlantic. She had completed eight grades in country school, alternating between Pymosa No. 7 and Benton No. 9, depending on which school had attracted the best teacher and whether the swinging bridge over Troublesome Creek between home and Benton No. 9 had been repaired after a spring flood.

I know little of her education beyond the country school. She once mentioned a private commercial college in Atlantic she had attended, and from other evidence, I deduce she completed one or two years of high school before that.

My father, William Clayton Acker, was also from a family of six siblings, a girl followed by five boys, including Dad and his identical twin. The twins' first names, William and George, were those of their grandfathers. Middle names Clayton and Clifton were considered their given names.

I was about six when, at a livestock auction, a man approached my father with the greeting, "Hi, Bill!" Dad had to explain. They had served together in WWI and my father's first name, William, had been used in all military records. He was "Bill" to his army buddies and Clayton to his family, the community, and in the local Masonic Lodge, an important part of his life.

My parents were likely apprehensive about my approaching birth. By early 1931, my mother was near her thirty-fourth birthday; Dad was thirty-five. Their first child, Maria, was stillborn in 1927, and within about a year they had adopted a girl, Virginia Lorraine. Adoptions were not generally talked about in those days. At school or on the school bus I would overhear a comment that Lorraine (again, the middle name and not the first was used) was adopted, but I took no stock in such a comment. She was my sister.

Lorraine's adoption was never mentioned to me by my parents nor alluded to until I was thirty-two. A childless uncle and aunt had died and left their estate in equal proportions to their nieces and nephews. My father commented to me, "I am so thankful they included Lorraine." No elaboration was given or needed.

At no time did I see any difference in the regard or esteem with which my sister and I were held or treated by our parents, other relatives, or teachers that could be attributed to adoption. As brother and sister, Lorraine and I probably had the normal range of disagreements, competitiveness for attention, and pride in each other that exists among siblings in most families. From my perspective, natural births are a matter of chance; adoptions are chosen.

My parents had been married in 1920, two years after my father's return from eighteen months' service in WWI, including six months in France. While he was in the service, Mother worked in the Atlantic offices of Shrauger and Johnson, a manufacturer of ventilation equipment and windows for farm buildings. They lived on and worked rented farms until the spring of 1924, when they moved to what had been her parents' farm.

Send Me a Person Who Reads

My sister Lorraine started school two years ahead of me and dreamed of being a teacher. When she got off the school bus in the evening, she wanted someone to teach, and I was available. She sat me down and drilled me enough with flash cards: 2+2, 2+3 and cat, dog, hen so I had a head start when it came my turn for the first grade. Today I thank her for that.

My parents received three daily newspapers and five or six farm publications. The six-day *Atlantic News Telegraph* kept them posted on local people and community. They never missed the back page local news briefs, and I picked up the habit. They knew Editor Ted Simpson and ad salesman Ray Neff and through them sometimes contributed to those briefs.

Less common in area homes was the *Des Moines Register*. Though the *Register* today can be called exceedingly liberal, Cowles family ownership in the 1930s and '40s kept it conservative in both editorial content and news tone. The *Register* was then also statewide in coverage and had its own Washington correspondent. Even the *News Telegraph* carried a Washington column. They were my early windows to the world, and, perhaps, among the roots of my fiscal and political conservatism.

The third newspaper, the *Daily Journal Stockman*, published in a little brick building perched above the Omaha Stockyards cattle pens, was likely sent courtesy of a commission company through which Dad sold fed cattle once or twice each year.

Dailies came by mail, the Sunday *Register* by a contract carrier. Saturday night a quarter went into a small tray outside our east porch door, and before Dad and I headed to the barn to milk at five thirty or six Sunday morning, the Sunday *Register* would be in a big clip above that tray.

Many evenings during my school years, when I should have been reading the next day's school assignment, I would have my knees on a chair and my elbows on the dining room table while reading those papers, perhaps while listening with one ear to *District Attorney* or other radio serials.

When I was old enough to join Dad in the milking barn, he moved the family's old tabletop radio to a barn shelf so I would not have to miss the fifteen-minute after-school episodes, such as *Jack Armstrong, the All-American Boy*. That barn radio also widened my window to the world. About five forty-five came World News, H. V. Kaltenborn, and reports from the WWII European and Asian theatres.

Most of the farm magazines, such as *Successful Farming, Farm Journal, Country Gentleman, Capper's Farmer,* and *Hoard's Dairyman* were monthlies. An exception was *Wallace's Farmer*, a biweekly Iowa publication founded in the 1800s by "Uncle Henry" Wallace, the father and grandfather of two USDA secretaries, Henry C. and Henry A. Wallace.

It was either *Country Gentleman* or *Capper's Farmer* that carried a series, *Little Black Sambo*. Not knowing any blacks (then called Negroes), I was fascinated by the series. Each installment told me more about that different existence, a society and life experiences far from my own. The evening that each issue arrived, I would be on the lap of Mother or Dad, listening to the latest adventures of Sambo.

Hoard's Dairyman was probably Dad's favorite magazine; he took pride in his milk cows and their production. Though he kept no numerical records, he could see how full the pail from each cow was morning and evening, and the biweekly check from the Exira Creamery gave him feedback incentive. *Hoard's Dairyman* was probably read cover-to-cover, but I would sometimes catch Dad asleep partway through one of the others.

During the 1960s, a major wood pulp supplier's advertisements highlighted the theme, "Send me a person who reads!" Few advertisements have been as constructive. Few gifts that a parent or teacher can give a child are as valuable as the skill, opportunity, and desire to read.

Roots

I believe it is important for each of us to have a sense of place, both geographic and in time. It gives us reference points; the more we know about our ancestors and the society and environment in which they lived, the more we may understand our own setting and bases for our future.

My geographic parameters were our farm, the neighborhood, the Kimballs and their kin on six farms contiguous with ours, the Wiota School and the school bus ride to and from, and gatherings at the several Acker farms in the county. Family acquaintances, as well as shopping, the courthouse, livestock auction, and doctors in Atlantic enhanced my sense of place. I knew where I was, where I belonged.

My sense of place was also enhanced by annual summer visits by Kimball cousins and my mother's uncle from Illinois, and my listening to reminiscences over sweet corn, fresh tomatoes, and fried chicken. Before I was eight, we would drive to visit the Ackers in Nebraska and the Noyers (my grandmother

Acker's brother) in Wyoming, as well as my father's Acker cousins in adjacent Adair County and his more distant Ibach cousins in Hardin County.

Over time I would discover deeper and branched roots, focused on the four surnames of my grandparents. A fifth surname, Ibach, that of my grandmother Acker's mother, is also mentioned, including Ibach linkages in South Dakota, as well as in Iowa.

The Ackers. In my youth, I would only hear the Ackers were "Pennsylvania Dutch" who had come to Iowa from Pennsylvania. In time I would learn the Ackers had migrated from Germany in the early 1700s, most through the Philadelphia port. The first of my line documented was Reverend Casper Acker, who became a citizen about 1730 in Chester County, Pennsylvania, just west of Philadelphia.

Some Ackers's spelling was changed to Ocker, Auker, Aucker, or Ocher. Though some name changes (and relocations) may have been prompted to escape bondage, more likely they were spelling errors by immigration officials at the port.

German tradition was that the oldest son inherited the farm, and from Reverend Casper, none in my lineage was the "first son." According to records I have found, each of my lineage had moved on west, if only to the adjacent county.

My great-great-grandfather Christian (a "second son") and his wife purchased a farm in Blair County, Pennsylvania, in 1823, and I have visited it several times. When Christian died in 1880, his oldest son inherited the farm, and George (the second son and my great-grandfather) and his siblings, their spouses, and families headed on west. George and his wife and family settled in Cass County, Iowa; a brother and sister and their spouses went on to the Geneva, Nebraska, area.

A late-1800s clipping lists George, my great-grandfather, and my grandfather Thaddeus Acker as members of a Cass County "corn club," a forerunner of the Cooperative Extension Service.

* * * * *

There was no mention in my youth of communication with the Ackers who remained in Pennsylvania. However, I later learned that about 1890, some of my grandfather's Pennsylvania cousins, then in their late teens or early twenties, had ridden their bicycles out to Iowa to visit him and his brothers. It had to be quite a ride, more than nine hundred miles on hard rubber tires, few marked or surfaced roads, and some tolls to be paid. According to the story told me in 1986 by the son-in-law of one of the Pennsylvania lads, who by then was in his late eighties, major roads were maintained by adjacent farmers and they charged a toll. The bicycling cousins would ride past a toll station single file, motioning that the last rider would pay the toll. The last rider would have only a five-dollar bill, the toll taker could not make change, and he was waved on. (Assuredly, for the return trip, the toll-takers were ready with change.)

When they arrived in Cass County and directed to their uncle's farm, they were not recognized. They said only that they were riding across the country and wondered if they might sleep in the Acker barn. My great-grandfather declined, but after a few minutes of friendly conversation, the boys identified themselves and "plenty of beds were found for them at the two Acker farms." My newly married grandfather lived on an adjacent farm.

My father and uncles had not yet arrived on the scene, and when I relayed this story to those yet alive, they were surprised. They had never been told of the visit.

* * * * *

My middle name is that of my father's apparently favorite uncle, Calvin, a Des Moines butcher. Another, Charlie, owned a sales commission firm at the Chicago Stockyards (the stockyards now long gone). On my wall is a photo of him and my grandfather, each on horseback in a pen of my grandfather's finished cattle. The cattle had gone by train from Atlantic, my grandfather provided a roundtrip ride in the caboose, and "topped the Chicago market" that day in 1915.

Grandfather Thaddeus was about twenty when he came with his parents to Iowa. He married Ida Noyer, then barely seventeen, who had been orphaned early in life. My father and his twin, Clifton, rode horses or drove a buggy to the Atlantic high school for parts of three years, interrupted by corn picking in the fall and spring field work. High school apparently came to an end after corn picking the third fall.

My father considered himself lucky in that, among the three brothers old enough, only his name was drawn for WWI military service. It exposed him to the world beyond the county, including Camp Dodge at Des Moines, Camp Pike, Arkansas, train travel to Camp Dix, New Jersey, and six months in France. It also gave him leadership experience and confidence; he was promoted to sergeant well before embarkation to France.

I did not know my grandfather; he died soon after I was born. My older cousins, who had worked for him in their youth, tell me he had a dose of impatience and a colorful vocabulary.

Dad told a story that illustrates the former. He and his brothers cultivated corn with single row, horse-drawn cultivators. One morning, Dad finished cultivating at home while two brothers started cultivating at their grandparents' farm a mile away. The brothers each rode their team home for lunch, and after lunch all three, with their teams, headed to the grandparents' farm. Dad forgot his cultivator. Embarrassed, he headed home with his team to get his cultivator and met his father on the road, at full run and pulling the cultivator.

The Kimballs. Nor did I know my Kimball grandparents; they died about the time of my birth. But the Kimball name was prominent because my mother's brother, Ralph, lived on the adjacent farm and because of August visits by Illinois Kimballs.

My mother's parents, Ed and Maria Jones Kimball, from their marriage in 1878 until they retired to Atlantic, lived on the farm we now occupy. The limited acquaintance circle of that era's farm youth is illustrated by the partners that each of their first four siblings chose to marry; all four lived within one-and-one-quarter mile of the Kimball home. My mother was not of dating age until after she moved to Atlantic with her parents.

Because my mother was by far the youngest of the siblings, all my cousins on the Kimball side were about twenty years older than me. One, Carl Keller, even had two older sons, Robert, three years older, and Ralph, a classmate. They were my closest "cousins," living just a mile away, riding the same school bus and exchanging help on the two farms.

* * * * *

Ralph Kimball and his wife, Mabel, had no children and were especially attentive to my sister and me. Ralph gave me my first paying job, leading a horse harnessed to a rope that, through a system of pulleys, pulled massive forkfuls of hay from the hayrack up and into the mow of his large barn. The pay was generous; after my three afternoons leading the horse, he gave me three two-dollar bills.

Ralph was quiet and steady but inwardly determined and with convictions. My father once related this story: Ralph had consistent problems with a new manure spreader. The chain driving the beaters or conveyor would break, and he would be seen in the field forking off his load. He had complained several times to the dealer but without resolution.

On a Saturday morning Dad watched across the field as Ralph repeatedly stopped his horses and worked on the spreader. This time, however, Ralph did not fork off the load; he just turned his horses toward home. At a fenced-off ravine near the farmstead, he stepped down off the spreader, kicked the wires off the fence posts, backed the spreader to the ravine edge, unhooked the horses from the double-trees, and let them roll the loaded spreader into the ravine.

Monday morning the dealer and his men were seen forking the manure off the spreader and then towing it back toward town.

Ralph also had a sense of humor. In a *Primer on Physiology and Hygiene* that he (and later my mother) used in their country school, I note his entry dated April 15, 1904: "Steal not this book for fear of life, for the owner carries a butcher knife."

* * * * *

Virtually all the Kimballs in the United States are descendants of a Richard Kimball, who had come at about age thirty with his wife and children to Boston from Ipswich, England, in 1634. From Richard, I am of the eleventh generation. Samuel, of the eighth generation, had moved from New England to Elgin, Illinois, northwest of Chicago, and that area became the home base of the Kimballs I would know.

Samuel's grandson, my grandfather Edward Kimball, set out from Illinois at age twenty-five and found a job clearing timber for John Jones in Cass County, Iowa. He soon rented some land from Jones, later bought adjacent land, and married Jones's daughter, Maria. My mother, Ruth, was born to Edward and Maria in 1897 on the Kimball farm.

The Noyers. It is of my grandmother Acker's ancestors that I know the least. I do know that William Noyer, my great-grandfather, attended a medical school in Illinois in the 1860s, and then followed or moved with his in-laws, the Ibachs, to Hardin County, Iowa, where he established a medical practice and where my grandmother Ida was born in 1869. By 1882 he had moved his family to the Atlantic area, and I only know he did not practice medicine after that move.

The early death of William and his wife left eight children, the oldest twenty-two and my grandmother at fourteen. She and her younger brothers and sisters were farmed out, the boys to local farmers, and the daughters, at least for a time, to Ibach relatives back in Hardin County. During my youth we made more than one trip to Hardin County, my widowed grandmother, Ida, accompanying us.

That Ibach relationship would emerge during our time at South Dakota State University. Some of my grandmother's Ibach cousins had moved from Hardin County, Iowa, to farms near Brookings, South Dakota, in the early 1900s, and even a descendent had worked in the dean's office that I was later to occupy.

*****

Though I know less of the Noyer ancestry, the extended Noyer family has provided some of our most interesting encounters. One of my dad's Noyer cousins who was about the same age, Del, was born with a malformed back that would make walking painful and difficult. He would have considerable impact on our lives.

From my first memories, Del was almost part of our family. Though he continued to live in his family home on the east edge of Atlantic after his parents' death in the 1930s, he was at our table many Sundays and often for weekday lunch. He would drive the seven miles in his Ford or in a cart at the reins of his driving pony. If by car, he would reach behind his seat, pull out a folding campstool outfitted with casters, flip it open, and push it ahead as he painfully worked his way up the walk and our porch steps. If he arrived by pony cart, Dad would lift him out to his camp stool and then unhitch the pony for water and shade.

Del's pony and cart was a familiar site on the then less-traveled US 71 in the 1930s and early '40s, headed east and north to our farm or south toward my uncle's farm, especially at threshing time. My cousins or I would hitch a ride on the back of the cart, Del taking us out to the field with jugs of cold water for the fellows pitching oat bundles onto racks, or unloading at the throat of the threshing machine.

Few expressions of satisfaction and achievement equal what I saw on Del's face when I was about eight, as he rolled up our driveway at the wheel of Dad's F-20. Del had always wanted to drive a tractor, and though he could handle the slightly modified clutch, brakes, and gear shift in his Ford, neither he nor anyone else assumed he could handle a larger and more cumbersome tractor.

Dad was renting the Prather 80, about two miles from home, and Del arrived there just as Dad finished raking hay. Dad decided "now is the time." He lifted Del up on to the tractor seat and instructed, "You take it home."

Dad drove Del's car back to our farm and was waiting, along with the rest of our family, when Del rolled up the drive on that F-20. He managed to push in the clutch and take it out of gear. His facial expression was the very definition of joy and satisfaction.

Later, during my high school years, two others would accompany Del in his Ford, all welcome at our Sunday or weekday table: Grace Roe, a former sister-in-law of Dad's and blind since her early twenties, and Fred Anderson, who had lost his meager railroad pension and was crippled with arthritis. Their inclusion in our family, extending through our two daughters' early years, taught us much.

It was in my dating years that I had picked up Shirley, Del, Grace, and Fred and brought them out to the farm for a Sunday afternoon and dinner. I yet recall Del's words as we left the farm and headed up the snow-covered road—Shirley and I would go to a movie after dropping the three at their homes—"This afternoon and evening with your family makes life worth living."

Del Noyer in his 1939 Ford on our way to visit the Ibach relatives in Hardin County. My grandmother in the rear window, sister Lorraine and me, my father, and his good friend Ted McDermott. This visit showed me Dad's respect for his friends; McDermott was working at the Eldora Reformatory, having been incarcerated for some financial irregularities in his Atlantic feed business. Dad believed McDermott had just been the "fall guy" for others in the business.

*****

Another of Dad's Noyer cousins, Hazel, and her husband, Merlin Dutson, came from southern Utah about 1940 to visit her Atlantic cousins. They were modest and friendly people, their visit a highlight of the season. A few years later one of those Iowa cousins, Arlene Wissler, middle-aged and single, left Cass County for Utah after the death of her father. In due time, her letters back to Iowa were signed Arlene Dutson. The family assumed she had met and married one of Merlin's brothers or cousins. Not so; she had married Merlin and become one of eight wives.

Of course the Iowa cousins did not know all that at the time. It became known, rather vividly, when the *Des Moines Register* and other major papers carried a news item and photo of five of the Dutson wives before a Utah magistrate. Though the Mormon Church had outlawed bigamy, the Dutsons considered themselves the "true Mormons."

When our daughters were about eight and nine, we drove my parents to California and had scheduled enroute a two-night visit with the Dutsons at their Mesa, Arizona, home. When we arrived Christmas night, several of the family's twenty-six children and a number of grandchildren were also there, many occupying trailers on the lot. Merlin and the five wives present, including my father's two cousins, were generous and hospitable hosts. We saw and learned that a family structure far different from our own was serving its members well.

The Jones roots and Talycoed. My mother's mother was a Jones, Maria, born in Wales on May 21, 1857. Maria came to the United States at age nine with her mother, Mary, and several siblings, more than two years after her father, John Jones, and two of her brothers had come. The family was united in Pennsylvania, moved to a farm near LaSalle, Illinois the following year, then on to Cass County, Iowa, and a farm on the north side of Turkey Creek between Anita and Wiota in early 1870.

That fall John purchased what became the "Jones home farm," about six miles over a ridge to the northwest, on the far side of Troublesome Creek and along the east edge of Pymosa Township. By the following spring he had purchased an adjacent farm across the Benton township line. That latter farm would be occupied by their eldest daughter, my grandmother, Maria, and husband. It is where their daughter and my mother, Ruth Fay, was born, and where I was raised and Shirley and I now live.

*****

I now flash forward to June 3, 2004, and am standing in a brick barn, midway between Monmouth and Abergavenny, Llantilio Parish, southeastern Wales, the very spot where 140 years ago my great-grandfather John Jones would be milking cows or forking cattle manure onto a horse-drawn wagon for spreading on the fields of Talycoed Farm. Bricks at the wide doorway's edge worn rounded and smooth tell me the barn is ancient, but it shows a bit of architectural flourish, with vertical ventilation slots and diamond patterns of bricks slightly projected from the outer walls. Rings anchored to one wall tell me where the cows had been tied for milking; more widely spaced rings on the opposite wall would have been for the horses. A well-worn hay manger hangs from a third wall. The rough-cut, heavy timbers above us are dark with age. Though the barn is no longer used, the smell of cattle manure is yet pungent.

Shirley, our daughter, Diane, and I had missed this spot by only a kilometer three decades earlier while searching for our Jones roots. We had begun then with only the names and birth dates of John and Mary Jones and their children born in Wales, and Llantilio Parish their starting point. We found a rural church and went to the vicar's home for advice. He told us that in a wooden cabinet behind the sanctuary pulpit we would find ledger books with handwritten records of christenings and baptisms. He added, "If you don't find what you seek, go to nearby churches, all parts of the Church of England. Churches often charged for baptisms and christenings, and farm workers would shop around for the lowest cost."

We moved back and forth among churches for an afternoon, confirmed John Jones's birth date, his father's and grandfather's birth or christening dates, and names of their spouses. In the entry of son Thomas's christening, we first encountered the word, Talycoed: Thomas was the "son of John Jones, a laborer at Talycoed." A nearby farmer directed us to Talycoed, a large manor house with barns and a formal garden in need of tending. We snapped a few photos and departed, believing we had found our Welsh roots. We had only been close.

Because our farm has been in the family continually since John and Mary Jones's purchase in 1871, we named it, after my parents' death and purchasing my sister's interest, Talycoed II. Years later, in searching for more information on Talycoed, I obtained from a Welsh agency CADW: Welsh Historic Monuments, photos of the manor house, barns, and garden we had seen in 1973, plus a site plan that showed Talycoed Farm, which was over the hill and perhaps a kilometer from the manor house. Outlined on the site plan were several plots within or adjacent to Talycoed Farm.

Recently acquired Jones family records had included an 1864 demand from "William Williams of Talycoed" for mortgage payment on a "cottage, orchard, and cider mill." Such had been common; a farm worker would purchase such a plot and home, the farm owner holding the mortgage. Talycoed Farm, including one of those plots, had to be the root.

This day, Shirley, Diane, now with her husband, Terry, and son, Clayton, and I were back in Wales to confirm and photograph the Jones's starting point. The current Talycoed Farm owners had recently sold this brick barn and another for conversion to homes, but there were conversion restraints. By coincidence, this barn's buyer and his architect were on site to assess what could and could not be done. We thought, *Would it not be fascinating to see, in a few years, the result?* A 2010 website search disclosed the result, and it is shown in an accompanying photo.

The barns at Talycoed on the left in 2004. On the right is the taller barn as shown on an Abergavenny realtor's website in 2010. Note the vertical ventilation slots, the diamond-shaped designs, and the main entrance location, all so clear in the 2004 snapshot.

*****

Back to my early youth, age five. Though I had crossed the Missouri River with my parents to watch Dad's cattle being displayed and sold at the Omaha stockyards, I had seen none of the world beyond. There was much to see.

Which Way, Son—Iowa or Wyoming?

We were en route in our 1931 Model A Ford to visit Dad's uncle and aunt, the Joe Noyers, in the southeast corner of Wyoming and had stopped for the weekend at the Homer Acker farm a few miles south of US 6 and Grafton, Nebraska. Homer's parents had been one of the two couples that had gone on to settle in Nebraska when Dad's grandparents and family had dropped off in Iowa.

After Saturday night and Sunday in far-away Nebraska, I was homesick. But on Monday morning we were to continue on to Wyoming. After breakfast we loaded up the Model A and headed north to join US 6 at Grafton. At the highway stop sign, Dad turned to me and asked, "Which way, son—east to Iowa or west to Wyoming?" My response was emphatic, "East!" He turned west.

By late morning we were in the sub-irrigated Platte Valley, and Mother tried to keep our minds off the heat by having Lorraine and me count haystacks. (In the late 1950s, with our daughters, we would count the alfalfa dehydrating plants as we drove that route. In flights over Nebraska in the 1970s, I would count the irrigation circles.)

It was a dry and windy day, temperature well above one hundred. It seemed we stopped at a gas station in almost every town to add water to the radiator and, once, a quart of oil. At our next stop for water, we discovered the flexible spout oil dispenser on the running board. In later years, I would often use that trip memento to draw oil for our Farmall F-20.

With our many stops for water and one for ice cream cones, it was dark by the time we crossed the Wyoming line and arrived for a late supper at the Noyers. Not until daylight the next day would I see Wyoming.

A month later, in early September of 1936, I would climb on a school bus for the first of twelve years at the Wiota School, having seen at least part of the world beyond Cass County.

Chapter II

The School Years

I could barely reach the step to the bus's only door, at the rear. The bus, a wooden body bolted onto a 1930 Chevrolet chassis, had a thinly-padded bench lining each side and single-pane wooden-framed windows that dropped down to let in air. My sister and I found seats next to neighbors Joyce and Byron Peterson, she a fifth grader and he a freshman. The bus rolled east, rumbled across the loose plank floor of the Troublesome Creek bridge, and proceeded on to pick up my two Keller cousins and more on the way to Wiota.

Our farm was in the far northwest corner of the Wiota Consolidated School District, four miles and across Troublesome Creek from Wiota, population about two hundred. The school, bus barn, and baseball field were on the north side of US 6; most of Wiota, including the Methodist and Catholic churches, homes, and a few businesses lay south of the highway, toward the Rock Island tracks. Reed's Grocery stocked schoolbooks and supplies; a saloon, post office, Mr. Line's barber shop, and the two-story Odd Fellows Hall were on the west side of Main Street. Across the street were an auto repair shop, Robinson's Hardware, and the Wiota Telephone Exchange, the latter in the front room of a local trucker's home. Beyond the end of Main Street, alongside the railroad tracks, were two grain elevators. Three gasoline stations along US 6—Mailander's, Sherm Beebe's, and Milt Bruner's—competed for the local and cross-country drivers' business. It was rumored one could buy other distilled products at Bruner's, and there was plenty of brewed product at Beebe's.

Lorraine and I on a frosty winter morning ready for the school bus and carrying our dinner pails. Note she was carrying some books. I felt it more important to help with chores morning and evening, so there was no use bringing books home from school.

Five wooden-bodied buses brought most of the students, boys in bib overalls and girls in simple dresses, arriving at the school about eight thirty. We dropped our dinner pails in the primary room (grades one and two) coat closet and headed out to play. I knew the routine, as I had visited school with my sister. At 8:55, one-armed janitor Pete Metz pulled the heavy rope just inside the school's front door to ring the big bell atop the building, and we lined up on the front steps. Our teachers would lead us to our rooms.

Among the twenty first graders, six of us would complete the twelve years together. Along the way we added a couple who were dropped back from the previous class, and we lost several to the class behind us. Changes might also come on March 1, when some tenant farm families relocated to new farms in or out of the district.

A few students dropped back more than once. Years later, home from college in late August, I encountered one who said he might not go back for his senior year. I urged him to continue. "After all, you have invested eleven years." His response was quick: "I've invested a lot more than eleven!"

* * * * *

I consider myself fortunate to have attended a small twelve-grade school where most teachers could call every student by name. Though it may have been limited in course options or extracurricular activities, the faculty was excellent.

Wiota Consolidated School

Wiota Consolidated was one of several hundred "Class B" schools (fewer than one hundred in grades nine to twelve) built in Iowa's small towns or the centers of rural townships during the 1920s or early '30s to both replace eight-grade country schools and provide a four-year high school. School district boundaries in most towns of more than one thousand in population were generally the city limits. Surrounding farm kids had to find their own transportation to high school, and their township paid their tuition. Wiota's twelve-grade district had been formed in the early 1920s, when a brick schoolhouse replaced both the town's ten-grade wooden structure and the country schools in a thirty-two-square-mile area.

The upper level of Wiota's brick structure had four classrooms for grades one to eight, plus a high school assembly room, all opening to the center hall. Behind the assembly were two classrooms, one with eighteen typewriters, a "ditto machine" (a.k.a. a "spirit duplicator," it was essentially a low-volume printer), and a mimeograph (a low-cost printing press). The second, with a roll-down wall map, accommodated economics, history, government, and shorthand classes.

The Wiota Consolidated School. Built in the 1920s, it served the area well for forty years. The school district was split between Anita and Atlantic in the early 1960s; the building had done its job and was demolished in the early 1970s.

Also off the central hall were the superintendent's small office and the science classroom. Science equipment was modest: a bell jar and a microscope. On the building's lower level were a shop with workbenches, tool cabinet, and a band saw; a home economics room with stoves and a refrigerator; a music room with piano; and two restroom/locker rooms. From that lower level we descended another ten steps to the gymnasium, perhaps thirty by sixty feet, with a wooden bench along each side and a recessed stage at the near end. Wiota basketball would attract such crowds in the late '30s that a two-row balcony had to be built by the shop class. It was suspended from the ceiling along the east wall, with access from the lower hall by a pull-down ramp.

Monthly PTA meetings were in the gym, with grade-school plays and school band or glee club as the program. The band was selective, those who had instruments. For a PTA meeting in my first year, parents had organized a play. I recall my sister and me watching Dad as Miles Standish and Mother as Pocahontas.

The small parking lot would be jammed with cars on PTA or basketball night; most every member of every family was there. Only once do I recall Mother, my sister, and me catching a ride with the Kellers; my dad was finishing his term as master of the Masonic Lodge in Atlantic and would come later. Although lodge was important in Dad's life, after he finished his term as master it would take a backseat to our school activities, PTA, class plays, and sports.

Wiota's ten-member faculty was consistently excellent, and I suggest two reasons: (1) few other professions, except secretarial work, welcomed outstanding young women; and (2) the school board had hired Joe O'Connor as principal and coach in 1934 and elevated him to superintendent in 1936 (at age twenty-three). The board had wanted good school discipline and a good athletic program and had consulted with Coach Henry Iba at Maryville, Missouri, the closest teacher training college. This was before Iba moved on to put Oklahoma A&M (later renamed Oklahoma State University) on the map in basketball. Iba recommended O'Connor, who had played for Iba.

There were three special days on the school calendar that stand out in my early years. A school Christmas party was on Friday morning preceding the two-week break. After some Christmas music by the band or glee club, every student was given a small bag of peanuts, hard candy, and, some years, an orange as we left the gym to put on our heavy coats and overshoes and climb onto the buses.

Grades three and up had a special duty in early May, digging dandelions. It was before the days of the 2,4D herbicide and no-weapons-in-school policies; each was to bring a knife, and at three o'clock, rows of students on hands and knees moved across the front lawn prying out dandelion tap roots.

Room picnics climaxed spring semester. I would have a paper sack with two hot dogs, buns, and an apple on my desk, ready to go. Miss Thoning led us in line down Wiota's Main Street, across the Rock Island tracks and the Turkey Creek bridge to the Christensen timber, adjacent to their farmstead. (At that age, proximity to a bathroom was important.) Third and fourth graders, taught by Janet Sutton, who would later marry O'Connor, might be in a separate section of that timber; higher grades at a more distant timber. For the high school, it was either the Dorsey or Bell timber, both more than a mile walk along US 6 and the latter timber complete with a bubbling spring at the edge a small pool. At this writing most of those timbers are gone, the land devoted to corn or soybeans.

Sometime after two o'clock we would file back to the school, pick up our report cards signed by O'Connor, and be on the bus home, free for the summer.

*****

I share on the following pages some of the move vivid school recollections. The first is of my marble bag, which was soon empty.

My Bag of Marbles

For many first-grade boys, his marble bag was a major possession. My bag was modest, perhaps a dozen multicolored marbles, three-eighths inch in diameter, plus a shooter, half inch or larger. We would draw a circle in the dirt before school or during recess, dump an equal number of marbles inside the circle, and try to win the opponent's marbles by knocking them out of the circle with our shooter.

I do not recall how I found myself competing with Duane Reed, the recognized room champion. He may have spotted me as a likely victim when I got off the bus, or I may have had a foolish air of confidence after winning a few marbles the day before. Regardless, Reed drew a circle in the dirt beside the sidewalk. I set down my dinner pail and emptied my bag of a dozen marbles. Reed counted out the same number from his vast store. We dropped to our knees and the game was on.

Reed generously let me shoot first. I took aim at one of his marbles, but my shooter only hit the mass and the marbles scattered, all still in the circle. Reed took aim at one of mine near the edge. Pop! It was gone. He took aim at another. Pop! It was gone. Reed was a dead-eye; from then on, I just watched as my marbles crashed against the schoolhouse bricks or flew over the sidewalk. I do not recall getting a second shot. Except for my shooter, I had only an empty bag and my dinner pail to carry into the schoolhouse.

*****

Haircut for a Quarter, Knife for a Nickel

An Atlantic haircut cost thirty-five cents, but in Mr. Line's Wiota shop it was a quarter.

If I needed my hair cut midweek, I would board the school bus with a quarter and during noon hour run the three blocks down to Line's shop. Even if Line's single chair was occupied when I got to the shop, there was no problem. He could do a haircut, with not much styling expected or provided, in ten minutes or less.

This Sunday morning, Dad and I were in Line's shop. I had spotted a schoolmate outside, and when Dad replaced me in the chair, I rushed out. My schoolmate had found a knife and would sell it to me for a dime.

I had wanted a knife, especially after Dad's hired man had shown me how he used one to make a whistle from a green willow branch. About an inch into a three-inch section, he cut a forty-five-degree notch halfway into the wood and then slipped out the inner wood from the green bark. The resulting hollow bark whistle yielded a mellow tone.

I rushed in to ask Dad for a dime. No luck. I returned to the sidewalk, reported the turn-down, and the price dropped to a nickel. With new hope, I was back in the shop and came out with the nickel.

As Dad and I left the shop, I proudly showed him my new knife. "That knife is new, worth a lot more than a nickel. Where did he get it? Why is he selling it?" I could not answer.

I began to understand. Had someone lost that knife? Had it been a gift? Was it right to buy a new knife for only a nickel? What would be the consequences? Dad drove us down to my schoolmate's home and we reversed the sale.

It was my first lesson in business: if a deal seems too good, perhaps it should not happen. And Dad handled it in such a way that two schoolmates remained friends.

* * * * *

There have been few personalities with which I would consistently clash. Some I would as soon avoid, but we could deal in a civil manner. Not so with Dorvin Elmquist, a first grader who had appeared on our school bus the first of March. I was a second grader, and his family had moved to a farm on our route.

The Beat-Up Dinner Pail

Though our animosity eventually tempered and the Elmquists later moved on, it had been sufficiently intense that a fellow bus rider reminded me of it years later.

Dorvin and I would daily disagree, usually on who had first dibs on a rear corner bus seat. First and second graders were dismissed at three thirty to run off steam before the higher grades were dismissed at four o'clock and the buses departed. When the drivers backed the buses up to the sidewalk, we would race to capture a rear corner. Of course Dorvin and I both wanted the same corner. Pushing and shoving ensued, usually climaxing with dinner pails swinging at each other's heads.

The fight subsided when a couple of juniors or seniors got on the bus; they might shove both of us to "where we belonged." But the fight would reignite in the two miles before we reached Dorvin's driveway, both of us standing and swinging our dinner pails. Driver Wes Morgan would bring that to a halt by slamming on the brakes, and we would roll halfway to the front of the bus.

Dorvin's head was hard enough that I had a few dents in my dinner pail, but mine was harder. By the end of the school year his pail was probably a total loss.

*****

My mother made several attempts to develop her children's musical talent. In my case there was continuous disappointment.

Musical Talent

Mother's search began with piano lessons from a Mrs. Taylor, in her Atlantic home. Every Saturday at twelve thirty, it was thirty minutes for my sister, thirty for me. For me, it was not the week's most enjoyable event, and fortunately, my lessons came to an abrupt halt when I fell off my pony and fractured an arm.

Sometime later, Mother suggested the cornet and took me to visit a local performer and teacher, John Fancolly. He was polite and encouraging, but his skill and long, agile fingers were intimidating to me. I took one look at my short fingers and rejected the idea.

Next came a Spanish guitar; I was a Gene Autry fan and this time I agreed. Mother found a used guitar and then a teacher, a fellow in his early twenties. My first Saturday lesson was in the armory basement, the next at his parents' home, a little square house a block west of the armory. Before the third Saturday he had left town.

The fourth effort, Hawaiian guitar, lasted almost a year. A new couple in town advertised for students, and my sister and I were enrolled. Mother likely used egg money for the up-front payment, sixty dollars for our sixty-lesson series. She negotiated for a used guitar for my sister and my little-used Spanish guitar was converted, with new strings and a metal fret bar.

I really got into that Hawaiian guitar; after my lesson, I would listen in on an advanced class with their electric guitars. I also tuned in at noon on Sundays to Alvino Ray, a well-known guitarist and for a time imagined myself in that advanced class with an electric guitar of my own.

Mother was proud that we were taking music lessons, was telling her friends, and one of those friends was Mary, a checker at Nord's grocery. One Saturday we had come from our lessons to meet Mother at the grocery counter. Mary suggested, "Bring your guitars in here and play for us." To me, that was over the top. But Mother was proud. Five minutes later, sitting on chairs brought from the rear, our music propped up against the cash register, and people standing in line with their groceries, Lorraine and I were picking and strumming through "O Sole Mio."

I do not recall if it was school and farm interests, my difficulty reading music scores, or fear of another grocery store concert, but my guitar enthusiasm eventually dwindled and died.

It was another Mrs. Taylor, my teacher in fifth grade, who found my true musical talent. She had moved a big console radio into our room; schools across Iowa had been invited by Iowa State's radio station WOI to tune in for a special program, to hear and learn to identify the sounds of an orchestra's individual instruments. One hundred miles from Ames, reception was not good; we could hardly hear the signal. Mrs. Taylor asked me to stand by the radio and grasp the short antenna wire. Reception was then remarkable; each instrument came through loud and clear.

She had found my talent, and in that one day I had reached my potential.

* * * * *

The USDA had taken some surplus food commodities off the market during the Depression years to help stabilize market price, and they were apparently available to schools at no cost. So, Wiota had joined the federal school lunch program, and we would now have hot lunches—no more cold sandwiches.

Spanish Rice and Peanut Butter Soup

The first day's main course was peanut butter soup. With surplus peanut butter and dried milk, that was logical. But it was hardly appealing or filling, even with bread or crackers and an apple. Washington nutritionists had no idea how many calories Iowa farm boys needed; nor did we have a taste for peanut butter soup.

For the second week, the plan changed. There would be no full meal, just one hot dish and perhaps cookies. Sandwiches and an apple or banana from home were suggested. I do not recall if there was a charge; it may have been ten or fifteen cents per week. Though the commodities were free, there was cost for cooks, fuel, and dishes. We were fortunate that Mrs. Hilda Jorgensen, the mother of classmate Juaquetta, and her partner found tasty ways to use those surplus commodities. Especially, they found a better use for the peanut butter: cookies. To this day, peanut butter cookies remain one of my favorites.

The cooks took over the home economics kitchen about ten in the morning, and at 11:50 Mrs. Taylor would send two students down to the kitchen. One would carry back to our room the bowls and spoons, the other a steaming pot of whatever the USDA's generosity and Mrs. Jorgensen's creativity provided.

Though most of my schoolmates did not care for a weekly mainstay, Spanish rice flavored with tomato sauce and butter, I took to it immediately. If others passed on it, I could get a second helping.

Wiota's school lunch program was short-lived. With the outbreak of World War II, USDA's commodity stores were needed for the mobilized troops. We were soon back to sack lunches from home.

*****

As students we had models, usually students a grade or more ahead. Among mine, in academic ability, were my sister and my older cousin, Robert Keller. I had watched each represent Wiota's junior high room in the county spelling contest. In time, as a seventh grader, it was my turn, and I was fortunate to win the county contest. I would compete in the state contest.

Divine or D*e*vine

It was midmorning on a Saturday in Des Moines's Scottish Rites Temple, with rows of folding chairs filling the main lodge room floor. I sat nervously in the third row. My parents and my seventh-grade teacher, Leona Tibken, were in seats along the side. A state champion speller would emerge from the one hundred or so county or city champions in those folding chairs.

The *Des Moines Register* sponsored the contest, which included a dinner the previous night at Younkers Tea Room, a commemorative medallion, and a lapel pin. Though nervous, I felt ready; Miss Tibken had drilled me for months. While on noon hall duty, and while my classmates were outside or in the gym, she had worked me through Eaton's little blue spelling book, she pronouncing and me spelling.

The written part of the contest, ten words pronounced each round, was over, and I had made it through five or six rounds before my number was called to go sit on the sidelines.

We were all now back in the chairs for the oral rounds, one word to each contestant, given in alphabetical order of the county or city represented. We would stand, and Drake University English Professor Mary Francis Boyd pronounced the word. If an incorrect letter was uttered, a bell rang. There was no backing up and starting over.

The first round words were rather simple and I was eager for my turn, in fact too eager. Professor Boyd enunciated my word, "divine," so intently I heard "d*e*vine." Out rushed, "D-e—d-i." GONG!

How about the next year? There was another contest in our junior high classroom, and then more noon hours in Wiota's central hall with Miss Tibken to prepare me for another county contest. Successful in that contest, I was now again in the Scottish Rites Temple. This time I was more cautious and deliberate and persisted to the later written and oral rounds but had been long on the sidelines when the final two were struggling with five-syllable words.

* * * * *

Now, as ninth graders, my classmates and I would be in the large high school assembly room alongside sophomores, juniors, and seniors, and with four different instructors each day. We were in new territory.

The High School Curriculum

Wiota high school's curriculum was fixed, with four years of English, two of math, including algebra, and one each of history and government for all. Freshman and sophomore girls took home economics, cooking one year and sewing the next. For the boys, shop and agriculture were taught alternate years, with freshmen and sophomores in one class. I was envious of those schools with four-year vocational agriculture, and I lobbied Superintendent O'Connor to consider it. But it was not in the cards.

Junior and senior boys took geometry and physics, which was also taught alternate years (long before engineering or physical sciences were considered women's work); the girls took shorthand and bookkeeping. There was no debate team, and I recall no mention of county or regional music contests.

Typing was taught our junior year, and in that class, as well as in our free time as seniors, we "published" the monthly school newspaper, *The Wiota Owl.* We typed the mimeograph masters, a soft, translucent film backed by harder pasteboard, then filled the mimeograph machine's paper tray, brushed the inside of the machine's drum with ink, clipped a master's film (minus the pasteboard backing) snugly onto the drum, and turned the crank. Just enough ink was pushed through the film's typewriter key impressions to yield readable copy on successive sheets of paper.

Basketball and Baseball

Wiota's basketball teams, drilled by O'Connor in the Henry Iba philosophy of tight defense and motivated by Iba psychology, would put Wiota on the map in the early 1940s. From 1940, girls' team would be in the state tournament seven years and win it in 1944 and '45, while the boys' team would make it to the state tournament in 1946. In baseball, Wiota played in the fall or spring state tournaments several times and won the state championship in 1946.

No Title IX was needed for equal treatment of men and women. Both boys' and girls' teams were coached by O'Connor, used the same balls in the same tiny gym, and practiced the same amount of time. Both teams rode to away games on a single bus (convenient for a bit of hand holding in the rear seats), where we played double headers, with the girls' game at 7:00 p.m. and the boys' at 8:10.

O'Connor and his girls' basketball team had gained enough respect by 1943 that they were chosen to demonstrate the finer features of the game at a statewide preseason coaching clinic in the West Des Moines school gym. Gasoline was rationed; the school could get barely enough for the bus routes, but Dad and other farmer parents each had a barrel of "tractor gas" they were willing to tap for basketball trips. For this event and most away games during the war's later years, I would be between my parents in the front seat of our '41 Ford two-door sedan, with Lorraine and at least three teammates and their gym bags squeezed into the backseat.

After this clinic, Dad took our carload downtown to Younkers Tea Room to celebrate their performance. For our family, a meal in a restaurant was rare. When the waitress asked Lorraine, "How do you want your steak?" she was puzzled; she had never been asked that question. Finally, her response, "Cooked!"

* * * * *

Even in later college zoology labs, I would not see tissues comparable to those of a human; there it would be mostly worms and crustacean. But this day, Miss Chapman's high school freshman science class would see close to the real thing.

Hog Lungs and a Tire Pump

I climbed on to the school bus this morning with a pair of fresh hog lungs in a sack and a tire pump. We were studying the human respiratory system in Helen Chapman's science class, and I had almost the real thing, what the class could see, feel, and watch function.

In early winter, Dad would butcher one or two hogs. After bleeding and removing the head, he would then skin the carcass, fix the rear legs to the end hooks of a singletree, and with the aid of a small block and tackle, hang the carcass in the corn crib driveway. He would then remove the head, cut open the front of the carcass, split the pelvis and breastbone with a heavy knife, pull out the offal (internal organs), saw down the center of the backbone to split the carcass, and leave it to chill overnight.

The next day, he and Mother would cut the two chilled sides. Hams and bellies would go into a salt brine for curing, while packages of pork chops and roasts would go to rented boxes at the Atlantic Locker. That evening they would grind the trimmings, mix in spices, and with a hand-operated sausage press, squeeze the mix into "natural casings," which were washed intestines purchased that day at Sauer and Dahlberg's butcher shop. Stuffed sausages, perhaps up to six feet long, would then be coiled into a large crock and the crock filled with lard, the latter cooked down from the internal fat and fat trimmings, and stored in an unheated upstairs bedroom.

Through the winter and spring, Mother would climb the stairs most mornings, and pry out and cut off a section of that sausage to fry with our breakfast eggs. The lard went largely to pie crusts and donuts.

Dad had just finished eviscerating a two hundred-pound hog when I got off the school bus the evening before and spotted those soft, pink lungs and extending trachea. For our class to see real lungs, the same size as a human's, would be fantastic!

First thing after dropping off the bus, I found Miss Chapman and showed her the lungs. Her lesson plan changed. A few minutes later, in class, I was holding the lungs, a classmate was holding the trachea tight around the tire pump hose, and another was handling the pump. We all watched as the pump induced "inhaling." The soft, spongy lobes expanded, and with the trachea released from the hose, they "exhaled."

* * * * *

In later years' work, I would often identify a student or a faculty member who had the energy to do more and needed another task. In this case, O'Connor thought that some of my energy should be given another task.

A Job and a Lesson

I had just given classmate Karl Aldag a jab in the ribs, typical noon-time behavior in the school gym, when my eye caught O'Connor up in the stage doorway. O'Connor always seemed to be in the right place at the right time, and would say the right thing to keep his two hundred students on the right track. He had likely seen my jab and would soon be facing me in the gym. But nothing happened.

At one o'clock we were back in our assembly seats. Three grades would soon leave for their classrooms; the last grade's class would hold forth in the assembly. O'Connor walked in. *Here it comes,* I thought. *He'll motion me out into the hall.*

O'Connor stopped, though, and spoke to the total assembly, "We have an opportunity to raise money for school activities by selling magazine subscriptions." He described the project, selling subscriptions to parents or neighbors. The school would receive a commission, and the top sales people would be rewarded with a prize. Then he said, "I want Duane Acker to be the sales manager."

His message was clear to me. "If Duane Acker has surplus energy that gets him in trouble, I will put it to work." And, more specifically to me, the message said, "Show me that you can do something worthwhile."

In the two-week sales effort, the high school exceeded the sales goal. Perhaps, as sales manager, I had helped. More important, I had learned an O'Connor technique for handling people.

* * * * *

Teaching faculty may come and go with little impact on students. Two other staff changes during my twelve school years do stand out, however. One was O'Connor's departure at the end of my junior year to become superintendent at Atlantic, the county seat. Arnold Christ, long-time principal, assistant coach, and whiz math instructor, took over, and Richard Bloomer, fresh out of Iowa State Teachers' College, now UNI, arrived as our new principal. An earlier staff change was the arrival of Sam Morgan as janitor after Metz had retired.

That Was Sam's Job

While Metz was a respected fixture of the school, Morgan quickly became a friend of every student and part of most every activity. Not only did he ring the big bell at 8:55 and 12:55 and keep the floors spotless, he waxed and polished the school's five basketballs every evening. Sam also umpired our home baseball games, sometimes quietly offering a word of encouragement to a player during the game. Earlier in the day, he would drag smooth the infield and mark the foul lines with lime, usually with help from a couple players pulled out of class. Among the total school staff, Sam may have been the most universally appreciated.

As principal, Bloomer had noontime gym duty; his presence kept rambunctious students under control, especially on rainy days. Sam would also usually be in the gym, just watching "his kids." Before climbing the stairs to ring the 12:55 bell for those playing outside, Sam would reach up to the gym light switch and blink the lights.

This day, Bloomer glanced at his watch; it read 12:55 and he didn't see Sam. Bloomer stepped over and blinked the lights just as Sam was coming down the steps. *But that was Sam's job!*

We glanced at Sam, saw his momentary grimace. For those of us who were in the gym, the balance of the day was unsettled and there was tension in the air. Just as Sam felt that polishing the floors and the basketballs was his responsibility, and his pride, so was alerting students that one o'clock was near.

A person's job, whether or not it is in the job description, is their pride. One takes it away only with caution.

* * * * *

During World War II, able-bodied men not in the service were all in day-long jobs, not available for an hour each weekday morning and afternoon to drive school buses.

School Bus Drivers at Age Sixteen

At Wiota, using senior boys for the job had become standard practice; at age sixteen we could get a special chauffeur's license. To save fuel, bus routes driven by farm boys were designed to start and end at their respective farms.

On home baseball days, the seven-inning game would start at three o'clock and be over by about four thirty. Our riders would be on the buses by the time we came down from the diamond. We would jump on the bus, toss our gloves under the seat, and go. Days of away games, our dads or a friend would drive our bus.

By this time, Wiota's wooden buses had been replaced and the bus for my route was a short metal body mounted on a 1939 Chevrolet chassis. It had five rows of seats on each side. Except for the width of a city lot before my turn into the school driveway, my circuitous seven-mile route was all dirt roads, not even gravel.

Each morning I would drive west a half-mile and then south on the "crossroad," to pick up three Pedersens (their farm was outside the Wiota district, so the township paid tuition). From there it was east over a knoll past the Both farmstead, across Troublesome Creek bottom and bridge to the Brown corner, south for two young Zellmers, and then backtrack to pick up Carol Brown. Then it was a quarter mile east, around the sharp "Devil's

Corner," north and east for three Johnsons, and then on east and south to pick up two young Urys. I would have half my load and only one stop left, just a half mile from Wiota.

Four Kinens would be standing by the road along with one or more of the Wedemeyers. In due time, five Wedemeyers would appear and climb on. Years later one of the Wedemeyer sons would tell me his mother's strategy. When she heard the bus approach and some were not yet cleaned up from doing the morning milking, she would release them one at a time to hold the bus while she washed the ears and put jackets on the rest.

Tire chains were essential many days. If it rained overnight, I would slip on the chains after milking, then wash up, change clothes, and speed through breakfast so I could leave home by seven forty-five. If it rained during the school day, we drivers would head to the bus garage after our last class, about 3:40, to put chains on the rear wheels.

My bus had been purchased with duals in 1939, but to save rubber during WWII, the outside dual had been removed and not replaced. With only single rear tires, I could quickly put on chains without getting my shirt cuffs dirty. The job was not so easy for the others, whose buses had duals wheels and heavier, more cumbersome chains.

* * * * *

It was a typical Troublesome Creek spring flood; snow melt coupled with spring rains brought more water than the creek would hold. Further, the creek's tortuous path, the little fall in elevation, and the heavy timber on each side of the creek caused the flood water to move so slowly that our bottom pasture would be covered with water for a week. In this case, that the water moved slowly was a good thing; there would be no risk in my driving the school bus on through the water.

The Annual Troublesome Creek Flood

For a quarter mile ahead the road was under a foot of water. The subsoil was still frozen, but the top six inches had thawed, and there were deep ruts in the roadway below the water.

This Friday evening, the thaw and a series of steep hills a mile north of Wiota had forced me to change my route. After delivering the Wedemeyers and Kinens, I had dropped the Urys and Johnsons at the top of the first hill (they would need to walk their half mile or more from there) and returned to Wiota. I then headed west on US 6. Irvin Zellmer was at the highway with his team and wagon to meet his youngsters. He had known I would come that way, that I could not make it up to his farm from either direction in the deep mud. I continued west on 6, then north across the Troublesome Creek bridge on US 71, and headed east a mile south of my home farm's road, again in the mud. I dropped off the Pedersens and had just one remaining student to deliver, eighth-grader Carol Brown.

Though the water ahead was shallow and with no current, I could not let Carol wade through it. Just east of the Both farmstead, I crossed a small tributary bridge and proceeded slowly into the water. Water seeped in the door to my right and covered the lower step, but I was not worried. The valley floor and road were level, the water would not get deeper, and if I drove slowly, there was no chance the bus would jump out of those deep ruts and slide off the road. Even if that should happen, the ditch bottoms were but a few inches lower than the road.

The approach to the Troublesome Creek bridge and the road beyond was up out of the water. I thought I could deliver Carol, turn around in the Brown driveway, and head back to the highway. But the road ruts were so deep that my front wheels simply pushed up against the bridge floor frame. I could not get the bus onto the bridge. Carol would have to walk across the bridge and the last few hundred feet home.

There was no way to turn the bus around; I would just have to back through that quarter mile of water, over the tributary bridge, up the knoll and turn around at the Both's driveway.

Through the water I had no problem. But in backing over that small bridge, the rear of my bus slid to one side, my rear wheels missed the ruts beyond, and the right wheel slid into the south ditch. I was done. The mud was so slick and deep there was no chance good neighbor Paul Both could pull me out. By morning the road surface would be frozen, solid enough for traction. Tomorrow would be Saturday, with plenty of time to do the job. I would walk the mile home across soft fields.

The Boths' pasture was easy walking, on grass sod. From there, however, through three fields of corn stalks, I stepped slowly and carefully, from corn stalk to corn stalk. It was long dark before I reached home and supper.

*****

It was the last four minutes of a late conference season basketball game in the tiny Casey gym, my senior year and my lowest point in twelve school years. I felt embarrassed, even ridiculed. Could I handle it?

Sixth Man Two Years

What I needed to handle was being left on the court as an apparent part of Wiota's "second team." It was the biggest disappointment of what had been, for me, a disappointing season. As a junior, I had competed for a starting guard position, but had had to settle for "sixth man." I got plenty of playing time, though, especially in bringing the ball up the floor against press defenses and setting up plays, and had felt good about the season.

Wiota's six-man "first team" for the 1946–47 season. I cannot explain the glum looks; perhaps it was the day after a rare loss. From the left, Center George Stuetelberg, 6 foot, 6 ¾ inches, forwards Ralph Keller and Mack Taylor, and Guards Dean Coomes, Duane Harris, and Acker.

We lost our two starting guards to graduation, so, as a senior, I felt I had a lock on being a starting guard. Not so. For the second half of our third game, at Exira, Coach Christ left me on the bench. My play had not been good enough. From then on, I was again the sixth man. That hurt, but I adjusted, still got a lot of playing time, and Wiota and Fontanelle were leading the conference.

In the perception of the student body and parents who never missed a game, I was an integral part of the all-senior first team. If I was on the floor when our score was safely ahead, I would be retired to the bench with the other seniors, recognition for a job well done. The second team, mostly sophomores and juniors, would finish the game.

Tonight, with a twenty-point lead over Casey and four minutes to go, Christ had put in three sophomores and one junior and left me on the floor. *So I'm now second team,* I thought.

In our furnace room early the next morning, while putting on my second pair of jeans and heavy coat for chores, I opened up to Dad. I was embarrassed and frustrated. "Should I quit?"

His response was simple. "Think it through. I'm guessing you'll stick it out."

In the end I swallowed hard and stuck it out. A week later, in the conference championship game against Fontanelle and played in the larger Anita gym to accommodate the expected crowd, I was glad I had.

Fontanelle's press defense was giving my teammates on the court a hard time. More than once, they got boxed in and lost the ball. After another costly turnover, forward Mack Taylor, racing by our bench in pursuit, yelled in frustration to Christ, "Put Acker in!" Christ did.

There were no more Wiota turnovers. We won the game 28 to 27, and the conference championship. And, I would be among the starting five for several of the tournament season games that followed. For Taylor and his words as he raced by our bench that night, I am forever grateful.

*****

On my bookcase shelf is a golden glove on a walnut base, an award from the Iowa Baseball Coaches Association. I assure my Wiota teammates it was given for reasons other than my performance on the diamond.

Fun on the Hot Corner

For me, baseball was fun, especially when I was playing the "hot corner," third base.

Grounders come hot and fast to a third baseman, little more than 90 feet from home plate, and the throw to first base could be 125 feet or more. My arm might not be the strongest, but I could react quickly, and once a grounder was in my glove, I could snap it from near my right ear toward first, low and straight. If our pitcher was in my line of throw, I could make him duck, and a couple such outs at first are etched in my memory.

From the batting box, my recollection is a different story, especially with Chuck Fredericksen on the mound for arch rival Exira. I never got a hit off Chuck. In fact, I do not recall seeing the ball! Fredericksen would go on to pitch for Iowa State, and still later, be the university's longtime director of residence.

Coach O'Connor or Christ would usually have me batting first or second in the lineup; I might draw a walk and be driven home by a heavy hitter batting fourth or fifth. Or, I would be listed eighth or ninth in the lineup; the game might be over before I came to bat the fourth or fifth time. I was therefore surprised years later when a classmate gave me an April 1948 *News Telegraph* clipping. Under the heading Wiota Nine Whips Cumberland 15–3, it included, "Duane Acker came up with three hits in five trips to the plate."

I do recall that in the next to last game my senior year, I hit a double. Perhaps to reward such unexpected performance, Coach Christ listed me to bat sixth in our final game.

* * * * *

An epidemic of senioritis might be excusable, but four school buses and their drivers being on the opposite side of the highway when the primary students were waiting by the schoolhouse to load was not excusable.

Senioritis

It was well after three thirty, when our buses were supposed to be in position beside the school. However, four of the five were across the highway at Mailander's station. Mel Mailander answered the ringing phone. We heard only, "Mack, George, Don, and Duane." We knew who had called, and the question. Superintendent Christ's office faced the highway and station. We were out the door before Mel dropped the phone.

Conscientious Ralph Keller had gassed up his bus and left; his bus was where it was supposed to be by three thirty. We all should have taken care of any maintenance in the morning, after dropping off our load and before nine o'clock classes. But that was also free time to shoot baskets, and we enjoyed a few afternoon minutes at Mailander's station. Owner Frank Mailander said little, but his sons Mel and Cliff were usually good for a few stories and laughs. Though we needed gas only about once a week, we would often find some reason for an afternoon trip to the station, perhaps to check the tire pressure or oil level.

Our four buses nearly created a traffic jam headed for the school drive. Once in place, we sat glued to our driver's seats, dutifully greeting the first and second graders as they climbed on. We hoped Christ by now was occupied with some other problem.

No such luck; we were his problem. From bus to bus he stalked, and at each there was a very short conversation. At least for that day, our senioritis was cured.

* * * * *

By 1963, fifteen years after my graduation, Wiota Consolidated School had done its job and would cease to exist. Farm population had declined as farms consolidated, so enrollment dropped. Other professions were competing for high ability women, and society demanded more breadth in school curriculum, including art, languages, and vocational courses.

Though school loyalty and community resistance made it difficult, the need to join either the Anita district to the east or the larger Atlantic district to the west became clear. By that time, both of these districts had expanded to include their surrounding rural areas.

With my parents' proximity and affinity to Atlantic, their preference was consolidation with that district. However, Lorraine's husband, John Rasmussen, was in the family's hatchery and feed business in Anita, he was president of the Anita school board, and Anita needed Wiota's enrollment. The topic of the Wiota School's future was therefore avoided in family gatherings.

In the end, the Wiota district was divided, with the west half attached to the Atlantic district and the east half, including the Wiota school buildings, to the Anita district.

Chapter III

The Farm and Community

Up to the day I first climbed on to that Wiota school bus, my main focus was the farm, with the livestock, the Farmall F-20 tractor, and what Dad and Mother and a hired man were doing each day. Though school was fascinating and I enjoyed it, my interests and attention were about equally divided between school and the farm.

From the time I could carry a half-bucket of milk, I would be helping Dad and the hired man with the milking, morning and evening. On Saturdays and during the summer I would be in the middle of whatever was on the agenda, on my pony carrying water to threshers at oat harvest or, from age seven, driving the tractor loading hay or leading the horse on the hayfork at the barn. When I was large enough to lift one row of cultivator shanks by bracing my foot against the tractor's steering post as I tugged on the lift lever, I would be cultivating corn. Even in the less pleasant task of walking the tall corn rows in search of and pulling Dad's nemesis, button weeds, I was part of the crew.

At age four or five, "helping" Dad as he forked silage off a wagon into a feed bunk for his cattle.

The Changes I Lived

My first seventeen years on the farm would bracket the Great Depression, the Dust Bowl, and World War II, all impacting what I saw and lived. During those years, tractors replaced horses on most farms, hybrid corn gained full acceptance, and electricity reached most farm homes.

Regarding the latter, our community had been ahead of time. My parents and their neighbors had built a line from Atlantic in the late 1920s and purchased electricity from the Atlantic Municipal Utilities' coal—and water-powered generating plant.

Dad's F-20 would still be the farm's major power when I finished high school in 1948, but an electric starter had replaced the crank, a hydraulic pump lifted the cultivator shanks and a manure loader, and an added "road gear" would let us speed to rented land at thirteen miles per hour instead of crawling along at five. A creation of WWII, a Willys Jeep, would replace the last team of horses and serve as a second tractor for pulling wagons, a hay rake, or rotary hoe.

My parents had rented from Mother's retired parents since 1924, and at their death, she was granted the home 130 acres, but a mortgage remained.

It was livestock and poultry that would pay off the mortgage. Milk, eggs, and finished animals are higher value products than grain and also provide a market for family labor. When Dad's corn crop was lost to drought or hail, Mother's eggs could at least be exchanged for groceries, and the cream check would cover the phone and electric bill.

In 1937, I watched carpenters double the size of Mother's hen house. She also found and bought three small "brooder houses," to quadruple the number of fryers—today we call them broilers—that she would raise and dress for town customers' Sunday dinners. Her ad would be in the Friday evening Atlantic *News Telegraph*; that evening the phone would be ringing. Early Saturday morning she would catch two dozen or more birds with a long hook and wring their necks, then dress them and cut the carcasses into legs, thighs, wings, and breasts. She would package them as three-pound fryers, delivered for sixty cents, twenty cents per pound.

Dad meanwhile more than doubled his eight-cow dairy herd, replaced his bull with semen from higher production dairy lines, started a ewe flock to produce market lambs and, early in the war years, began purchasing western lambs for finishing. All of this required more forage, so he would purchase and harvest standing hay on neighboring farms and, in time, rent nearby farmland to grow both grain and forage.

In the thirties we had a hired man, who was given room and board plus thirty dollars per month in the summer, fifteen in the winter. With all that livestock, help was essential. After the prewar draft started in 1940, there were few men to be hired; a series of older school boys filled the role. One would drop off the school bus at four thirty with my sister and me, help with morning and evening chores, share my second-floor bedroom, and climb on the bus with us after morning chores and breakfast. By the end of the war, except for day labor and exchanging work with neighbors during hay harvest, threshing, or silo filling, it was usually only Dad and me.

Hay handling would change from a hay loader, a late 1800s invention that lifted windrowed hay off the ground and, with reciprocating rows of long tines, pushed the sun-dried forage up to drop onto a horse-drawn or tractor-drawn rack, to an engine-powered field baler. The loose hay or bales were lifted into the barn via a large fork at the end of a rope. Later came a field chopper that chopped and blew dried or green forage into a wagon, plus a companion blower that was stationed at the barn or silo.

Ear corn harvest moved from husking by hand, with Dad or the hired man tossing the ears against a high "bang board" on a team-drawn wagon's far side, to a one-row tractor-powered corn picker. Hand husking would yield a wagon load before lunch, a second before evening chores. In the corn crib driveway, he would drop down the wagon's rear "scoop-board" and hand-scoop the corn ears into the crib. For extra help, in one case two Kansas farmers with total crop failure due to drought, Dad assigned a team and wagon and paid one cent per bushel plus room and board.

In contrast to two loads per day with hand husking, that one-row picker could fill a wagon in thirty minutes. At the crib, a Model A Ford motor and differential mounted on skids powered a long, sloping elevator with paddles on an endless chain that pushed the ears up and through a hole in the crib roof.

Corn silage harvest advanced from a single-row, ground-driven binder that cut and tied the corn stalks into heavy bundles, to a tractor powered two-row binder, to that field chopper mentioned for hay harvest. We removed two stud bolts and disconnected a drive shaft to remove the hay pick-up mechanism, and replaced it with the "corn head," which cut off and pulled the stalks into the chopper.

Hired man Wayne Johnson standing on the Farmall F-20, about 1939. The lack of a power-take-off (PTO) shaft above the trailing tongue tells me the F-20 was pulling the one-row, ground-driven corn binder in the tall forage sorghum for silage. The crop was so heavy that the wheels on the binder would slide, which prompted Dad to replace that binder with a used PTO binder.

Doubling the milking herd without a hired man during the war prompted Dad, with my strong encouragement, to try a milking machine. He chose a low-cost innovation, an electric motor and piston pumps on a three-wheeled frame that we could roll behind the row of cows. It worked but saved little time, and we would eventually go back to hand milking. The day before I departed for college, though, I would help a technician install a proven and popular Surge milking machine system.

What about the roads? It would not be until I was away in college that the roads past our farm and west a mile to US 71, or across Troublesome Creek and southeast to Wiota, were graveled. Even then it would happen only in sections where neighbors agreed to pay for half the gravel. More than once after spring thaws, my sister and I were shuttled home from school in a series of parents' horse-drawn wagons over deep-rutted mud roads, conditions the school bus could not handle.

Unlike the higher clearance Ford Model A, with its twenty-nine-inch diameter wheels and open fenders, the lower-slung cars of the mid-1930s, equipped with sixteen-inch diameter wheels and snug fenders, were of no value after a rain. Pasty "gumbo" would pack the space between tires and fenders, making the car virtually immovable.

Wiota women's basketball teams in the early forties consistently made it to the mid-March state tournament in Des Moines, and with my sister on the team, we could not miss the games. It was not uncommon to go by tractor and wagon to meet friends at US 71 for a ride to Des Moines in the late afternoon for an evening game. It would be near midnight when we arrived back at the highway's edge for the tractor and wagon ride home and a couple hours sleep. We would then need to be up early for milking, so we could also milk early that afternoon and be in Des Moines for that night's game. More than once I fell asleep with my head against a cow's flank and my limp hands on the edge of the bucket between my legs at six in the morning.

Our grandsons might ask, "Who were your babysitters?" I do not recall hearing the term until I was in college and Veterinary Professor Alan Packer and his wife asked me to sit with their children one Friday night. When our parents went to a neighborhood party or to dances, the latter every other Friday night at a community hall south of Atlantic, we went along. We played outside or in the basement kitchen with the other kids until the dancers broke for a ten o'clock lunch, likely sandwiches and cake or cookies that each family brought, plus coffee. After the lunch we would go to sleep on chairs in the cloak room off the upstairs dance floor and wake up the next morning in our bed at home.

The one place I could say I had a real sitter, other than in my grandmother Acker's Atlantic apartment or my aunt's home, was next to the county jail. Sheriff Pat Edwards, Dad's good friend and WWI buddy, lived in the adjacent courthouse apartment so he could supervise the jail and his wife could prepare the prisoners' meals. Their teen-age daughter, Imogene, took care of me in that apartment several times, and I recall her holding me up so I could see the prisoners through the tiny jail door window. I would ask, "Are they dangerous? Should we be standing this close?" Seeing the bars on that tiny window and prisoners on their cots in cells just a few feet beyond was far more exciting than Grandmother's apartment.

* * * * *

Among my vivid recollections are stories of family and neighborhood happenings that I had missed while in school. Here is one.

Peddling Eggs in Des Moines

Compared to the twenty-five shrink-wrapped pallets of eggs (about twelve thousand dozen) that now daily leave our Southwest Iowa Egg business in an eighteen-wheeler, the three thirty-dozen cases my parents hauled to Des Moines in the backseat and trunk of their 1936 Ford did not amount to much. However, Mother's four hundred-hen flock was a significant part of our farm business, and it was by far the largest flock in our community.

If Dad could sell those ninety dozen eggs, the last three days' production of Mother's four hundred hens, at a good price in Des Moines, that would cover the cost of the allergist's appointment for my sister, plus gas for the trip. Then nine, Lorraine had long suffered asthma, and allergies had been suggested as a possible cause. The eggs might bring seventeen or eighteen cents per dozen in Des Moines, compared to twelve cents at Joe Moore's produce or in exchange for groceries in Atlantic.

At the supper table, I would hear about their Des Moines trip, especially the sales pitch Dad had made to grocers after he cajoled them out to the car to see those large, fresh eggs. Working daily on the farm, Dad had a ruddy complexion. One of his favorite stories was the response of a grocer near the north end of Des Moines' Sixth Street, "What makes you think you can get eighteen cents; just because you've got a red face?" That may have helped; it was clear both Dad and the eggs were fresh off the farm.

* * * * *

Anytime during the summer that Dad left the farm for a routine trip to town, for feed, repairs, or other business, I would go with him. This time we saw some excitement.

The Runaway Truck

Dad and I had just come from Cloyd Jones's law office in the former Farmers Bank building, northwest corner of Fifth and Chestnut, and were walking west on Fifth Street toward our parked car. That bank had failed in the Depression, and the building's main floor had been divided into offices for two lawyers and a realtor; the second floor housed two dentistry offices and an apartment.

A truck rolling out of the alley to the south caught our attention. A second glance told us why: no driver! The truck rolled across the street, jumped the curb, and with a crash, came to a stop with the cab mostly inside the Blue Goose café.

A trucker had been unloading at Mayor Joe Burnea's grocery, uphill on Sixth Street. Apparently he had not set the brake, or it had disengaged while he was inside the store. No one was injured, but a midmorning coffee group would remember the day, with the truck's radiator up against the counter and its right fender alongside the booths.

Thirty-five years later I was in Minneapolis to speak to the presidents and directors of the banks that were part of the Northwest Bank Corporation system (now Wells Fargo). Northwest had just purchased a major bank in eastern Iowa, and I fell into a conversation with a member of that bank's board, an attorney in his midsixties. When he learned that my hometown was Atlantic, he recalled, "When I was just starting my practice, I had a case in Atlantic, defending a wholesale grocery company. One of their trucks had broken loose and run downhill into a café."

I could confirm his story. "I was there."

*****

Probably the most "colorful" language in the neighborhood came from Bob Woods. He was sincere and friendly, but his vocabulary would sometimes "turn the air blue."

Blocks for the Baler

Woods owned the only hay and straw baler in the neighborhood. It was a small, stationary machine, powered by an air-cooled Wisconsin engine, and equipped with a foldout table to the side of the bale chamber. Hay or straw would be forked from a wagon or stack onto the platform and Woods, standing at the table, would slide a forkful into the chamber in synchrony with a reciprocating tamper. The tamper shoved the forage down into the bale chamber, and a horizontal plunger from the front would pack it into the forming bale. In time, a tied bale would emerge from the far end of the bale chamber.

Woods was busiest in oat threshing season. He would follow the threshing machine from farm to farm, to bale up the loose straw around the edge of the stack, perhaps two hundred or three hundred bales at each location, for inside storage.

The forty-five-pound finished bales would be bound by two wires. A pay job for neighborhood boys was on either side of the bale chamber, one to poke the wires, each cut to length and with a loop at one end, through the chamber and a second, on the opposite side, to tie the wires.

A wooden block between forming bales in the chamber accommodated the wires. When a block emerged to where those two boys worked, the "poker" would send through its channels the remaining wire ends for the bale then in the chamber, and his partner would tie those two wires. The poker would poke the looped ends of two new wires through the channels on the block's opposite side to start the next bale. The tying job was clearly the senior position; beginners started by poking.

This afternoon, Woods had arrived at neighbor Bert Scarlett's new straw pile; Roy Theede and his threshing machine, plus the rest of the threshing crew, each with tractor and rack, had left for the next farm. I had stayed behind to drive Bert's little Farmall B to his granary with the last load of oats.

Unfortunately for me, Woods needed a wire poker more than Bert needed a tractor driver. I had heard Bob swear when a poker's wire caught in those blocks. The boy would yell "stop" to prevent an untied bale dribbling in pieces out the far end of the chamber. The baler mechanism would idle while Woods waited, his fork poised. Sometimes he would need to step down and do the poking.

Straw baling got underway with me sitting on a bale beside the chamber so I could poke wires. I had no trouble with the wire ends for the bale in the chamber or pushing through the looped ends of the next pair of wires. But a minute later the remaining sharp end of a wire got caught partway through, either in the straw or the block itself. I had to yell "stop." Woods stepped down and helped me get the wire through.

Through the balance of the afternoon I had to yell stop too many times, sorely testing Woods's patience. He would jump down, grab the wire, perhaps straighten the end, and work it through. I did hear a few muttered words, but my inexperience constrained him.

With the dew off the next morning about nine o'clock, I was back at Bert's straw pile, ready to face the day. Woods roared up in his 1939 Pontiac and pulled open the trunk. He reached in and threw down in front of me three new blocks made of clean white pine, each of its four channels lined with tin. "Damn it, Acker, see if you can get a wire stuck in one of these!" Though Bob's words were fierce, there was also a hint of a smile behind them.

* * * * *

The next year, Bob had added a pickup attachment to his baler. Farmers were shifting their hay harvest to bales. Bales were easier to handle than loose hay from the traditional hay loader, and more hay could be stored in the same space.

Bob had salvaged a ground-driven pickup mechanism off an old Allis Chalmers combine and somehow attached it to the front of his baler's feeding table. He had also built for himself a platform, suspended by chains, plus benches on each side of the bale chamber for the boys who would poke and tie the wires. He had even attached a section of drain pipe to hold the bundle of wires.

Perhaps thinking I would be better at driving a tractor than poking or tying wires, Bob had me on his little John Deere H, pulling his self-fashioned "pick-up" baler over acres of windrowed alfalfa or clover for Dad and neighboring farmers. More than once, from my safe and comfortable tractor seat, I would hear the wire poker yell, "Stop." I would reach for the hand clutch, and over the idling pop-pop of that little two-cylinder H, I would hear Bob's familiar words.

*****

Little did I know at the time that these farm experiences would make my college courses more meaningful, provide illustrations for classes I would later teach, and help provide an experience base for some of the judgments I would make years later as a dean or as a director of an agricultural experiment station. This next item is but one example.

Before the time of anhydrous ammonia or ammonium nitrate, animal manure and atmospheric nitrogen fixed by legume crops (such as alfalfa, clover, or soybeans) were the only nitrogen sources for enhancing corn yields. From our several livestock and poultry enterprises, we had plenty of manure to spread on the fields and, in our four-year corn-oats-alfalfa-alfalfa crop rotation, the alfalfa would leave some nitrogen for the following corn crop.

More Nitrogen and More Forage

Dad's drive to produce and more corn and forage for the growing livestock numbers on our 130 acres included an attempt to grow sweet clover for silage. Taller, with thicker stems than those of alfalfa, and with yellow blossoms, a single stalk of sweet clover in a field of purple-blossom alfalfa was considered a weed by some of our neighbors. However, sweet clover would fix more nitrogen than would alfalfa. As is true with most trees, there is as much root mass below the ground surface in crops as there is vegetation above ground, and the more root surface, the more bacterial nodules to fix nitrogen.

Dad's cattle-feeding program was based heavily on silage. Our two vertical silos would be filled with corn silage every September, and by summer at least one would be empty and Dad would fill it with chopped alfalfa or sweet clover. Often he would add one or two temporary silos, which amounted to a circle of picket snow fence, the inside lined with heavy sisal paper. As that circle filled with silage, a second and third circle of snow fence and paper would be added.

One of those temporary silos, in this case four rings of snow fence and sisal paper filled with corn silage. The three men posed for the photo tells they were proud of their work.

*****

Dad had long been part of a silo filling "ring" of five neighbors, each with one or two silos built for corn silage. Collectively they owned the stationery silage cutter and pipe, and functioned, as did the threshing ring, with the total crew moving from farm to farm as corn matured in September. The tedious job with each move was raising the pipe into its vertical position, with its curved hood over the top edge of the silo, and then securing that top end. After the silo had been filled, one could climb up the silo ladder, walk across the silage, disconnect the top end of the pipe and help those on the ground guide it down to its wheeled carrier. At the next farm, though, someone had to climb the ladder, "shinny around" on the narrow edge of the empty silo to the opposite side, catch a rope thrown up from the ground, pull up and fasten a block and tackle to a ring, and then guide the ascending pipe into place and secure it.

Dad was not afraid of heights, so it was his job at every farm to climb to the silo's top. If he was the last to arrive at the next site, his neighbors would all be doing a minor repair job on their racks or checking their team's harness, anything to keep from climbing to the top of the empty silo.

His move to alfalfa and sweet clover silage was not matched by his silo ring neighbors, so for several years, he paid more into the silo ring for the hours or days he used the collectively-owned cutter. Eventually, he purchased a used cutter and pipe that could remain at our side-by-side silos through the season.

* * * * *

That used cutter and making sweet clover silage would mean a new and difficult job for me.

My Own Heavy Words

My uttering of swear words was rare—perhaps when our universal tool, the crescent wrench, slipped and I skinned a knuckle, or when a cow swished her wet tail in my face during milking. This day, Dad had given me a job that might warrant more generous mutterings. He had put me at the feeder of our stationary silage cutter at sweet clover harvest time.

We then handled sweet clover for silage as we had handled alfalfa, windrowed the sweet clover soon after it was mowed and before it had dried. However, the taller plant with longer branches made the harvested material coming off the hayrack more difficult to handle.

My job was to feed that wet, heavy, and wadded rope of material evenly into the cutter. If too much went in, it would overload the spinning cutter/blower wheel, and the tractor engine would lose rpm (revolutions per minute), or the drive belt from our F-20 would slip off the pulley. The cut silage would not get to the top of that thirty-two-foot pipe, would fall back, and the pipe would be plugged. We would have to disconnect that pipe from the cutter, and then dig and shake ten to twenty feet of chopped silage out onto the ground.

If a big wad was on the way in, I would hit the reverse lever, tear apart the wad by hand, and then ease it forward. About the time I would get a portion feeding through well, the frustrated men on the rack would let a large wad roll down on both the apron and me.

Yes, I did use a few heavy words. Fortunately, the noise of the cutter and tractor, plus more experienced words from the men on the wagon, drowned out mine.

* * * * *

Though my story underlines the rigor and perhaps discomfort of the work, I am reminded now of sweet clover's pleasant smell. It was subtle but certainly distinguishing and no doubt the reason for the species' common name. What filled my nostrils at the cutter, with the juices exposed by the spinning cutter wheel, was even sweeter than that of the mass coming down off the rack.

There were other smells that I recall, each an element of my farm life that few people have the privilege of encountering. As I drive today past a field of newly mowed alfalfa, I will have the car windows down; I want to inhale that fresh aroma, the aroma that filled the air when I was mowing or windrowing in my youth.

Gardeners may know what I am describing as I also write of the smell emitted from newly turned soil, perhaps a combination of freshness and fermentation, mostly consequences of the microbial breakdown of the organic matter, corn stalks, or alfalfa plowed under a year and two years before, and perhaps of the earthworms and their body metabolism.

* * * * *

Dad was not ready to give up on sweet clover; there had to be an easier way to handle it. For the next harvest, we tried our ground-driven grain binder, designed for oat harvest; sweet clover in tied bundles should be easier to handle.

Dad would ride the binder to watch the mechanisms; I was on the F-20, driving carefully to cut only half the binder's cutting width. Even then, the mass in the binder's elevating canvasses would be so heavy that the machine's mammoth drive wheel would sometimes slide along the ground. I would stop and Dad would step down and roll the canvas with a hand crank to move the mass on up and through to the tying mechanism.

We still needed a better way, and Dad's search led us to a side hill near Panama, Iowa.

A Black Market in Farm Equipment

As we topped a hill on a country road a short distance out of Panama, Iowa, we stared in amazement at a side hill covered with shiny, new red, green, and orange farm equipment. There were tractors, corn pickers, combines, discs, and what we were looking for, several field choppers. It was the summer of 1945, near the end of WWII, and new farm equipment was scarce. For four years, most auto and farm equipment manufacturing facilities had been building trucks, tanks, and planes for the war effort.

Most farm equipment dealers had only used equipment on their lots. Any new equipment produced had been rationed to dealers, either by federal edict or voluntarily by the manufacturer. Dealers could only offer to put your name on a list for a possible allotment, or for the end of the war when production might renew. The allotments did not necessarily mesh with demand in dealers' areas and a robust "black market" had developed. Dad had read about field choppers for both hay and silage, and we followed a rumor that one might find new farm equipment near Panama.

The next week a new rubber-tired John Deere field chopper and a companion blower to be stationed at the silo were unloaded in our farm yard. The chopper had two "heads," one for picking up windrowed forage and a second for cutting one row of corn stalks and feeding the stalks into the cutting wheel.

Both pulling and powering the chopper, our Farmall F-20 had a big load; I often had to drive in low gear, to avoid losing rpm or killing my tractor engine. Two years later, the war over and farm equipment in full production, Dad traded the PTO chopper for a newer model with a mounted, air-cooled Wisconsin engine. Though the same size machine as the earlier model, it was a dream to operate.

* * * * *

This black market of WW II illustrates two life lessons. The first is the economic concept of supply and demand and that an open market balances the two. That side hill represented the market; the equipment had come from dealers where the supply exceeded demand, to western Iowa where demand exceeded supply.

The second lesson is that people, in this case the party who gathered that equipment, had both motivation and ingenuity to make a profit, even when perhaps afoul of government rationing or manufacturers' quotas. That lesson applies today to every *government payment program*, such as Medicare, food stamps, or loans and grants. A potential recipient may have both motivation and ingenuity to achieve maximum benefit, even if beyond the program's intent. The other party to the transaction, the government, per se, has no motivation and no ingenuity to limit the benefits to those intended; it has only the law, regulations, and salaried employees, plus the usually low chance for catching violators and imposing penalties.

* * * * *

When I would later, in my dating years, get permission to drive my parents' 1941 Ford two-door sedan instead of my 1929 Model A or the yellow Jeep that replaced it, I would note the back portion of the driver's seat tilted back an extra five or six degrees, and a pillow filled the void. What could have been a neighborhood tragedy was, except for several pain-induced chiropractic visits by my mother, a rather funny story.

John Holding the Crank

Mrs. Henry Arp continued to live on the farm that fronted on US 71 after her husband's death. She did not drive, but her brother, John, who came to live with her, had a 1930 Chevy coupe.

My parents had just turned south from our dirt road onto US 71 toward Atlantic when they noted John's Chevy coupe roll out of the Arp driveway at the top of the next hill and turn toward town. Then, John's coupe stopped; the engine had apparently died. By the time my parents got to the top of the hill, John had stepped out with his crank and gone around to the coupe's front to insert the crank and restart the motor.

Dad beeped his horn to alert John that he would just give him a push. John caught the message and, holding the crank, came around toward his door. He had one hand on the door handle and a foot poised to the running board when *bang!* Our '41 Ford was rear ended, and it punched John's Chevy coupe down the highway, Mrs. Arp yet in the right seat.

Two more cars were on the way. One swished by on the right shoulder; the next swished by on the left. My folks '41 Ford was at a standstill, and the Chevy coupe was several yards down the highway. John was still standing in the middle of US 71 holding the crank!

*****

An ambitious city boy or girl might be up early to handle their paper route before breakfast. And there could be an afternoon version to deliver. What was a typical day for me on the farm? Did work give me pride?

Work, Pride, and a Typical Day

At nine years I had been a steady hand for some jobs: in the summer, driving the Farmall F-20 pulling the hay rack, or leading a horse on the hay rope. In the evening, I would be balancing on a one-legged milk stool (a short piece of 2x4 nailed across the end of even shorter 4x4), squeezing and pulling milk from the teats of a Holstein while listening to the barn radio.

From the age of ten I would often be cultivating corn, and in time I would learn that if I pulled the levers to lift the cultivator beams "on the go," the beams would lift more easily. I could hold the steering wheel with my knee while pulling the levers, and once the cultivator sweeps were out of the ground, I could grab the steering wheel, spin the tractor 180 degrees, and drop the sweeps over the next two rows.

As I write this, however, I am reminded that I soon departed from that "spinning 180 degrees" to the next two rows. I had noticed and was impressed by an attractive pattern in a neighbor's field at cultivation time. He skipped a pair of rows each time he turned around, leaving a striped pattern as he worked his way across the field. Two rows of freshly tilled black earth were followed by two rows of gray, undisturbed surface. I adopted that striped pattern and felt a bit of pride as I looked back on my work. If cultivation was interrupted and I was up on a hill windrowing alfalfa, my eye would gaze down on what I thought was really rather neat, that striped pattern I had left earlier in the day. Yes, that F-20 was rather central to my life, an instrument that provided both challenge and pride.

Animals were another source of challenge and pride. Dad could milk six cows in a half hour, a full pail in five minutes from each cow. To do that became my challenge.

* * * * *

What was my typical day late in those WWII years? Sometime before six in the morning I would hear Dad's broom handle tap the floor register of my second-floor bedroom from below. If late fall or winter, that bedroom's cold was tempered only by heat that rose through that register from the dining room below. The house's first floor was heated by a wood—and cob-fueled furnace in the basement.

I would jump out of bed, discard my pajamas to a chair, and step into my shorts and jeans on the floor. In two other quick moves my undershirt and flannel shirt would be in place. Then it was down to the basement for a sweatshirt and bib overalls from the nail on a support post. In January, that second layer was essential, and over those I donned an insulated "army surplus" jacket. (I always thought it strange that army surplus clothes were available well before the war was over.) I then grabbed a lined, corduroy cap, complete with ear flaps.

Dad and I would each carry two washed milk pails to the barn, slide open the barn's driveway door just enough to squeeze in, flip on the light, and greet my dog, Sandy, stretching from his warm spot in a pile of hay. Dad would turn on the radio for the morning war news, grab a milk stool, and sit down beside the first cow. I would open the door of the small grain bin, fill a bushel basket with ground corn, and drop a hand scoopful in front of each of the twelve cows that had spent the night in the barn.

By six thirty we would be carrying four buckets of milk down the house basement steps to the cream separator. By seven o'clock the freshly separated cream poured into a five-gallon can and the skim milk carried to the hen house, we would be washed and at the breakfast table, usually for fried potatoes and two eggs, sometimes also sausage or bacon. The cream was destined for cheese-making at the nearby town of Exira, a five-gallon can picked up three times per week by a contract hauler.

At seven forty-five my sister and I would be at the end of the driveway waiting for the school bus. Through the war that bus was still a wooden body on a mid-1930s Chevy chassis. Those near the front of the bus got whatever heat passed by our gregarious driver, high school senior Lester Phillips.

About four thirty, my dog, Sandy, would greet us as we stepped off the bus. In the house I would grab a couple of chocolate chip cookies, change into my chore clothes in the basement, and head to the silo shed, a lean-to between the north end of our cattle barn and those two cement silos. During the day, Dad would have forked down from one of the silos a big pile of corn silage. I would open the east shed door and anchor the upper end of an eight-inch plank to the near end of a fifty-foot-long cattle feed bunk. Then I would fork perhaps four bushels of silage into a wheel barrow, push it up that plank, and starting at the far end, shake about four or five wheelbarrows of silage out for Dad's thirty or so feedlot cattle, by then finding their way to the bunk.

The next step was from a wagon stationed at the far end of that long feed bunk, filling a bushel basket with ground ear corn and spreading two or three bushels on top of the silage. For those cattle to finish well, they needed more grain each day than was in the corn silage.

Again, though my story is largely of the task, I recall my fascination in watching those calves' noses plunging into the tart and pungent silage, how they relished it, and when one thought he was not getting his share, would nudge his neighbor's nose away from his space in the bunk.

My next task was to feed the one hundred or so lambs in an adjacent lot. Because lambs seem to insist on feed that is fresh and dry, bunks had to be cleaned of any snow or residue from the previous feeding. Dad had designed and built reversible bunks that made the job easy. They were but twelve feet long, a foot wide, and low to the ground, so I could just roll them over, spread bushel baskets of chopped hay from a wagon inside the bunk, and then add shelled corn from a nearby bin on top of the hay.

By the mid-forties Dad had doubled the number of milk cows, and by the time I finished feeding the lambs, he or he and a helper would have the second group of twelve in the stanchions. H. V. Kaltenborn would be reporting war progress or other news on our barn radio as I helped finish the milking. That radio, the European and Pacific area maps Mother had pasted on the kitchen wall, and the daily *Des Moines Register* had kept us fully abreast of the war. At the same time, it alerted me to the size and scope of the world beyond Troublesome Creek valley, the Wiota School, and Atlantic.

By six thirty that second batch of cows given their dessert, a forkful of alfalfa for each, bedded down for the night, and the milk and cream handled, we would be washed and at the supper table. Supper might also be fried potatoes and eggs, sometimes pork chops or a roast. As a special treat on Saturday night, there would be a plate piled high with hamburgers.

A summer day's morning and evening schedule differed little, except that it usually started earlier and ended later. After breakfast, I may head to the machine shed, check the oil and water in the F-20, fill a five-gallon can with gasoline, climb up onto the F-20's drawbar and axle to fill the tank, and then head out to cultivate corn, mow alfalfa, or windrow the alfalfa cut earlier.

As I write this, I recall the viewing pleasure I had those days, the same pleasure I would have in later years, viewing terrace patterns as I would fly in a college plane over eastern South Dakota, Nebraska, or Kansas, or descend in a commercial plane toward the Sioux Falls, Omaha, or Kansas City airport. It was the simple pleasure of viewing a field pattern of windrowed alfalfa. Depending on the thickness of the crop and shape of the field, it may be one continuous, rectangular "spiral," having started at the field gate and raking one mower swatch around and around the field until reaching the center. Or, if the crop was light, it might be two widely spaced windrows around the field, and then similarly spaced windrows made back and forth across the field. Regardless, I saw beauty and felt pleasure and pride in the scene, whether I was on the tractor making those patterns, or if I was viewing the pattern from high on another field.

My favorite times were when we shared work with the neighbors or at oat threshing or silo filling time. Involvement of neighbor men and boys, and their jokes and stories, would make life so much more interesting. My concern on Monday and Thursday summer afternoons was that chores got done and supper over in time to get to the free movies before sundown, across the road from the Lorah store on Monday night and in Wiota's town park Thursday night.

* * * * *

During the war years, hired help was hard to come by. In the summer months, as well as before and after school, I helped fill the need. This summer an opportunity came along that increased both my role and my pride.

Doubling the Farming Acreage

I had not known there were Benton Township hills that were so steep. I was on newly rented land two miles east of our farm, with our Farmall F-20 pulling two ten-foot discs that would chop up last year's corn stalk residue. One disc was attached to each end of a heavy beam bolted across the tractor drawbar, the beam fashioned from pieces of an old auto chassis.

School was out for the summer; we had finished planting corn and had been cleaning our feedlot of manure the day before when the farm manager for an insurance company had stopped by. Insurance companies had been the major lenders on farm real estate in the 1920s, so when the Great Depression hit and owners lost their equity in the land, the mortgage holder became the owner.

The previous tenant on this nearby farm, 240 acres of mostly steep hills, had moved on to better land, and the farm manager had found no buyer or replacement renter. Would Dad plant corn on some of the better land, on a crop-share basis, and pay some cash rent for the hay ground?

With our traditional spring work done, Dad agreed. He called a neighbor, Vern Pigsley, to learn if he was available to plant the corn with his two-row lister. It was mounted on a small 8N Ford tractor, made two six-inch deep channels and planted the corn seed at the bottoms of the channels. No plowing was needed; we would only need to disc down last year's corn stalks ahead of the lister. Near Memorial Day and fewer than one hundred days growing time before expected frost, it was important that we get the seed in the ground quickly. On our way to the movie in Wiota's town park that night, we stopped by a seed corn dealer to pick up bags of "short season" hybrid corn seed.

After morning milking and breakfast, I was on the road with the tractor and discs. It was an exciting new venture for me; this would double our farming acreage. Dad followed in his Model A "farm car," and once I was in the first forty-acre stalk field, he helped me bolt that heavy beam on to the tractor drawbar and hitch the discs in place.

I took off for the first round, and when I got to the far side of that field, a ridge-top, and peered over the edge, I better understood why the last three tenants had each stayed only one or two years. Fortunately, that steep slope beyond was not part of the deal; it would lay untouched for the year.

Generous spring and summer rain brought good growth for three cuttings of alfalfa and two of red clover in the hay fields. There was an unexpected bonus; ten acres of timothy grass, intended for hay, was setting a good crop of seed, a high-value product. In late July, we cut the timothy with a grain binder, let the bundles dry and cure, and hauled them home for threshing the day we threshed oats.

Thanksgiving morning we finished corn harvest and calculated the yield, more than fifty-five bushels per acre. Fifty-five bushels today would be embarrassing, but for the time, the soil, and the fact it was second-year corn with no nitrogen from manure or previous legume, it was a yield to be proud of. It was an exciting year for me, and my enthusiasm for farming had grown.

Eighteen years later, using an inheritance of about $7,000 from my uncle and aunt, Shirley and I made a down payment on that 240-acre farm. In the intervening years, the eventual owner had built some terraces, seeded considerable of the land to grass, and in 1955 had enrolled all the land that was eligible in USDA's soil bank program.

* * * * *

Apparently Dad thought that at fourteen I was old enough to operate the corn picker in his absence. We had borrowed a tractor and disc from a new neighbor, Robert Wheatley, to help work that rented ground in the spring, so we were helping him finish his corn harvest.

Corn on the Ground

Our corn picker was called a "snapper" and was the lowest cost ear corn harvester on the market. It was a light, two-wheeled machine with twin rollers that squeezed or "snapped" the corn ears from the stalk. The ears fell into a pocket left of the rollers, were elevated up about four feet, and then dropped through a blast of air to the bottom of a second elevator, which carried the ears up and into the trailing wagon. There was no husking bed, a feature of more expensive machines, to rub and pull the husks off the ears. There was only a fan to blow away any loose shucks as the ears dropped from that first elevator to the second.

Every stalk had an ear, but the ears were small; most were what we would call "nubbins." (Wheatley's predecessor had little livestock, so there had been no manure spread on the land.) I was cautious and drove slowly, my eyes focused on the pointed snouts of the picker. A snout could easily get caught in one of the many "washouts" we crossed and get bent under. Or, if I turned too short at the end of the field, the near snout might catch and puncture a tractor tire.

I was just finishing my first round when Wheatley came out to the field. I stopped, and he stepped up on the tongue of the wagon trailing the picker. I heard him exclaim, "Where's the corn?" While he certainly had not expected a full load, only a few bushels were in the wagon's bottom.

We both then noticed a dangling clean-out door at the bottom of that loading elevator; a pin had fallen out, and a trail of those nubbins extended back up the row. Had it been me in my first year of farming and needing every penny, I might have used some of those words Bob Woods was known for. Not Wheatley. His only words, said with calm and evident patience, were, "I know there isn't much corn here, but I sure hate to lose what there is."

Two obvious lessons here: Pay attention to output, not just process. And when young people err, consider tolerance and constraint.

* * * * *

Farming is considered a high-risk occupation, and the next situation illustrates.

Three Thousand Pounds on a Loose Pin

If the hitch pin holding the hayrack load of clover bales dropped out there would be nothing between the rack's three thousand pounds and us. We were only halfway down the steep "Wheatley hill," with cousin Ralph Keller driving the little 8N Ford tractor. I was standing on the drawbar, leaning on the fender. The hitch pin was upside down, with its head on the bottom.

Bob Wood had baled the clover, with me driving his John Deere H, and we were hauling the bales home. Dad was cultivating corn with the F-20, so we had borrowed Pigsley's 8N so Ralph and I could get the bales home before night.

How a hitch pin could become upside down requires some explanation. Our hayracks and wagons had been designed for horses, and the long tongue had provisions for a double-tree at the rear to which the horses' harnesses could be hitched for pulling. The front end of the tongue was blunt, but with a lower projection about six inches back. The horses' neck-yoke, clipped at each end to a horses' collar, had a ring suspended at the middle that slid over the front end of the tongue. That would keep a rack or wagon from rolling into the horses going downhill.

To adapt that long tongue for tractor use, we would pin a clevis with a suspended ring to the tractor drawbar, back that ring over the end of the tongue, and then string a log chain snugly back to the double-tree pin. We had not considered that the Ford's drawbar could rotate; it was secured at each end only by round projections into the Ford's hydraulic lift arms.

As we had come over the top of that hill, perhaps while shifting down to the lower gear or as a rack wheel had rolled over a rock, the rack had lurched and pushed the clevis ring forward hard enough to flip the drawbar, and the clevis pin was upside down. No matter how it had happened, it had our attention.

If Ralph kept steady the weight of that loaded rack on the pin, friction would keep the pin in place. But should there be a momentary slackening of that weight, from a rack wheel hitting a rock or dropping into a washout, the pin could drop out, and we would be in trouble.

Ralph throttled down and we both scanned the roadway for rocks and washouts. He sought the smoothest route for both the tractor and rack wheels. We perspired, from more than August heat; it was a long hill.

A few days later, Dad modified the front ends of our rack and wagon tongues, replaced the blunt ends with upper and lower irons through which a pin could be inserted, the lower iron with a projection to catch a team's neck yoke ring.

* * * * *

There were few secrets in our family, but here is an event neither Dad nor I wanted Mother to learn about.

Mother Never Knew

It was a Saturday morning, and we were converting a gully on the newly rented Cornell farm, a mile north of our home farm, into what would become a grassed waterway. I was on the F-20, building a small dam at the head of the gully being plowed in. Our baseball team was to play in the district finals at Harlan that afternoon and the team bus would leave Wiota at eleven. Mother would pick me up at ten thirty to take me to the bus, and I wanted to finish the dam before then.

Dad and Don Albert, an Atlantic youth who worked for us, were plowing in the gully. Don was steering our newly acquired but used Farmall Regular, with Dad manhandling a walking plow at the end of a chain. My small dam would divert rain water to furrows along the edge of the waterway until newly seeded grass could get established in the waterway.

With a hydraulic-lift loader mounted on the front of the F-20, I would scoop up some of their freshly plowed dirt, raise the loader, back up the slope, turn left, and drop the dirt to form the dam. This load of dirt was extra heavy, so my rear tires had too little traction and began to spin. Impatient, I shifted from reverse to third and pulled opened the throttle. I would do a complete circle, to the right and uphill to the forming dam and drop my load.

I had the wrong combination, a tricycle-type tractor, third gear, throttle open, front wheels turned sharply in loose soil, and the loaded bucket raised too high. In seconds, my front wheels pushed into the loose dirt and my right rear wheel was off the ground. No time to clutch; it was rolling!

I jumped, the only way to go, over the left wheel. Unfortunately, that is where the tractor was rolling, though perhaps balanced for a moment on that left rear wheel.

From that point I have just two memories, two visions. The first is a split-second later, lying in the waterway and seeing that tractor rolling toward me. The next is a few seconds later, a few feet "downstream" in the waterway, trying to walk, but bent over and with a jeans cuff clutched tightly in each hand. How I had moved or rolled between those two visions, I do not know.

Neither Dad nor Don saw the tractor roll; they were plowing away from me. I caught up with them and grabbed Dad by the arm. He turned to see the overturned F-20 with one rear wheel still spinning freely.

After the shock and seeing I was okay, his first words were, "Let's get that thing back on its wheels before your mother gets here!" Mother continually worried about a tractor roll-over.

There was no damage to the tractor, and no fuel or radiator water lost. Only the tool box had emptied, and one cable guide had snapped off a hydraulic cylinder of the loader. The tractor had been righted no more than two minutes when my mother's car came over the hill.

I do not recall how much or how well I played that afternoon at Harlan. But we did win and were on our way to the state tournament.

To my knowledge, the incident was never mentioned in the community. Not until well after my mother's death thirty-one years later was it mentioned by me.

*****

It was not until fall of my high school junior year that I joined 4-H. Dad had reservations about 4-H's most visible activity, the county livestock show. Our animal operations were focused on converting forage, grain, and labor into milk, eggs, and livestock to sell, not for show-ring honors. We did not have the short-legged, blocky calves that would win blue ribbons.

4-H and Money under the Rug

My 4-H experience all started on a Sunday morning, helping unload several hundred sixty-pound feeder lambs from a railroad stock car into pens on Atlantic's North Linn Street. Though I was fifteen, I had just joined 4-H, and some of those lambs would be my first project. Finishing western feeder lambs, in units of sixteen, was a new project in the Iowa 4-H program, and our enthusiastic county Extension agent, Cliff Hardie, had latched onto it. More significant, it had gotten both Dad and me interested in 4-H.

Dad had another motive. Don, little older than me, had dropped out of high school after the death of his father to help support his mother and younger brother. Dad saw this project and 4-H as something tangible for Don. The lambs would need to be fed and managed separately from Dad's; 4-H required detailed records on the ration, weight gain, and handling.

By the first of January, with the lambs doing well, Dad's interest in 4-H had grown, and he took me in search of some good quality calves for a second project. We found three, two steers and a heifer. To buy my lambs I signed a note at the bank, but Dad financed the calf purchase, $180.

After we had finished our fall corn harvest, Dad let me help neighbor Ted Anderson finish harvest with our picker. I put the forty dollars I earned under the linoleum rug in my upstairs bedroom. Mother paid me ten cents a day to feed her hens and fryers, and Dad paid me a few dollars for Saturday farm work. Whenever I had accumulated a few bills, they went under the rug.

After the lambs were sold at a statewide event in Des Moines in mid-February, I paid Dad for their grain and hay, paid off the bank note, and had nearly one hundred dollars' profit. I could now pay off Dad's loan for the calves.

That night I went upstairs, pulled the accumulated bills from under the rug, and along with the lamb profit, handed Dad a stack of bills. I still recall his surprise, and, I think, some pride.

Earning and saving those dollars, and the resulting satisfactions, set my pattern for future years. We now hold only two credit cards, use them only for convenience, and the monthly bills are paid in full. I believe there is little merit in paying interest unless borrowed funds lead to a profit. There is rarely any merit in borrowing money for consumer items.

*****

The heifer calf won her class at the County Fair in August and 4-H gave me other good experiences. I traveled with Hardie to Iowa State for a livestock judging clinic and to Omaha for a marketing clinic, and competed two years at the state fair as a member of the county livestock judging team.

It was on a frigid February Saturday at that statewide lamb sale on the State Fairgrounds that I first met several Iowa State faculty. Animal husbandry extension specialists were appraising the lambs, and state 4-H leader George Boehnke was reviewing our project record books for completeness. These experiences would eventually help me decide I wanted to study animal husbandry at Iowa State.

A far more significant reward: At my first county 4-H fair, in August 1947, I spotted a cute and enthusiastic blonde and learned her name. Though she had no idea who I was, I found the opportunity to say, "Hi, Shirley."

*****

The gold border along the bottom of my left front tooth came with some pain. This is how it happened.

Look, Mom: No Tooth

My first years driving the F-20, I was not strong enough to turn the crank. If the tractor died in the field, perhaps from a too-heavy load, I could only walk to the farmstead or over the hill to ask Dad to come crank it. Later, when I could handle the crank, he taught me the risks. If the timing was a bit off, a spark plug could ignite too early, drive its piston backward and the crank would "kick" in reverse. If I held the crank as a baseball bat, the kick could break or sprain my thumb. I should hold my thumb alongside my index finger.

The second risk was a crank not fully engaged on the shaft. When the tractor started the crank could spin up and hit you in the face. Dad had secured the crank with a bent nail. However, during the winter I had run the tractor and crank into a feed bunk, bending down the shaft and the hanging crank rubbed the front tires. So I removed and stored the crank in the steering post bracket. Big mistake!

This day I was raking hay purchased from neighbor Lester Louis, just across the fence from our farm's north end. It was near noon, and I had just one round to go. Throttling down for a sharp turn, I killed the engine. I jumped down, grabbed the crank, rushed around to the front, slipped the crank onto the shaft (but not securely enough), and gave it a twist.

As the engine started, the loose end of the crank flew up and hit my mouth. My right front tooth and the back half of the left fell out in my hand. An hour later I was in Doc Knarr's dental office, where he affixed a bridge to the back of the left tooth remainder and pasted on an artificial tooth to fill the void.

The Acker farmstead about 1954. Note the Holstein cows and heifers and the two vertical silos. Beyond the barn on the left, expanded from twelve to twenty-four milking cow stanchions while I was in college, is a Jeep pickup that had replaced the post-WWII yellow Jeep. Beyond that is the henhouse for Mother's layers and several smaller brooder houses where she had raised pullets for the laying flock and fryers for dressing and delivery Saturday mornings during my youth.

* * * * *

It was the day I would see the great Satchel Paige pitch. But another experience, well before the game, would have a more enduring impact.

Never Give Up

The Kansas City Monarchs, in one of their last years, were playing in Council Bluffs and local attorney John Budd, sponsor and coach of Atlantic's "Junior Legion" summer baseball team, was taking his team to the game. Farm work had kept me out of the Junior Legion program, but there had been an empty spot for the trip, and somehow I had been invited to join.

Paige was said to be one of the greatest pitchers ever, but few had seen him play. Paige was black, and thus barred from the major leagues. By the time Jackie Robinson had broken into the majors, Paige was well beyond his prime. Several times I have visited the Black Baseball Museum, near Eighteenth and Vine streets in Kansas City, Missouri. It features not only Paige but hundreds of black players and dozens of black teams.

Today we would see Paige pitch. We were to leave from the courthouse parking lot at ten o'clock. I rode in with cousin Ralph Keller, a regular on the Legion team, and my mother was to meet us on our return.

I asked Budd what time we would be back in Atlantic so I could call that to my mother. I rushed in to Court Clerk "Skip" Skipton's office and asked to use the phone. Our party line was busy. After a minute I tried again; line busy. By the fourth time, it was near ten; the team would be loading, ready to leave. The line was still busy. I dropped the phone with disgust. "I give up."

Skipton heard me and would not let that comment stand. "Young man, never give up. *Never* give up!" I made one more try and heard our home phone ring.

I would not forget seeing Satchel Paige pitch. Nor would I ever forget Skipton's admonition, "Never give up!"

*****

That cute and enthusiastic blonde I had discovered at the county fair would soon become the major focus of my life. What was her heritage, and what had she been up to during my early and school years? Here is a glimpse.

In the Meantime

About the same time my ancestral Kimballs, Jones, Ackers, and Noyers were finding their way from England, Wales, Germany, and perhaps France to the

United States, and then through Pennsylvania, Ohio, and Illinois to Iowa, Shirley's ancestors were also settling in Iowa.

Her paternal grandparents Carsten and Christina Johansen Hansen had come to America, at different times in the late 1800s, with their parents and siblings from near Bredsted, Germany, just south of what is now the Danish border. Both families came directly to western Iowa and settled on or near the Wisconsin Ridge, high quality land northeast of the town of Walnut, Iowa. Carsten and Christina raised two sons and three daughters; their oldest, Henry O., was Shirley's father.

Less is known about Shirley's maternal grandparents David and Alice Kite Longnecker. Shirley's mother, Lula Longnecker, was but sixteen when her mother died. Her father relocated to Nebraska, and Lula went to live with her older sister Ada and her husband, who also farmed northeast of Walnut.

Henry O. and Lula married in 1922, and by 1929 they had saved enough for a down payment on an eighty-acre farm south of Walnut and west of Atlantic. Shirley, the second of three daughters, was born January 29, 1932. The farm depression and Henry's health forced the family back to Walnut, where Shirley started school in the fall of 1937.

By the following spring, the Hansen family was back on the farm, where the third daughter, Marilyn, was later born. Shirley and her older sister, Norma Jean, walked nearly two miles to Washington Township No. 4, a typical one-room country school.

After completing the eighth grade and a high school qualifying exam, Shirley and the township's two other graduates headed to the Atlantic high school. She and Norma Jean arranged room and board in a house on South Chestnut, about six blocks from the high school.

By the following spring, 1946, Henry had taken a job assembling farm equipment at Cappel's, a new John Deere dealer in Atlantic. They sold their farm and moved to a house on Atlantic's Walnut Street. The family would now be together weekdays as well as weekends.

Though it was not easy for farm kids to enter the town high school's social structure, Shirley's enthusiasm and humor made for some good and close friends, and observing teachers put her enthusiasm and skills to work. She typed and made copies of algebra and geometry tests for her math teacher, helped the secretarial instructors, and did art work for the school yearbook, *The Javelin*.

Her teachers recommended Shirley for summer jobs after her junior year, in the offices of the Atlantic hospital and the local popcorn factory. Her senior year, after school and on Saturdays, she was the lab and office assistant for a local dentist.

Washington Township had a strong 4-H program, then separate boys' and girls' clubs, and Shirley had participated in 4-H demonstrations and other activities. However, "town girls" were not allowed in township clubs, and no town clubs existed.

Though she was no longer a 4-H member, she had chosen to spend an afternoon at the county 4-H fair. I am glad for that.

*****

Shirley was not Dad's reason for trading in two Model A Fords, my 1929 dating car and his 1930 farm car as down payment for a new yellow Jeep in November of my senior year. But Shirley was delighted; the Jeep should be safer than my Model A.

Shirley and the Yellow Jeep

We had been dating since late September. It had started at a dance at the Grove Community Hall on US 71 south of Atlantic, with some matchmaking by mutual friends. They named the two of us, along with another couple, to plan the next dance.

This dance group had been an outgrowth of a county junior Farm Bureau organization called Link and Linkettes. Members wanted to dance more often than at their monthly meetings, and they needed more participants to justify renting the community dance hall.

Starting with the Link and Linkettes membership, all beyond high school age, they added names of some high school seniors and juniors across the county, many of them current or former 4-H members. The organization structure was simple, a shorthand notebook of names and addresses and a rotating four-member committee.

The committee would rent the community hall, borrow the county Farm Bureau record player, arrange a nearby couple to chaperone, and mail postcards announcing the next dance. The committee would provide a light lunch at the dance intermission, perhaps chili or hot chocolate and cookies, collect twenty-five or fifty cents from each to pay the bills and, after lunch, name the next committee.

My "Hi" to Shirley at the county fair and our dancing a few times in the group mixers that night had been the limit of our acquaintance. A week later, with that second couple, we set the date for the next dance, decided the refreshment menu, and addressed postcards. The night of the dance I picked her up in my Model A, and we headed to the dance.

It was on our second dance date that, from her home on Walnut Street I drove east to Olive, turned left and coasted downhill toward the stop sign at US 6. No brakes! I double clutched into second gear, slowed us enough to make the corner onto the highway. Fortunately, there was little highway traffic, but she was not impressed.

Dad had many reasons to consider and eventually purchase a Jeep, with two Model A Fords as trade-ins. His farm car had had a rough life, including a small fire from shorted wiring. Since it was our usual transportation from home to the rented farms, there were usually two five-gallon cans of gas or bags of protein supplement behind the front seats. I had used it to carry baby calves home from the pasture, their small body on the seat beside me and their mother following behind.

My '29 was in good shape. Dad had purchased it for me only in January and I was proud of my repaint job, black with red wheels. However, I was also pushing for a Jeep, the civilian version of the vehicle that WWII made famous.

Dad's major rationale was that a Jeep would be "another tractor." It was advertised as such, and with its low-range, four-wheel drive and solid frame, we used it to rake hay or pull grain and hay wagons. Where it really shined, though, was pulling a rotary hoe. At nine mph, the hoe did a great job of kicking out those small weeds in and between the corn rows, before the corn was tall enough for cultivation.

Dad added an aluminum top for winter work and for summer shade, and I added a radio. For serious dating, there was a problem; the two front seats were at least ten inches apart. I had spent my money on the radio, but Dad had sensed the need and bought a cushioned insert that bridged the two seats.

We would remove the aluminum doors and the cab's rear panel for summer field work, and the tail gate so we could watch trailing wagons or implements. For dating on warm summer nights it was a farm boy's convertible. For the next several years, summers and weekends home from college, the Jeep would be our dating transportation, whether to the community hall, a formal dance, a friend's wedding, or the skating rink.

That first summer, Shirley expressed interest in driving; she had had no chance to learn, and the Jeep was ideal. Sunday afternoons we would be out in our pasture, the Jeep in low range and Shirley behind the wheel. Little did we know where those driving lessons would eventually lead, from the cinder streets of Iowa State's Pammel Court to Germany's autobahn and Washington's packed freeways.

Chapter IV

The College Years

In later years, speaking to high school assemblies about careers and university preparation, I would use the pinball machine to illustrate my theme. Just as the ball bounces off the pins as it makes its way down the sloping machine table, so does a young person bounce off his or her experiences. His or her path is determined by what he or she encounters along the way. (Yes, there are electronic pinball games, so the illustration remains apt.)

From a positive experience, one may carry away success, praise, recognition, and satisfaction, and the "bounce" will certainly be different than from a negative experience, failure, embarrassment, or belittlement. Many experiences are a matter of chance, but good experiences can also be provided or sought.

Following are some of those experiences, or pins, of my undergraduate and master's degree years at then Iowa State College. There were many courses completed, including botany, zoology, math, physics, a year each of economics and English, rural sociology, journalism, scientific report writing, speech, several courses in crops and soils, a long list of animal husbandry courses, and at least seven quarters of chemistry. After that it was a year each of graduate nutrition courses, both animal and human, animal physiology, and several courses in statistics.

Each course had value. However, as in a work experience, factual knowledge is usually not the differentiating factor in one's success. A person's growth in his or her college years may be as much determined by personal interactions, pursuit of opportunity, persistence, and response to problems.

* * * * *

During my high school years, I had considered college out of my realm. But circumstances had changed that.

College Is Possible

My first exposure to the Iowa State campus had been just two years earlier. Dad and I had driven to Ames for a forage field day, and not knowing where it was held, drove through the campus searching for a clue. It happened to be summer term graduation, and graduates in their caps and gowns were posing for photos with their parents. That sight made a positive and lasting impression.

4-H experiences, though limited, had also exposed me to Iowa State staff at livestock judging clinics on campus, state fair competition, judging my calves at our county fair and the 4-H lamb sale in Des Moines. I began then to think about enrolling in Iowa State's winter quarter Herdsman Course, which a previous Wiota graduate had attended. However, after classmate George Stuetelberg mentioned interest in the four-year college program, my aspirations changed; maybe I could also do that.

I knew a sizeable debt remained on our 130-acre farm, so I was reticent about pressing the issue. One evening while milking, the time seemed right, and I told Dad I would like to go to college for the degree program. He was supportive, saying, "I would sure like to see you go if that is what you want, but we can't help much financially." That was all I needed. "I'll find the way," I said. But I had no idea how.

A May piece in the *Atlantic News Telegraph* announced that two Alice Graham scholarships would be available for Cass County residents graduating from high school that year or the previous year and attending or planning to attend an Iowa college or university. Competition for the scholarships would be by written examination.

The Graham scholarship could be the answer. The exam was scheduled in the courthouse the first Saturday in June and would take about eight hours.

Wiota classmate and cousin, Ralph Keller, and I joined about a dozen graduates of Atlantic, Griswold, Anita, and Cumberland schools. Could we, from the smallest high school in the county, compete with those from the larger schools, especially those with a year of college under their belts? We had good grades, especially Ralph, and our superintendent, Arnold Christ, had loaned us several scholastic aptitude tests for practice and experience. Still, we were not confident.

It was a Saturday morning when the call came from Cass County Superintendent Georgia Byrne, and Mother came rushing out to the farmyard to tell me, "You won!" With $500 per year for four years, college was assured.

* * * * *

Byrne's call had not disclosed the second winner, but by evening we had learned it was Ralph. He was heading to Simpson College, with arrangements already made. I could now go to Iowa State, but I had not yet applied for admission. There would also be the problem of finding a room.

A Visit with Coach Sutherland

Stuetelberg and I were in Iowa State Basketball Coach "Chick" Sutherland's office in mid-July; perhaps he would be interested in George, and if so, help us find a room. During the state 4-H convention in early June, I had submitted my application for admission. But campus dorms were full, and we had found only a few available spaces, in the basements or attics of Ames downtown homes.

At nearly six feet, seven inches, George would get any college coach's attention and certainly had Sutherland's. Sutherland hardly acknowledged my presence until we were ready to leave, and then it was only, "Anything I can do for you, young man?" He then mentioned a friend, owner of a cement block plant on South US 69 who just might have a room. We headed to the plant. The owner had no room for rent but called in one of his workers, Buzz Stewart.

We had hit pay dirt. Stewart and his wife lived in a two-bedroom bungalow ten blocks north of Ames's main street, 1521 Douglas, just two doors from the north edge of Ames's residential area and three blocks from a bus stop. We could have their front bedroom for five dollars per week each. We could use a bath in the basement, reached by a stairway beyond their dining room and kitchen.

In the end, George was not able to enroll, and I arrived at the Stewarts alone. They gave me two options: either seven dollars per week, or they would look for a roommate. I opted for the seven dollars. The Stewarts were gracious landlords, but by the time of my arrival in September, Buzz had started to replace the basement's north wall. Until Thanksgiving, as I shaved and showered each morning, a canvass tarp was the only thing between me and the neighbors—or, as winter came on, between me and the North Pole.

* * * * *

Not knowing how well I could handle money, the Graham scholarship administrator, a Council Bluffs bank, had issued the first $200 check jointly, to Iowa State and me. I had endorsed the check for deposit at the treasurer's office, so the university held the money, and I drew out twenty dollars weekly.

Mrs. Anderson

I pulled the deposit receipt out of my billfold, stepped to the counter in the Iowa State treasurer's office, and handed it to Mrs. Anderson. She gave me two ten-dollar bills, marked the amount and date on the back of the receipt, and handed it back with a smile. "I hope you are enjoying Iowa State, Duane; I know you will do well."

Most every Saturday morning my first two quarters, I would repeat that ritual with Mrs. Anderson and always left with a good feeling. Along with the twenty dollars, she gave me an encouraging smile, and in calling me by name, showed her personal interest.

With that I would buy a ten-dollar Union Cafeteria coupon book for $9.50 (the coupon book discounted to encourage its use) and pay Mrs. Stewart seven dollars rent. With eleven city bus tokens for a dollar, I could get along until the next Saturday.

After the Council Bluffs bank learned my first quarter grade average had been 3.33 (4=A, 3=B), and that I had enrolled for the second quarter, later checks were issued just to me. Each went to my personal checking account, so after my second quarter, I did not see Mrs. Anderson again until my junior year, when I was working part time at the meat lab. When I stepped to her counter to pick up my first payroll check she was ready. "Why, hello, Duane."

* * * * *

I was among about fifty freshmen and transfer students our adviser, Professor Bill LaGrange, had urged to join Block and Bridle, the student club for those majoring in animal husbandry, and we were being initiated.

Pucker Up!

"Pucker up now, for your reward!" The words came from a sweet, female voice that I assumed to be that of Norma (Duffy) Stong, a vivacious blonde and one of the few girls in animal husbandry and its student club, Block and Bridle. Though yet blindfolded and having suffered such indignities as slogging barefoot through what we were told was pig manure in the animal holding pens of Iowa State's meat lab, the invitation was captivating and I puckered. I figured Duffy would not be part of further indignities. I was wrong.

Several of my fellow initiates would become lifelong friends. Corby Fichter, from a farm near Shenandoah, and I would become fraternity roommates and best man at each other's weddings. Dan Merrick would become Cass County's longest-serving county extension director, national president of the County Agents association, and, after retirement, mayor of Atlantic. Packy McDonald would establish a successful meat brokerage business in Wichita, Kansas, and we would reestablish our friendship after I moved to that state. Bill Dubbert would later earn his doctor of veterinary medicine degree and be assistant administrator of the USDA's Food Safety and Inspection Service at the time I joined USDA.

My experience with those hog lungs I had taken to the high school science class, plus the texture and wetness that hit my lips, told me what I had puckered for—a fresh hog lung!

We forgave Duffy, of course; she had played her part well, and in time I came to love her. Duffy dated and married my fraternity pledge father, Joe Lyon, they raised a wonderful family, and she gained fame as the butter cow sculptor at the Iowa State Fair.

* * * * *

As I walked toward Beardshear Hall from lunch at the Union, I had fallen in step with a kindly, gray-haired gentleman who turned out to be Iowa State's dean of the junior college, M. D. Helser.

Descendent of a WW I Veteran?

Though I did not know it at the time, Helser had been a professor of animal husbandry and had authored the textbook I would use a year later for the meats course. Maybe that is why, after he learned I was majoring in animal husbandry, we had such a good visit.

As dean of the junior college, Helser was responsible for Iowa State's freshman and sophomore student advising program, as well as scholarships and student discipline. In fact, my formal advising visits with LaGrange, such as scheduling courses for the next quarter, were in a room below Helser's Beardshear office.

As we walked, I mentioned to Helser that I had a merit scholarship (I had applied for that when I applied for admission) which paid my first year registration fee and wondered if there might be other scholarships that could cover later-year fees. His response surprised me. "Would you happen to be a descendant of a World War I veteran?" His wording suggested he would be surprised if I were. Thirty years after the war had ended, most WWI veterans' children would have graduated, and their grandchildren would not yet be ready.

"I sure am!" My father had served eighteen months and was thirty-five when I was born.

Helser described the LaVerne Noyes scholarship, established in honor of a Noyes son killed in WWI, and added, "Come on with me to the scholarship office; we'll get you an application."

I was in luck; Noyes money paid my registration fee the balance of my undergraduate years. (Lake LaVerne, where Iowa Staters watch the swans in summer and skate in winter, is also named for LaVerne Noyes.)

* * * * *

It was midnight, cold and clear, as I walked along Lincoln Highway across snow-covered Squaw Creek bottom toward downtown Ames. A half mile ahead, I would walk north on Grand Avenue to Thirteenth Street and then east five blocks and north to the rented room I would soon be leaving. I felt good.

I Belong

By the time I had broken away from the FarmHouse Fraternity Christmas party, the first event I had attended since pledging just after Thanksgiving, and walked to the bus stop on Lincoln Way, the city buses had quit running for the night. That had not bothered me; my jacket and cap were heavy, and I would enjoy the three-mile walk.

Compared to what may have occurred in other fraternities or elsewhere in Ames that Friday night before final exams, it had been a tame party, with members and pledges playing cards in the library and pool or ping pong in the basement before a late lunch of loose-meat sandwiches, potato chips, and Cokes. Nearing the end of my first quarter at Iowa State, I felt I now really belonged, to a living group as well as at Iowa State.

At the September Block and Bridle Club initiation and barbecue, the ticket-taker had been club president, Dewey Lyon. I had learned he was also FarmHouse rush chairman, and as I handed him my ticket, I told him I had heard good things about FarmHouse and would like to learn more. Dewey was a bit taken aback; how would this green freshman know about FarmHouse? But Dewey was a poised person and quickly said he would be glad to tell me more.

Nothing I had read or heard about fraternities in earlier years had been good. News items covered only pranks, drinking parties, and initiation incidents that got out of hand. However, a week before I left home for Iowa State, local veterinarian Dr. Jim Bailey had come out to vaccinate several litters of pigs; I caught and held the pigs for him. We talked about Iowa State and after we finished the job, he asked if I had given thought to joining a fraternity. Though I had been contacted by members of two fraternities and had finally agreed to visit one during "rush week," my response was negative, and I told him why.

"There is one up there at Iowa State that is different, and it is called FarmHouse," he said. "It puts emphasis on scholarship, does not allow any alcohol in the house, and there is no smoking above the basement." That got my attention. My parents did not serve alcoholic beverages, except perhaps a cold beer after a hot day of oat harvest, and had not allowed smoking in our home because of my sister's asthma. Having grown up in that circumstance, I saw no redeeming value in either alcohol or smoking, and found no comfort or pleasure in a smoking environment.

Equally important, this information was from a person our family admired, a quiet, sincere, and highly respected Atlantic native who had returned to practice with his father after earning his DVM two years earlier. My first week on campus, I checked out FarmHouse, at least enough to know it was located at 311 Ash Avenue, south of the campus, and that Dewey Lyon was its rush chairman.

In the one fraternity I had visited during freshman days (time for aptitude tests, fraternity and sorority rush, registration for classes, and a senior-led campus tour to locate our first quarter classrooms), I mostly watched and listened. Smoking was common, but the sophomores, little older than me, were still learning and visibly awkward. The officers, especially the rush chairman, emphasized to me the fellowship value of fraternity membership, but I also heard several brag and joke about how much beer they had consumed at last year's big party.

FarmHouse did not participate in rush week; instead, the members would quietly identify a student who might fit, whether freshman or upperclassman, and invite him to the house for dinner. Recruitment was a cautious and considered process.

A few days after that Block and Bridle meeting, I was contacted by Dewey and invited to dinner Wednesday evening at six. In suit and tie—I was not sure a sport coat would be proper—I was welcomed by several members, some in suits and others in sport coats but all wearing neckties. Others gathered from upstairs; all introduced themselves. In a few minutes the dinner gong sounded, and I was guided by several members to one of four tables.

My impressions: Ages from mid-twenties, including WWII veterans who were likely seniors, to eighteen-year-old sophomores, and all well groomed. There was some kidding among members, but most conversations focused on me or the campus. I had recognized several from Block and Bridle meetings or Curtiss Hall, which housed animal husbandry, agronomy, agricultural education, and forestry. There were also agricultural engineers and veterinary students, who spent their days in other campus buildings.

One of the most vivid impressions: Al Zmolek's necktie with a perfectly centered dimple. *How does he do that?* I wondered. Mine, tied in "four-in-hand," the only method I knew, skewed to one side.

After dinner, several members excused themselves for a basement smoke or to go to campus for a club meeting, while others lingered for a brief visit in the living room (a lighted FarmHouse badge was above the fireplace, so it was also called the Chapter Room). Three or four members who earned their meals waiting tables at nearby sororities, Thetas or Tri Delts, then arrived; they wanted to meet the prospect. All were impressive, but it was Jim Thomsen's personal enthusiasm and good humor that stuck with me in the days that followed.

Two weeks later I was invited back for another dinner, and the week after that, I was invited to join as a pledge. The pledgeship would be a trial period, learning FarmHouse history. (The fraternity was started in 1905 at the University of Missouri. The key organizer had been Howard Doane, who later started Doane Farm Management Company.) There would also be two hours every Saturday of "pledge duties," such as washing windows or repairing carpets or lamps. If all went well, the "active chapter" members would vote on my full membership in the spring quarter.

I had briefed my parents of course, but they had to overcome the same negative perceptions of fraternities that I had carried. At Dewey's suggestion, my folks drove to Ames the Sunday before Thanksgiving for dinner with me at FarmHouse. They could not believe what they saw, heard, and felt. Could this really be a fraternity? By the time I arrived home on Wednesday for Thanksgiving break, they had fully accepted the idea of FarmHouse.

With three other freshmen, Bill Dubbert of Laurens (son of an Iowa chapter founder), Bill Myers of Beaman (whose sophomore brother was a member), Dale Hoover of New Sharon (state president of boys' 4-H), and several sophomores or juniors, I would move my belongings into FarmHouse before departing for Christmas vacation.

Tonight, as I walked those three miles, I felt good; I felt I belonged.

* * * * *

I was a seventeen-year-old, fresh from a Cass County farm and seventy-student high school, living with two veterans who had seen the world. Their maturity and common sense put the FarmHouse motto, Builder of Men, into action, and I was their subject.

Builders of Men

My first FarmHouse roommates were Guy Flater, veterinary medicine, and Bob Skinner, animal husbandry, both seniors and WWII veterans. Desks, chairs, and bureaus for each of us, plus a double-bunk bed were crowded into a third floor L-shaped room no more than 150 square feet. Temperature control was by a hot-water radiator and a swing-out dormer window. I had the top bunk and Skinner the bottom, while Flater preferred the sleeping dorm, a third-floor back porch with double and triple bunks wall to wall.

From 137 pounds at the end of basketball season, I had bulked up to more than 160 pounds, and Flater started calling me "Chub." Skinner, meanwhile, challenged me to get involved in the Block and Bridle club. From both I gained a few tips on dress; they showed me the "half-Windsor," the tying process that gave Al Zmolek's necktie the perfect dimple. Skinner even sold me a lightweight suit he had outgrown, so now I had two.

All but seniors moved their books and clothes each quarter, with room assignments made by business manager Al Bull. For spring quarter, I was assigned a second-floor room with agriculture (ag) journalism junior Dave Bryant, editor of the college student magazine *The Agriculturist*, animal husbandry junior Deane Rinner, member of two judging teams with workouts every afternoon, and animal husbandry senior Chet Randolph, public relations chairman for Veishea, the all-university spring open house and celebration. There were four desks and four bureaus, but only three chairs.

Though a pledge, I was never without a chair. Rarely were any of those three at their desks; they were too busy with their activities. They continued the "Builder of Men" effort and were good examples for me. They also briefed me on college activities of value, told me of both good instructors and those to avoid, and we talked often about life goals.

My spring 1949 FarmHouse roommates thirty-five years later. To my left are Chet Randolph, then host for Iowa Public Television's Market to Market, Deane Rinner, retired head cattle buyer for Wilson and Company, and David Bryant, retired editor of a Missouri farm publication.

* * * * *

With my first college year over, I was back on the farm for the summer. Bluegrass harvest would soon begin, and a company contracting for the seed had advertised for people with tractors to pull seed harvesting "strippers." Our Jeep would work, and the harvesting would be between first and second alfalfa cuttings, so I had responded to the ad and was among six hired. Pay was $3.50 per hour for the Jeep, fuel, and me.

Harvest Bluegrass or the Company?

It was Saturday night, the end of the first week of bluegrass seed harvest. Ricks of seed heads covered the closely trimmed vegetation in a "seed-gathering yard" just beyond the cemetery east of Atlantic. With our Jeep pulling two lightweight and simple seed harvesters over many acres, I had contributed to those ricks. So too had my partner, a fellow in his mid-fifties pulling three units behind his Farmall M.

Each harvester was an eight-foot-wide wooden box with hundreds of twelve-penny nail points protruding from a spinning drum across its open front. The nails on the drum stripped the heads off the bluegrass stems and into the box, so the harvesters were called strippers. The drum was driven by a chain from a large sprocket on the outside of one wheel. Compared to equipment for harvesting other crops, it was crude and simple.

Pulling two strippers, the second offset behind the first, I covered a sixteen-foot swath. I carried large burlap bags in the Jeep and periodically would stop, open the lid on each stripper, gather up the accumulated heads by hand and stuff them in a bag. Each evening a company truck would pick up the bags; at the seed yard, the heads would be dumped out to form the ricks. After two or three weeks of curing and drying, with the ricks turned and reformed several times by hand, the tiny seeds were threshed from the heads and re-bagged for shipment.

It was a refreshing change from college. The doors, back cab panel, and tailgate were off the Jeep so I could feel the outdoors and watch the strippers. I could even enjoy the radio I had installed.

My partner and I had covered many acres on several farms that week and had a good many hours to turn in at the yard. As we helped each other through a bluegrass pasture gate that evening he caught me by surprise. "Since we keep our own hours, let's just add five more for the week." I told him I could not do that and considered it a closed issue.

I had turned in my hours, had my first week's check in my pocket, and was greasing the strippers for the next week when my partner pulled into the seed yard. He shut down his tractor and walked over to the manager's pickup. I soon overheard a heated conversation. *Was he foolish enough to turn in more hours?* I wondered. I concentrated on the grease gun.

He stalked back to his Farmall M, pulled the pin and dropped the front stripper tongue, yelled a less-than-kind message to me, opened the throttle wide, and tore out of the yard at full speed. He and his Farmall M were not around the second week.

Postscript: Four years later, Dad was sidelined by surgery a couple weeks in late winter. He had hired a fellow to do the milking and keep the hog feeders filled but asked if I could get away from my graduate school duties a couple of days to be sure things were going well.

Whom did I encounter when I arrived? You guessed it—my bluegrass-stripping, tractor-driving partner. For two days we worked together. He said nothing about that Saturday night in the seed yard. Neither did I.

* * * * *

It was late summer, and I was at Camp Miniwanca, on the eastern shore of Lake Michigan. What an experience it was proving to be!

Cold Water and Clear Thinking

Though mid-August, it was cold at six in the morning as we did calisthenics on the sand shoreline. After a dip in the lake, we would be even colder. We would shiver all the way up and over the sand dunes to our tents, where we would grab a towel and head for a hot shower. Only in the shower would we quit shivering.

Camp Miniwanca was a project of the Danforth Foundation and our host for these two weeks was William H. Danforth, founder of the Ralston Purina Company. Danforth had invited each land-grant college of agriculture to select an ag freshman and a to-be ag senior to spend two weeks at the camp, with all expenses paid. Somehow I had been chosen during the spring to be Iowa State's ag freshman.

Iowa State's ag senior, Richard Schoenhair, Ralston Purina Founder William H. Danforth, and me in front of the "I Dare You" cabin at Camp Miniwanca, August 1949. Danforth's inspirational book I Dare You is prominent on my study bookshelf.

After riding the Rock Island from Atlantic to Chicago (my first-ever train ride), Saturday night in Chicago's YMCA, and a Greyhound bus to Muskegon, Michigan, on Sunday, I had joined the rest of the Miniwanca-bound ag freshmen and ag seniors at a Muskegon hotel. Monday morning there had been a fifty-mile bus ride north to the pole-framed camp entrance.

We disembarked and carried our belongings, in my case a big duffle bag, up the narrow and winding drive, over a sand dune and down into camp. In view were a rustic headquarters building, a sandlot with volleyball net, and a dining hall. Off to the side and among the few trees were tents on wooden platforms, similar to those I had seen in my dad's WWI Camp Dodge and Camp Pike photos. I joined five others in one of those tents and stuffed my duffle bag under one of three double-deck bunks.

The calisthenics and dip in the lake readied us each morning for a full schedule of inspirational speakers, good food, and Mr. Danforth's four-square-living philosophy: physical, social, mental, and religious. Perhaps as important, time had been set aside for deep thinking about our lives ahead, what we wanted our lives to be. My thinking, often while alone among the few trees, or in my bunk after hearing a good speaker, focused on college, Shirley, FarmHouse, career options, parents, beliefs, and convictions.

Both the lake's cold water and the inspiration of the camp environment induced clear thinking. I would leave Miniwanca more mature, more confident, and with more purpose.

Shirley and me in front of FarmHouse, fall of my sophomore year. She had flown to Ames on a mail plane from Atlantic for the fraternity fall party, the Farmers' Frolic.

*****

The FarmHouse policy of no smoking above the basement was one of the reasons I had pledged the fraternity less than a year before. Now, a departure from that policy was to be voted on, and it appeared I would have the deciding vote.

The Swing Vote

The circumstance had its beginning in September when FH treasurer John Patterson did not return for fall quarter. To my surprise, although I was only a sophomore and activated the preceding spring, I was elected to replace him and moved to join the chapter business manager, Harry Lowe, in his southeast corner room of the second floor. As business manager, Lowe was responsible for house maintenance, including the Saturday afternoon work projects our pledge class had handled. He was a junior in veterinary medicine, and spent most evenings studying in the room.

As treasurer, I would issue members' monthly house bills, collect and deposit the money in an account at the College Savings Bank, and write the expense checks after Lowe approved each item, including the housemother's and cook's salaries.

My only real visit with Lowe had been at the pre-Christmas party before I had moved into the house. He and I had gotten along well, until today, the day before Farmers' Frolic, the fraternity's annual fall party. Shirley would be in Ames for the weekend.

The pre-party talk about Farmers Frolic was the "passion pit," the basement pool room with light bulbs removed and the floor covered with straw. Dancing, food, punch, cards, and singing would be on the main floor. It would be up to each member or pledge to entice his date to venture downstairs to the passion pit (although in terms of passion, I suspected there was more talk than "action").

A suggestion had emerged midweek in the planning committee that the policy of no smoking on the main floor of the house be set aside for the frolic. Straw in the passion pit would preclude basement smoking. Several who smoked had said that on past frolic nights they had felt too constrained.

By Friday morning, the idea had generated a head of steam among several of the smokers, and strong resistance among others, both nonsmokers and some smokers. Such an issue would normally be settled in a Monday night chapter meeting, but it was too late for that. President Bob Crom decided the fraternity's executive committee should make the decision after Friday noon lunch.

It was only then that I learned the executive committee, specified in chapter bylaws, was comprised of the president, Crom, a nonsmoker and assumed opponent, the business manager, Lowe, a smoker and vocal proponent, and the treasurer. Having been in the house only two quarters, members knew little about my feelings on smoking and I was lobbied by both sides, especially by Lowe.

There was no way I could vote yes. I felt obligations not only to my own beliefs, but to those who had pledged the fraternity under its basic tenets and presumptions, as well as to their dates. My vote in the brief meeting was not difficult, but I knew discomfort would follow.

As I would experience in later roles, those who agree with one's action may give some quiet words of support; those who disagree will often be more vocal, more public, and more strident. Though I received some words of appreciation for my vote, there were also some bitter words, and, at the party, a few "cold shoulders." For the balance of my brief term as treasurer, through late January, Lowe and I were able to work together, but our relationship never warmed.

*****

Come January fraternity elections, there would be more fallout.

The Fallout

Election of chapter officers had begun with anticipation but had become painful and discouraging. But I would survive, and Joe Lyon, who had been my pledge father, would help ensure that.

The nominating committee had put forth a slate of officers, one person for each of a dozen positions, from president to sergeant-at-arms. Nominees for the top two were, for president, Deane Rinner, a senior scheduled to graduate the following December, and I for business manager. To move from treasurer to business manager was logical, and the previous year all committee nominees had been elected, so I anticipated the move.

Before discussion and a vote, each nominee was escorted upstairs from the basement meeting room. For president there were no nominees from the floor, and Rinner was quickly elected and returned to applause. After my name was advanced by the committee, animal husbandry classmate Bill Myers, a smoker, was nominated. Bill and I climbed the stairs to the main floor and time went by, enough for considerable discussion. Eventually we were escorted back down to applause for Bill. It hurt, but I could only swallow hard and accept it.

More pain followed, however. The committee's nominee for treasurer was advanced, and I was nominated from the floor. We climbed the stairs and were soon called back to applause for the committee nominee. That sequence was repeated for what seemed to be position after position, I was nominated from the floor and the committee's nominee was chosen.

Though I had empathy for each of the committee nominees, in that each had anticipated unchallenged election, I also had pain from repeated defeats.

Sergeant-at-arms was the final position. With so many members well schooled in Roberts Rules of Order via 4-H and FFA membership, the major role of that officer was to issue the call to breakfast or song practice. The retiring sergeant-at-arms had probably done more that night, escorting nominees up and down the steps, than in the previous twelve months. I do not recall the committee's nominee, but perhaps empathetic to my continued embarrassment, he may have left a message of withdrawal. On return to the meeting room, I heard my name and applause.

Still, the pain remained. As the meeting ended, Joe grabbed my arm. "Let's go talk." It was what I needed, and Joe was the right person—straight, clear, and supportive. Our visit in his room was short but substantive, largely his advice, "There is no value in focusing on the root cause of the election challenge; just be the best sergeant-at-arms you can be."

In the history of the Iowa FarmHouse chapter, I doubt if there has been a sergeant-at-arms who called members to Tuesday and Thursday 10:00 p.m. song practice more loudly, more clearly, and with more authority. Members would snap their books closed and rush down to the piano room just to save their ears from a second call. Nor, I doubt, has there been another year when no one missed breakfast because they did not hear, "Seven o'clock! Last call to breakfast! Doors close at seven ten!"

Myers did an excellent job as business manager, and a year later, I was elected to the post.

* * * * *

Though our family had not been regular church attendees, they did get my sister and me to Sunday school at the Wiota Methodist Church in our earlier years. From the fourth grade on, however, I had more interest in Sunday morning farm chores with Dad. After morning chores in the summer, I might be in the field raking hay or cultivating. In winter, I might be on the frozen pasture bayou, ice skates clamped on my work shoes, playing solitaire hockey with a walnut and a stick.

Religion in Life Week

If only my Wiota Methodist friends could see me now. This day there were a couple thousand students in Iowa State's men's gym for Religion in Life Week's centerpiece convocation and, as the week's general chairman, I would be introducing the speaker. What had led me to this role? Probably two things: (1) the penetrating speakers and discussions at Camp Miniwanca the previous summer; and (2) encouragement by my early FarmHouse roommates to "get involved" in student leadership.

Rev. Roy LeMoine, a philosophy instructor and faculty adviser to the annual event, had called in early fall for planning committee applications. Though I had not taken LeMoine's class, I had met him and was impressed, so I submitted an application. Perhaps I could be part of the planning committee. But, for some reason, LeMoine asked me to be chairman. With his help we assembled a very good planning committee. (One member, Ray Underwood, would later join Atlantic's Walnut Grove Products Company and, after we returned to the Atlantic area years later, become a close personal friend.)

Following the pattern of previous years, we had arranged, in addition to the centerpiece convocation, a full week of what were called matins. At seven thirty each morning in the Union's South Ballroom there was a fifteen-minute matins program, including a prayer and a short message, in most cases by a local minister or an upper class student. At seven forty-five we would be on our way to class.

Knowing and working with such a thoughtful and supportive person as LeMoine, observing the work of a productive committee, and being part of inspirational interludes in the lives of fellow students was a fully rewarding experience.

This group would spend three days with livestock buyers and commission salesmen at the St. Joseph Livestock Market, an award for placing high in sophomore meat and livestock judging contests. To my left are David Flint, who would become long time Vo-Ag instructor at Hampton, Iowa; Bill Dubbert, later assistant administrator of USDA's Food Safety and Inspection Service; Bob McKensie, who would return to his family farm in north central Illinois, Instructor Al VanDyke (who had been my first quarter animal husbandry instructor and a model for me); and Harry Earl, who later was in charge of buying all the potatoes for Pepsico's FritoLay. Flint and Dubbert were also in FarmHouse, and VanDyke was a Michigan State FarmHouse alum.(Reprinted with permission from Drovers/Cattle Network.)

* * * * *

Several of my FarmHouse brothers had worked with 4-H members and clubs as extension youth assistants the previous summer and had shared with me their experience. It was an experience I wanted, so I had followed up with the Southwest Iowa extension supervisor and had interviewed during spring break with the Audubon County extension director. The county office, in the basement of the Audubon Court House, was only twenty miles from our farm, so I could live at home and perhaps help with evening chores.

4-H: Are My Kids Eligible?

County director Dave Fenske and I had set three goals for my summer's work, develop a livestock judging team to compete at the state fair, get some boys involved in demonstrations, and, if time permitted, increase 4-H membership. The girls' 4-H activities had been taken over by two club leaders in the absence of a county home economist.

By late July I had spent time with each of the nine boys' clubs, in most cases both a monthly club meeting and a Sunday or weekday evening tour. The tours were family events, including visits to every member's calf or pig project and ending with a picnic or ice cream.

Of the county's twelve townships, two pairs of townships had combined clubs, and there was no club in Sharon Township. Sharon should be an opportunity to increase membership; I would spend a day or two scouting the township. I first asked Fenske and others about the township. Not only did Sharon have no 4-H club, it had no representative on the county Farm Bureau board, which then also served as the county Extension Council. (A decade later that would change. Iowa would make Extension a unit of local government, with an elected council of citizens.) Though I had become acquainted with community leaders in the rest of the county, I did not recall having met anyone from Sharon Township. My only "database" was a township map showing names of farmstead residents.

Sharon farmsteads were modest. There were few sizeable animal enterprises, and few roads were graveled. I would stop at farmsteads, ask about the family, especially youngsters of 4-H age, and make a brief sales pitch about the value of 4-H projects and membership. People were friendly and felt complimented by my visit, but I never received a "you bet!" response to 4-H.

At my third stop, I was taken aback by the father's response, "4-H? My kids aren't eligible. I'm not a Farm Bureau member." Though I rushed to say that 4-H was open to all farm youth, it was clear he was not convinced, and I could understand the perception. In my home county, Cass, we had referred to Extension agent Cliff Hardie's office as "the Farm Bureau office;" two Farm Bureau staff, insurance agent Jim Braman and field man Don Trumbo, also headquartered there. This Sharon Township father saw Farm Bureau, Extension, and 4-H as one. Neither he nor most of his neighbors were Farm Bureau members, so 4-H membership by his children was not something to consider.

I changed my strategy. By mid-August I found a Sharon township Farm Bureau member who, after some encouragement, was willing to become a 4-H leader.

My three-month assignment would soon end, and I would not be around to see a Sharon Township club. However, I had found the right person to take the lead.

* * * * *

4-H leaders and local farmers will always have my respect. In my three months as Audubon County youth assistant, they "saved me" several times. Our half-day livestock judging clinic was an example.

Let's Go

We had scheduled the judging clinic at Harvey Johnson's farm south of Gray. Harvey's sons, Keith and Lynn, were active 4-H members, and the family had top swine and Hereford cattle herds from which we could select four-animal classes of both mature and younger breeding stock for the clinic. I had cajoled a Johnson neighbor to loan four breeding ewes and four market lambs for the clinic and arranged a truck to transport them to the Johnson farm. The clinic was publicized to club leaders and in a weekly newspaper column, and more than twenty members came to participate.

It was a productive afternoon. The members would place or rank the four animals in each class and turn in their placing cards. Harvey and I would make the official placings, and one of us would then explain why we placed them as we did.

All went well until it was time to take the sheep home, and the truck I had arranged had not appeared. The sheep had been loaned with some misgivings, for fear they might be injured by the youngsters as they assessed thickness or finish with their probing hands. If those sheep did not get home in good shape and on time for evening feeding, I would be in trouble.

I knew the Henriksen family had a truck, and they lived only four miles away. Henriksen sons Dale and Norman had been at Iowa State my freshman year, and Dale was a club leader, so I headed to the Henriksens.

Neither Norman nor Dale was on hand, but their father, Clarence, was at the shop repairing a combine which had broken down with only a few acres of oats left to harvest. Dark rain clouds threatened in the western sky, and it was clear he did not need an interruption, but I told him my problem. Clarence did not hesitate. He just dropped his tools and said, "Let's go."

In my next forty years' work in Iowa, Oklahoma, Kansas, Nebraska, and South Dakota, I was never turned down by a farmer when I asked for help. Regardless of the request, whether a 4-H effort, a committee assignment, or lobbying legislators or the governor on behalf of university programs, the response was always, in essence, "Let's go."

* * * * *

To get at least a few boys involved in 4-H demonstrations was another of my summer's goals. Can there be satisfaction if your top participant does not win the blue ribbon?

Satisfactions of a Red Ribbon

It was not a purple ribbon, not even a blue, but that red ribbon Don Lauritsen earned at the Iowa State Fair was rewarding for both Don and me. Don's workmanship and clear oral presentation, in competition with participants from counties with long records of blue ribbons and with a demonstration project outside the norm, Don had won the judges' respect.

Choosing and building an item for demonstration, then telling an audience why and how they had built it and what they had learned, is a valuable experience. However, few of my Audubon County 4-H club leaders could recall having been involved with demonstrations. With the help of club leaders, I had identified ten boys I thought would gain the most from such an experience, and drove to visit each one. Six were willing to give it a try. Several chose to build a pig brooder, a triangular box with a heat lamp in the top and that would fit in the corner of a sow's pen. The newborn pigs would be attracted to the warmth, and there would be less chance the mother sow would lie down on one or more.

Don had a demonstration project in mind, but it was more complex than 4-H specifications suggested. He would build a model of a redesigned family farmstead, with buildings and drives rearranged. In contrast to the pig brooder project, the implementation would take many years. However, he was enthusiastic about the idea, and it seemed to me it would qualify, so I encouraged him to proceed.

We arranged a July evening event where each of the six would demonstrate their work. A local publisher, a teacher, and a Farm Bureau board member were asked to judge the demonstrations, award ribbons, and choose the winner to go to the state fair. Attendance was good, especially by parents, grandparents, and club leaders. The participants did well, Lauritsen's demonstration was the chosen winner, and the local paper gave the event good coverage.

Six county boys had gained demonstration experience, several club leaders had become involved, and a few weeks later, a state fair ribbon had come to Lauritsen and Audubon County. Yes, there was satisfaction shared by several. (As I now drive by the Lauritsen farmstead, two miles north of Exira on US 71, I see Lauritsen's demonstration plan implemented, and far more.)

* * * * *

I once asked South Dakota friend Bob Best, who owned office supply stores in Sioux Falls, Aberdeen, and Rapid City, how he came to start such a successful business. His response: "I got fired from the clothing store down the street." I did not get fired from Atlantic's new radio station, KJAN; the station just could not afford me.

My Radio Career

Though my college major was animal husbandry, I had always been fascinated by radio and had met several farm radio personalities, including WHO's Herb Plambeck. Further, three FarmHouse brothers had been successive recipients of Cedar Rapids' WMT farm radio summer fellowship, helping WMT farm editor Dallas McGinnis.

I considered applying for that fellowship for the summer after my junior college year, but knew other applicants would be far more qualified. Perhaps more important, I wanted to spend the summer in the Atlantic area, where Shirley worked in the Walnut Grove office.

Atlantic's new station, KJAN, might be my chance. Licensed for only daytime broadcasting, KJAN was started by a Nebraska minister who wanted to share the gospel. Perhaps the station could also use a farm reporter. I managed to arrange an interview during spring break and was asked to meet at the Tomlinson funeral home on East Sixth. Why at a funeral home? KJAN broadcast Sunday afternoon organ music and the funeral home had the organ; the station manager was handling that end of the connection.

I had made a list of some likely interviews, including 4-H clubs, extension field days, or outstanding farmers. The manager liked my ideas and agreed to give the farm program a try. A few minutes after six on the Monday morning after Iowa State's final exam week, I was at the station door. Ferne Anderson, one of those advanced Hawaiian guitar students I had admired years earlier, was the station engineer. He had switched on the power, turned a few knobs, and put a wake-up record on the turntable for the 6:30 sign-on. After the record, Anderson announced the time, 6:31, welcomed the listeners to another day of good listening from KJAN, Atlantic, Iowa, and the Nishna Valley, and pointed to me. I was in a little soundproof booth only six feet from his chair.

There had not been much orientation. Anderson had led me to the teletype machine in a closet off the lobby, where I tore off printed-out news stories that had some relationship to agriculture, and handed me some envelopes addressed to KJAN farm editor Duane Acker. I had asked the Omaha and St. Joseph Livestock markets to send me reports of livestock sales from the Atlantic area, and Iowa State's Extension office for their releases. With those materials, some clippings I had accumulated, and local farm and 4-H news I had picked up over the weekend, I was able to keep going until Anderson gave me the thirty-second signal just before seven.

KJAN's staff was small; Anderson and his engineer colleague split the weekdays and the weekends, Skeet Preston was the ad salesman and also gave some of the news, and there was a secretary/office manager. Bill Baxter, an Atlantic classmate of Shirley's and also back from college, had been hired for the summer to help with sports and news. Baxter was destined for a career in communications, first in the military and later in universities. His humor and antics, egged on by Anderson, would keep the place lively.

Soon after eight in the morning Preston took me to Atlantic's main street to introduce me to potential farm show sponsors as the station's "new farm editor." But no one we talked to had heard my show! Most still had their radios tuned to Des Moines, Omaha, or Shenandoah's KMA. "Listen this noon," Preston would urge. "I'll check back tomorrow to see what you think."

Regardless of Preston's difficulty in finding sponsors, I was having fun. My mailbox was full every day, the clattering teletype disgorged plenty of useful material, and there was local news that I could use.

What I enjoyed most were the interviews in the country. I took the station's portable tape recorder (the size of a large carry-on suitcase) to an Audubon county 4-H club meeting, the local Franklin township club tour, a drainage tiling machine at work on the Turkey Creek bottom south of Atlantic, and a drainage ditch being blasted southwest of Marne. Turning up the recorder volume, I caught the clicking and scraping of the tiling machine or the full thunder of the dynamite blast.

The recorder's power source in the field was a transformer that I would set on my car fender and connect to the car battery. I would remove the recorder lid, place an eight-inch reel of tape on one spool, and thread the tape through the recording mechanism to a take-up reel on the second spool. Back at the station, I would hand the tape to Ferne, who would rethread it on his equipment.

This was to be my summer job, but at the end of the first week, Preston had found no sponsor for my 6:30 a.m. and 12:30 p.m. farm news and interview shows. I was cut back to half time, to just the 6:30 program. As the end of the second week approached, sponsors were still not standing in line. The first and only sponsor to sign on was local veterinarian, Dr. Ross Bailey, a contemporary of my dad's. No doubt his sponsorship was more a generous gesture than a need for advertising. I had to consider, "Should I hope to stay on half time or start looking for another job?"

I called for a visit with E. A. Kelloway, president of Walnut Grove, the local feed manufacturing company. It was fortunate timing; Walnut Grove had just purchased eighty acres southwest of Atlantic for a research farm, and Kelloway needed someone to dig postholes and build fence.

* * * * *

It was probably fortunate that KJAN could not afford me. Building fence at Walnut Grove's research farm was a valuable step on a track toward eventual graduate study in animal nutrition, and from there, a university career.

The Birth of 4x4

We were in the office of Walnut Grove's assistant sales managers, Clair Becker and Darryl "Wag" Waggoner (who had been Atlantic's vo-ag instructor and had also refereed many of our Wiota basketball games). It was the only room in the Walnut Grove headquarters on Atlantic's Linn Street that would comfortably hold eight people. In addition to Becker and Waggoner, there was President Kelloway, sales manager Howard "Herb" Herbert, new director of public relations Joe O'Connor, my former school superintendent and coach, and two men from an Omaha advertising agency. We were there to find a name for a new line of livestock and poultry feed supplements that Walnut Grove would manufacture and market. It would be a brainstorming session. Hired to build fence, I felt especially privileged to be invited.

Being connected to Walnut Grove was "a natural" for me. At the end of Dr. Damon Catron's animal nutrition course the previous fall, he had offered class members the opportunity to do a "special problem" for college credit at the swine nutrition farm, and I followed up. Catron assigned me a batch of pigs and three pens and guided me in formulating three different rations to demonstrate progress in swine nutrition since the 1930s. I would be at the farm part of almost every day the balance of that year, working with graduate students and gaining experience in what was essential for valid animal research.

Walnut Grove (the company) was started in the early 1920s by Warren Kelloway on his farm east of Anita. He had found that extra minerals improved hog performance, had formulated and marketed a mix of minerals to neighbors, and eventually established an office and mixing plant in Anita. As demand grew, the company needed both financing and larger facilities, and several Atlantic residents agreed to invest if the business moved to Atlantic. In early 1949, Kelloway's son, Everett (E. A.), had "come back home" from his job as head of the Omaha Livestock Market Foundation to run the company. Kelly, as he was called, was leading it into new territory.

My first day with Walnut Grove, Waggoner and I drove out into the middle of the previous landowner's remaining oats crop on that newly acquired land, and with a spade, we marked where we would place the corner posts for four pigpens.

By early August, Kelly's son and my partner, Pete, and I had four pens of pigs on experiment, with two being fed corn and the new supplement the company would market and two on a simpler "control" ration.

My first weeks at the farm, I carried my lunch, but when Pete joined the project, Kelly and his gracious wife, Dottie, invited me to have lunch with them and Pete each day at their adjacent home. One day at lunch, Kelly suggested that the next morning I should come to the office rather than the farm; their advertising agency people would be in town to help find a name for that new line of feed supplements.

* * * * *

It did not take long for the group to get down to business. The first step was for Kelly and others to educate the two agency men on the new product, a line of supplements high in protein but also containing other valuable components. The agency men suggested ground rules for brainstorming: "Toss out a lot of ideas, no criticizing or rejecting, and let more ideas build on those already on the table. Don't rush it. It will evolve."

Discussion progressed through the morning, encompassing attributes of the product, quality control in manufacturing, value of the Walnut Grove name, what farmer customers look for, and farmers' reservations about new products. It became apparent that Kelly had been through such a process before. Neither he nor the agency people rushed things. They let ideas flow. I listened.

Lunch break in the Whitney Hotel tea room was another thrill. At nearby tables were some of Atlantic's business leaders and lawyers; I had delivered my mother's dressed fryers to their homes on Saturdays, never visualizing myself sitting in the same dining room as them.

Back at work in Wag's and Becker's office, things began to crystallize. Four major attributes of these new supplements that would "ring important" to farmer buyers were highlighted: protein, vitamins, antibiotics, and minerals. Discussion then moved to items that farmers respect, that do not fail, that are sturdy and dependable. Maybe there was a "hook" of some kind there. The brainstorming ranged from dependable draft horses to durable equipment to heavy barn beams. Another focus was balance and the term, four-square, or the four legs of a table.

By mid-afternoon the suggestions and discussion had crystallized into the term "4x4." Every farmer has respect for a 4x4. It is solid and dependable. It is balanced, with the same dimension on all four sides. Most important, in terms of the new Walnut Grove product line, it would highlight the products' four major attributes.

Years later, as I would spot Walnut Grove's large delivery trucks with the Walnut Grove "4 x 4" logo emblazoned across the front on Iowa, Kansas, Nebraska, or South Dakota highways, I would recall this day with considerable pride and appreciation.

I later learned that Shirley, known by her Walnut Grove coworkers as a budding artist, had been asked to do some sketches of a "4x4" bag design for the new supplements. She disclaims any credit, though, for the final logo design that would appear.

(The Walnut Grove company was purchased by W.R. Grace in 1964, in large part for Walnut Grove's large and effective sales force that might handle Grace's fertilizer products as well as livestock and poultry feed. In 1991, Walnut Grove was purchased by Cargill and became part of that company's animal nutrition business.)

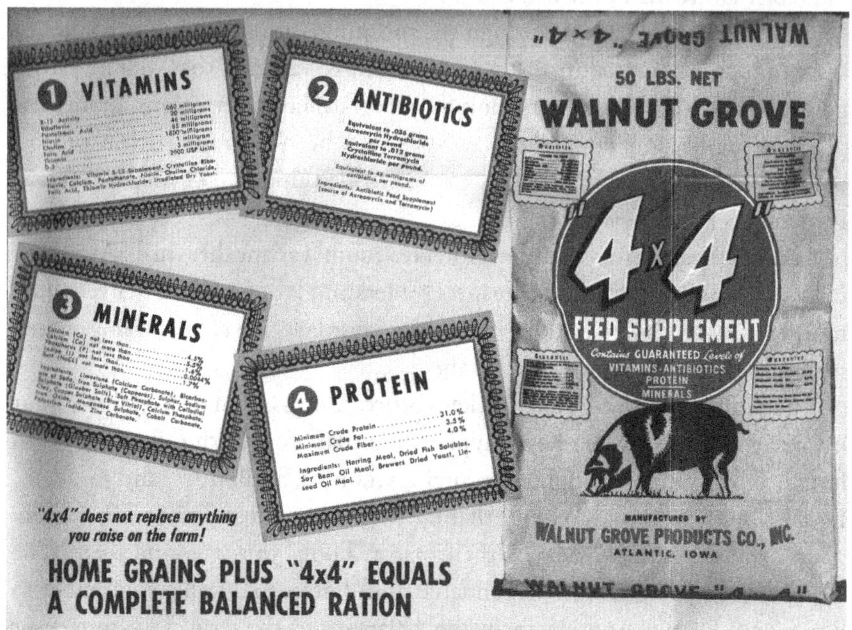

A portion of a fold-out brochure announcing Walnut Grove's new line of 4x4 supplements for hogs, cattle, and sheep, and highlighting the attributes of the products. It had been mailed to Shirley and me at our Ames Pammel Court address, likely in April of 1952, about six months after the brainstorming session. (Reprinted with permission of Cargill, Incorporated ©)

Another portion of that brochure. The left photo includes Shirley at her desk and typewriter in the Walnut Grove office where she calculated salesmen's commissions. Shown in the right photo are the pens and watering platforms Pete Kelloway and I had built, the hog houses we had put in place, and the scale house we had designed at the Walnut Grove research farm. (Reprinted with permission of Cargill, Incorporated ©.)

* * * * *

Monthly house bills in FarmHouse showed separate charges for room and meals. Because some members living outside the house took their meals with us and several in the house earned their meals waiting tables at sororities, treasurer Corby Fichter and I, as business manager, had projected input costs for each and billed members accordingly. In the process, I may have tightened up too much on the food budget.

The Beans Go or Acker Goes

Though that statement by Ted Hutchcroft in our Monday night fraternity house meeting may have been made partly in jest, it summarized with clarity the recent complaints about meals. Beans are high in protein and vitamins, but Iowa farm boys want more meat with their potatoes. As business manager, I had been cautious with the food budget. Even more cautious was our housemother, Mrs. Hazel Anthony, who, with the cook, planned the menus.

Mrs. Anthony's caution with our food money was not new. I had landed a table-waiting job my second quarter in FarmHouse. Boxes of cereal, quart cans of juice, and three-gallon cans of milk our cook had placed on the dumb water would be pulled up from the basement kitchen. We would set the table with spoons, a small plate, and a glass of juice at each plate. Bowls, cereal, and glasses for milk were on a separate table. We would open the dining room door at 7:00 a.m. and close it at 7:10, guaranteeing we could wash the dishes, clean up, and make it to an 8:00 class.

Mrs. Anthony had spotted a special on sauerkraut juice. When head waiter Joe Lyon saw the cans of sauerkraut juice, he predicted this would be a fun morning, and it was. The fellows filed in, poured out a bowl of cereal, found a place to sit, nodded a sleepy "good morning" to others, and then it was "down the hatch" with what each assumed was grapefruit juice. After their shock, each would watch new arrivals and their wake-up surprise.

Soon after I became business manager, our cook had to cut back to handling only the evening meal. I mentioned this to Bob Nipp, a fellow student working at the swine research farm (and who would later be Atlantic's vo-ag instructor). Bob offered, "My mother-in-law just arrived from Latvia; maybe she would help, at least temporarily. She does not speak English, but my wife could come a couple days and translate." I was grateful for the suggestion; it was worth a try.

The first morning's breakfast was great, a big pot of steaming oatmeal. It was like home. However, at noon the main course, piled high on large serving plates at each table were hot, gray patties that did not appear to be salmon cakes or hamburger. There were also plates of butter, bowls of sugar, and pitchers of syrup.

Yes, it was oatmeal cakes—good food but unfamiliar. Having worked in the serving room, I knew the waiters were watching and smiling behind that serving room door window. However, I had hired the cook, and my fellow members at the tables were not smiling.

After Hutchcroft's comment about beans and the applause that followed, I arranged time with Mrs. Anthony to review the food budget and menu. And I did find a full-time cook.

* * * * *

For the Little International Livestock Show three years earlier, I had chosen to fit and show a Holstein cow and learned that showmanship competition was not my forte. This year I was having more satisfaction as the show's general chairman and was confident the show would go well, but I was in for a big surprise.

A Horse with a Big Foot

It was near nine thirty on a Monday evening in the college's small livestock arena. The Little International's draft horse showmanship class was the last to be judged before the winners in each species would compete for the evening show's grand champion showmanship trophy. Dairy competition had been held that afternoon at the college dairy farm. Since six thirty, the student contestants had been presenting college-owned sheep, hogs, beef cattle, and horses they had fitted. The small arena was packed, and the seats were getting uncomfortable.

My committee, with superintendents for each species and subcommittee chairs for publicity, prizes, and other functions, was fantastic. At weekly coordinating meetings, each superintendent and subcommittee chair had reported good progress, and everything had happened on schedule. I was especially proud we had attracted Mal Hanson, the popular farm editor of Omaha's radio station, WOW, as master of ceremonies. My parents and Shirley's parents had driven to Ames for the show.

Superintendents had arranged judges for their species, each experienced in judging showmanship. We had hosted them at a five-thirty dinner in the Union and briefly reviewed their tasks, especially the need to handle each class with dispatch.

The draft horses were in the ring, stretched and poised by their showmen, for Mr. Good, a long-time Belgian breeder and judge from nearby Ogden. His experience was evident; though well along in years, he worked quickly, studied each animal, and then had each student move his or her horse to the far end of the ring and back. Differences were evident in how the students handled their animals. Mr. Good directed the animals and showmen into what appeared to be a reasonable order. He took the microphone to explain his placing to the audience, but then walked to the far end of the line!

What is going on? I thought.

When Good spoke his first words into the microphone, "I like a horse with a big foot," I knew. He had judged the horses instead of showmanship!

In short order, Good completed his comments and ribbons were handed to mostly stunned competitors as they led their animals out of the ring.

In a show ring, the judge rules. Though Good made some generous comments about the fitting and showmanship by several handlers, it was clear to all that he had had a lapse regarding his job and the show's purpose; he had judged the animals. There were some gasps in the crowd and some astonished looks on contestants' faces, but there was nothing the horse superintendent, MC Mal Hanson, or I could do.

Two management lessons for me: (1) regarding my committee, pick good people and they will do the job well; and (2) expect the unexpected.

*****

My name was not on the posted four-man squad for the international meat judging contest in Chicago, the World Series of the meat judging year. The previous January, I had placed high in several classes at the Ft. Worth contest and had done well in the Kansas City contest early in the fall, but I had now been replaced on the team.

Is Life Fair?

It was probably my own fault. During recent workouts in meat coolers at Morrell's in Ottumwa, Wilson's in Cedar Rapids, or Iowa Pack in Des Moines, I had sometimes focused more on the antics of a classmate than on the cuts or carcasses being judged.

In a typical contest, we would judge classes of four meat cuts, such as hams, pork bellies, and beef chucks or loins, plus classes of four pork, beef, and lamb carcasses. On a small card we would rank the four according to ratio of lean muscle to fat, abundance and dispersion of "marbling" (fine flakes of fat in the lean), and, especially with pork, firmness, the degree to which the cut or carcass held its shape. Then we handed the card to our coach, Ed Kline.

We would also record on a grading sheet our judgment as to the USDA grade (prime, choice, standard, etc.) for twenty numbered beef carcasses and ten lamb carcasses, including whether high, medium, or low within its grade. Judgment precision was the goal. We had studied colored photos for each grade and federal graders in the plants would spend time with us during workouts.

In the long rides home from the Ottumwa, Des Moines, or Cedar Rapids plants, we would discuss the classes and our placings and grading. Early in the season, one of my classmates had difficulty getting his carcass grading sights "calibrated." If he got on target with the first carcass, he would have almost a perfect score. Some days, though, he would miss the first carcass by as much as a full grade, and the rest the same.

In later weeks, as we studied a class of meat cuts or started down a line of carcasses to grade, he would inch his way behind Kline's shoulder as Kline recorded his "official" placing or grades. He would then back off, and his eraser would be at work on his grading sheet.

Others also noticed, of course, and for several of us it became an obsession. We could not figure out why Kline did not notice. But Kline was a kind and trusting soul, concentrating only on his own grading or placing.

My heart sank as I read the Chicago list. Not only was I absent, the fellow who had spent so much time behind the coach's shoulder was on the list. *Is life fair?* I wondered.

Besides my disappointment, I knew that a few years earlier at the Chicago contest, Iowa State's team had been disqualified because a team member was seen looking over the official judge's shoulder. Neither Kline nor Iowa State could afford another disqualification. Should I convey to Kline our observations? If I told him, it could be interpreted as "sour grapes" or, at least, jealousy. If I did tell him, should I identify the person? I struggled with that, and in the end, I decided I could not keep quiet.

Monday afternoon I went to Kline's meat lab office. "You know I am disappointed I'm not going to Chicago and you might assume what I will say is sour grapes, but you need to know that one of the four team members, and I will not tell you which one, has been getting some of his carcass grades and class placings over your shoulder during the workouts."

It was an awkward visit, of course, and brief. Kline thanked me for being willing to come in, and I wished him and the team well in Chicago.

How did the team do? They won the contest. Not only that, the object of our obsession in team workouts ranked high; he had accurately calibrated his sights early in the contest. I have no doubt the team did better than if I had been a member.

Postscript: Years later I encountered that classmate as I walked through one of my state's major meat processing plants with the plant manager. It was near the rear of the plant, in a fifty-degree meat cutting room, an environment where I certainly would not want to spend my day. He was foreman of a production crew and apparently had been for some time.

As I drove back to our beautiful campus, with the stimulation of university faculty and students, and rewarding relationships statewide, I thought, *Maybe life is fair.*

*****

Back on campus after the summer with Walnut Grove, I had enrolled for another three credit "special problem" under Catron.

The Next Step

Catron assigned me four pens of pigs for comparing the feeding value of high-oil corn versus regular corn, two pens on each. In addition, along with graduate students who abstracted pertinent research papers from journals, I abstracted papers that appeared in the *Journal of Nutrition*. The abstracts were then typed, reproduced, and distributed to related faculty and graduate students. Catron also invited me to attend the Monday four o'clock graduate nutrition seminars. He was getting me on a path toward graduate study, and I was enjoying it.

Catron consulted for Walnut Grove as well as other feed and ingredient companies and by midwinter had convinced Walnut Grove to finance a graduate research assistantship, and he offered it to me. It would pay $125 per month and, with Shirley and me planning our wedding immediately after my March graduation, Catron topped it off with an offer to Shirley as a secretary in his office at $135 per month. An important plus was that Shirley would know my fellow graduate students and the discipline; she would be typing and reproducing the abstracts.

My goal was to become a feed company nutritionist, formulating rations or supplements to complement grain and forage, for Walnut Grove or some other company. Only the larger companies, such as Ralston Purina, then had a staff of trained nutritionists, and I saw growth for the profession.

Our wedding party including Shirley's sister Norma Jean as maid of honor and Corby Fichter as my best man.

* * * * *

Less than two hours after Shirley and I had exchanged wedding vows, my bride was sitting on the counter of a little café on the west edge of Atlantic, with FarmHouse brother Regis Voss and brother-in-law Glen Jones telling her she had to bark like a dog in order to be taken back to her new husband.

My Bride Kidnapped!
Sunday, March 23, 1952

After the reception, we had driven back to Shirley's parents' home. I let her out at the walkway cleared of snow and drove ahead so others in the party would not need to wade through snow. Big mistake!

Glen and Regis drove forward, Regis grabbed Shirley, and they were off. By the time I retrieved the car keys from my pocket, they were around the corner and gone; no way could I catch them. We would be headed to Des Moines over snow-covered roads, so I drove down to a gas station to have chains installed on my 1949 Ford.

It was a memorable day, not only for the ceremony that united us but for the beauty of the bride, the friends who attended us, and the more-than-generous congratulatory gifts. We appreciated even more the many who had overcome snow-packed roads to join us for the ceremony.

By the time I got the chains on our car, Shirley was back at her parents' home, her wedding gown had been put away, and she was dressed for the honeymoon. We made it only to a motel on the west edge of Adel.

Among highlights of our two-day honeymoon in Des Moines were a Guy Lombardo concert, visiting with some of the band members on the Fort Des Moines Hotel elevator, and spending twenty dollars for two unfinished chests of drawers for our new home in Iowa State's veterans' village, Pammel Court.

* * * * *

We had a million-dollar view for eighteen dollars per month. It was the west half of a Pammel Court Quonset hut, with two bedrooms, bath, kitchen, and living room in less than five hundred square feet, and it overlooked the first fairway of Iowa State's Veenker golf course. It would be our home for eighteen months.

Life on the First Fairway

The previous occupants had sold me a five-dollar couch too heavy to move, and I had spent several evenings in early March, just before my winter quarter graduation, cleaning and painting. An oil heater in the middle of the living room/kitchen area would heat the place. I turned on the fuel line, lit a match, and tossed it into the chamber. Nothing happened. I fiddled with the air intake, the "draft," and tossed in another match. Nothing happened. Another match and, finally, I saw a bit of glow in the chamber. By that time, there was a deep pool of oil in the bottom of the chamber, and I shut the valve.

I felt the heater warm; the fire was going. What about that pool of oil in the chamber? The fire began to roar; the lower chimney pipe took on a glow; then the pipe began to vibrate! At least the Quonset was metal; I could only cross my fingers and wait.

It was either the roar of the fire or the flames coming out of the chimney that attracted neighbor Lloyd Dumenil, who stepped in to see if I needed help. In time, the fire slowed to a steady pace, I reopened the fuel valve, and accepted his invitation to coffee with him and his wife, Lualis. Painting could wait another night.

The Pammel Court office furnished gallons of paint in two colors, cream and a light green, but I could add pigments. For the living room I added a tube of green. For the "ceiling," differentiated only by a masking tape line on the Quonset curvature, and the kitchen, I splurged on a gallon of white at Carr Hardware.

Those two unfinished chests and wedding gifts of a kitchen table and chairs, upholstered straight chair, lamp, hassock, and a card table with four chairs pretty well furnished the place. Shirley's $200 in savings had paid for a 6.2 cubic foot International Harvester refrigerator (which we still have), and my parents had given us a metal-frame bed. Our bookcase was three eight-inch white pine boards supported by bricks.

Life in Pammel Court was comfortable and easy. We walked to and from the animal husbandry department in Curtiss Hall. Afternoons that I mixed feed or weighed pigs at the nutrition farm, I would drop Shirley at Curtiss and drive to the farm.

The community phone was in a booth a half block away. With no air conditioning, we would leave open the tilt-out windows most summer days. Should a strong wind come up during the day, we would come home to a thick layer of cinder dust from the Pammel drives on the furniture. Saturday or Sunday mornings, being on the slice side of the golf course fairway, we would sometimes hear the rat-a-tat-tat of a golf ball rolling down the Quonset siding.

Our largest purchase, encouraged by Diane's birth the following February, was a Kenmore washer. It barely fit into the kitchen's northwest corner, and with borrowed tools, I tapped into the hot and cold water lines under the sink. The floor sloped so badly that when the first load finished the wash cycle and the tub began to spin, the machine danced out toward the middle of the kitchen. We had to put shims under the outer corner of the washer.

* * * * *

While studying specific gravity in high school physics, I considered it just another scientific concept that would fade into my bin of useless knowledge.

Now I was using it to estimate the proportion of lean muscle in a pork carcass, an important matter in the swine industry.

Specific Gravity of a Pork Carcass

I dusted off my recollection of specific gravity—that it is a measure of density, and to measure it, one first weighs the object in the atmosphere and then in water. Weight in water divided by the weight in air is the specific gravity.

Fat is lighter than water; lean muscle and bone are heavier. Therefore, a very fat carcass will float, a leaner carcass will sink. For precision we had to take both weights at the same temperature, and the carcasses were held in a forty-degree cooler. After weighing the carcass on a platform scale, we used an electric hoist to lift and then lower it into a water-filled stock tank. Perched above the tank on a small platform was another scale, connected by a light chain to each of the carcass' four legs.

Consumers in the early 1950s wanted leaner pork, and processors had less market for lard, so swine producers wanted to select breeding stock that would produce lean offspring. Leanness is highly inherited, and research had shown that probing for back-fat thickness (inserting a thin ruler through the skin and down to the surface of the loin muscle) gave a good indication of relative leanness in breeding stock. However, Iowa State scientists wanted to learn, with some precision, the "mathematical correlation" between the probe and more precise indicators of leanness. Specific gravity was already recognized as a precise indicator of relative leanness.

The central purpose of my thesis research was to learn the influence of protein level and/or antibiotics on growth, feed efficiency, and carcass leanness of hogs. I had fed 144 weanling pigs, two gilts and two barrows in each of thirty-six pens. I mixed rations with six levels of protein, half with and half without antibiotics, and had three replicates of each.

But these 144 hogs were also serving this second purpose, helping determine the degree to which the live probe was a valid measure of leanness. Every pig was probed for leanness before slaughter; having probe measurement and specific gravity data for each of the 144 let us calculate the mathematical correlation between the two.

Yes, high school physics has economic application to animal husbandry.

*****

When I began the masters degree, Catron had laid out a program that could let me complete both it and the doctorate in three years. Now, a year later, with a child and Shirley tending her, we would need more income than my $1,500 annual assistantship.

For the Doctorate: Stay or Go?

"Oh, he offered it to you too?" That statement, from my fellow graduate student and evening's host, Charlie Lewis, changed the plans Shirley and I had made. Along with other graduate students of Catron's, we were at Charlie and Norma Lewis' one-bedroom apartment in East Pammel for Charlie's birthday party. East Pammel apartments, with vertical walls and a larger living room, were a step above our Quonset.

Charlie, who had come from North Dakota State, was enthusiastic, quick, and candid, and his comments were usually tinged with a bit of humor (some of the reasons I would later hire him as head of animal science at SDSU). Other students were from England, Florida, Kentucky, and elsewhere, and there was good esprit de corps among us. We had much in common, including limited income, a boring physiology course sequence, weekly seminars, abstracts to write, and pigs to handle and rations to mix at the swine nutrition farm, where Catron generously shared with us his feed industry consulting experiences on Saturday mornings. From him we gained much.

Catron was also a super salesman who sometimes embellished circumstances and often made unduly optimistic commitments. He was a workaholic, tireless and persistent, and usually delivered, if only at the last minute.

My master's degree coursework would be completed during the summer session, and by late summer so would the last of my thesis research. I had a tentative job offer from Walnut Grove and feelers from two other feed companies. However, I had begun to think, *If I take a nutritionist job now in a growing company, within an industry that is increasingly science-based, that company will eventually hire a PhD to lead its product formulation and research, and I'll be Number two*. I would rather be that PhD.

On a weekend trip to help install a new FarmHouse chapter at the University of Kentucky two years earlier, I had stayed in the home of Dr. Dwight Seath, an Iowa State FH alum and head of the UK Dairy Department.

I was impressed with the Seaths modest but comfortable home in an attractive community a few blocks from the campus.

Seath's son, Don, was now a senior in Iowa State's FarmHouse chapter, and I had encountered him the morning of daughter, Diane's, birth when I went to FarmHouse to call my parents. A new baby had prompted more consideration of our future, and after the call, I fell into conversation with Don, especially about how he viewed his early years in a college-oriented family and community. Don's response was all positive, and another seed was planted in my mind.

Just that afternoon, the day of Charlie's birthday party, Catron had come up with an attractive solution for me to continue at Iowa State for my doctorate. I could have a new $2,500 fellowship that he had just obtained. Sensing my impatience to get on with both a good job and family, he reassured me I could wrap up the PhD in the originally planned three years.

Several of my freshman and sophomore instructors had also been pursuing graduate degrees. As full-time instructors limited to enrolling themselves in five credits per quarter and little time for thesis research, they might count on three or four years for the doctorate, after the master's degree. That did not appear attractive to me. Catron's offer would solve our problem. We could stay in Pammel and get by on $2,500 a year. I could earn twelve credits per quarter and have my doctorate and be in a feed industry job by my twenty-fourth birthday. I could not wait to tell Shirley that evening about Catron's offer, and we had gone to Charlie's party in high spirits.

We were having a good time at the party, exchanging anecdotes about the physiology class and happenings at the farm. We also talked about our next steps, what we hoped or expected to be doing after our degrees. I felt so good about Catron's fellowship offer that I could not resist sharing it with the group.

There was a short silence, and a couple of smirks. Then, from Charlie: "Oh, he offered it to you too!" Charlie and another student, both close to completing their master's degrees, had had an identical conversation with Catron. To our knowledge, there was but one $2,500 fellowship, and it had been offered to each of us.

Driving home, Shirley and I made our decision. Back at the Quonset, I put a sheet of paper in the typewriter and began writing letters to heads of animal husbandry departments at eleven universities, expressing interest in pursuing a doctorate in their department if they might have an academic year instructorship open.

* * * * *

My letters had yielded two instructor openings, one at the University of Illinois and the other at Oklahoma A&M (now Oklahoma State University). Illinois had an excellent reputation, but its research focus and corn belt environment would be too much like Iowa State's. I wanted new experiences in a different environment, so followed up with Oklahoma A&M, and we drove down in early August to interview.

Good Morning, Duane

"Good morning, Duane." It was A&M president Oliver Willham, and he had called me by name! That he recognized me and called me by name told me a lot about him, and it paralleled the friendliness of the faculty I had met the day before.

It was seven forty-five on the second morning of my campus interview, and I was walking through the student union on my way to the animal husbandry building. Willham was an animal scientist who had earned his PhD at Iowa State and by chance had been in the animal husbandry building the previous day, and we had been introduced.

Department head Glen Bratcher, an A&M graduate and former judging team coach, described the position, teaching sections of a freshmen course and helping with a junior level meats course. Based on my interest in working with beef cattle and sheep nutrition for my doctorate, he introduced me to Dr. Bill Pope, a Michigan native apparently in his early thirties who would be my PhD adviser. Until a second desk could be found for senior meats professor Lowell Walters's office, I would share an office with a former Minnesotan, Dr. Arnold Nelson.

I had met all ten department faculty. Dr. Jim Hillier, in charge of the swine production and nutrition work, was an Iowa State and FarmHouse alum and brother-in-law of Russ Plager, who had often hosted our Iowa State meats team at Ottumwa's John Morrell plant. Jim Whatley, senior geneticist, had his PhD from Iowa State.

Mutual respect and positive relationships among the faculty were evident. Bob Noble, also an A&M graduate and an instructor doing graduate work, and Joe Whiteman, who had just finished his doctorate and held the rank of assistant professor, would share their notes for the introductory course that I would teach.

I was reasonably confident about helping teach the meats course, another of my likely duties. After completing a comparable undergraduate course, I had worked in Iowa State's meat lab, processing pigs from nutrition and genetics research projects. Back home I had also skinned a few lambs from Dad's feedlot and my 4-H projects. But I would need some help with the cattle.

Bratcher offered me the job and I readily accepted. With the academic rank of instructor, my pay would be $400 per month, September through June, plus $100 per month for July and August.

While I had been interviewing, Shirley, along with my parents, had been looking at housing. Before we left town, we rented a two bedroom bungalow two blocks northeast of the animal husbandry building.

The path toward my doctorate was now set, and I felt good about the people with whom I would work. The latter was perhaps best illustrated by President Willham's greeting, "Good morning, Duane."

On the Road with Green Tomatoes

We had been packing boxes for the move to Oklahoma A&M. Everything had to fit in Dad's Jeep pickup, the six-by-eight-foot U-Haul trailer he would pull, and our 1949 Ford.

On a Monday afternoon in early September, as Dad and Shirley's father finished packing the U-Haul and Jeep pickup, I was answering questions before my master's degree examining committee. By five o'clock, my examination over and committee signatures certifying that I had passed, we were headed out of Pammel Court. My degree would be formally conferred in December.

We had one more stop to make, our garden at the swine nutrition farm. We picked all of our yet unripe tomatoes, put them in paper bags, and stuffed the bags in the corners of our Ford trunk.

Chapter V

Teaching and Learning at Oklahoma A&M

Shirley, Diane, and I pulled into the drive of that rented Stillwater bungalow late on Wednesday afternoon. Shirley's parents followed in their car, Dad in his pickup and the trailing U-Haul arriving an hour later.

The Campus Plan and My Plan

A&M's campus was impressive, though different from Iowa State's. Iowa State's open central campus was of natural beauty, with deciduous species and conifers randomly dotting the bluegrass lawn. At A&M, we saw a formal central mall, with paired structures of Georgian architecture framing the east and west, and a stately brick library overlooking the mall from the north. Connecting crosswalks and hedges were in a geometric pattern, with several walks leading to the rather new Union/hotel building, also brick, at the southeast corner.

I would later learn that the library and mall were on the earlier route of now intercepted Washington Avenue. The original A&M campus, a collection of older brick buildings to the east, was still serving the growing institution.

The animal husbandry building, a block north of the library, was one row of offices and classrooms on three levels and fronting a large judging and show-ring pavilion. The meat lab, which stood beyond a small pasture west of animal husbandry, was a small brick building dwarfed by a major addition yet under construction.

My doctorate plan: Major in animal nutrition, with minors in biochemistry and veterinary physiology. My first course would be graduate-level biochemistry, taught by a recent Wisconsin PhD, Bob Sirney. Next would be two more biochemistry courses, vitamins and enzymes, both taught by Dr. Bob MacVicar, head of biochemistry and dean of the graduate school (later to be president of Oregon State University). I had cited MacVicar's research in my master's thesis and so had been thrilled to meet him during my interview visit. I had already completed my second minor, veterinary physiology, in a three-quarter sequence at Iowa State.

How about graduate courses in animal nutrition? Those too I had completed at Iowa State, swine nutrition under Catron, ruminant nutrition under Dr. Bill Hale, and poultry nutrition under Dr. Elton Johnson, the latter during my senior year. (I would, though, take another graduate poultry nutrition course at A&M.) Most of my earned credits in nutrition at A&M would be a seminar each semester, plus "thesis research" under Pope. His "instruction" would be visits in his office or the hallway and, especially, on day-long trips to the El Reno research station, west of Oklahoma City. Most of my research would involve calves and lambs in projects that Pope directed there.

Having completed the physiology and nutrition sequences, I had free space in my graduate program, so I scheduled Dr. Jim Whatley's population genetics course. That was unusual for one majoring in nutrition and perhaps of questionable wisdom, considering my modest math background. Whatley was such an outstanding instructor, however, that I would have little difficulty.

Most important, Whatley's course and two in that field I would later audit or take for credit under Dr. Jay Lush at Iowa State, along with A&M experience in meats and my farm livestock background, would give me full subject matter breadth and confidence for what would become my specialty, introductory animal science, and to eventually write the textbook *Animal Science and Industry.*

I would teach two sections of the freshman course, with about thirty students in each. Each section involved two one-hour lectures and a two-hour laboratory, the latter largely judging classes of swine, sheep, and cattle. A graduate assistant would help me in the labs. Spring semester I would teach two sections of a second freshman course, feeds and feeding.

For the meats course, Walters would do the two lectures each week, and the students would be divided into five lab sections, a four-hour lab each afternoon. I would be Walter's lab assistant Monday afternoon, and handle the Wednesday and Friday labs with graduate assistant help. We would have up to twenty students in each lab section.

This was an exciting time for Shirley and me. At ages twenty-one and twenty-two, respectively, she was a "faculty wife," and I was a college instructor, on the first rung of the academic ladder. We assumed this would be our home and our life for at least three years; the long term was not a concern. We would get that doctorate and good teaching experience; the future would take care of itself.

* * * * *

Dad and I had come to a hardware store on the west side of Stillwater's main street for items Shirley and I would need in our two-bedroom bungalow.

Anything Else, Sir?

As we entered the store, a female clerk greeted Dad as the apparent customer, and then added, to me, "And how are you, son?"

As I walked the aisles gathering the items we needed—silverware tray, picture hanging wire and hooks, and curtain rods—I overheard Dad sharing with the clerk the fact that I, his son, would be on the A&M faculty. He was proud of that fact and had to share it.

I had paid little attention to the conversation details, but as I approached the counter with an armload of items, I heard its impact. "Anything else I can help you with, sir?"

* * * * *

It was my first day as a college instructor, and I had thirty computer-generated cards, each carrying the name of a student who had enrolled in my section of the introductory animal husbandry course. The cards, about three by eight inches, had been spewed from a mammoth IBM computer during the night and hand-delivered to the department office early that morning.

A Colonel in the Front Row

Though a bit nervous, I was also confident. I would call the roll from these cards; a few would not yet have found the meat lab classroom where my section was scheduled. I would introduce myself, including my background on an Iowa livestock farm and my study at Iowa State, and distribute the sixteen-week course outline I had prepared. I would then have about thirty minutes to lecture on the scope of the US and Oklahoma swine, beef, sheep, and horse industries. (Dairy and poultry were in separate departments, so not included in this course.)

As I walked through the room's rear doorway, I saw caps and cowboy hats resting on some empty chairs, then sun-tanned young men in jeans and short-sleeve shirts, most four to five years younger than me. What I had not expected but spotted in the front row as I strode to the lectern was a forty-five-year-old in a neatly pressed army uniform that had silver oak leaves on the shoulders. (After class he would explain that he was on the ROTC staff and would soon retire to a cattle farm in his home state of Arkansas. His assignment at A&M provided a chance for him to take some classes in animal husbandry.)

How would I handle this? Perhaps as important, how would these new freshmen, themselves enrolled in ROTC, react to an officer among them in class discussions?

I decided that humor might be the best way to begin. I introduced myself, started calling the roll, and, as he responded, I interrupted, smiled at him, and said, "Ever since my days in ROTC, I've been waiting for an opportunity like this!" He and the rest of the class broke up.

We would get along well.

*****

Had the federal Occupational Safety and Health Act (OSHA) then existed, its agency compliance staff would have had a field day in A&M's new meat lab addition.

Twenty Students with Sharp Knives

Twenty students with sharp knives, guided by a novice instructor and a graduate assistant with even less experience, were set to hold, kill, scald, lift to a rail, and eviscerate four 220-pound hogs, and there were no hardhats in sight. Because of both money limitations and delayed construction, there were also no chute to hold cattle for stunning, no restraining pen to hold pigs for bleeding, and no hoist to lift the bled pigs into the scalding vat. In fact, there was not even a scalding vat; a metal stock tank would temporarily fill that need. (The lab's remaining older structure was now exclusively dedicated to converting young cow carcasses purchased weekly from Oklahoma City processors to roasts, minute steaks, and hamburger for residence hall cafeterias. Three skilled butchers, plus student help, handled this work under Walter's supervision.)

I knew the risks. I once had a close call in Iowa State's meat lab, rolling a 150-pound pork carcass suspended by a long hook from a heavy steel trolley toward the cooler; I was unaware of an open rail switch ahead. Clang! The carcass, hook, and trolley hit the floor, the steel trolley having missed my head only by chance.

We would process hogs and lambs the first weeks. Each lab section would roll their dressed carcasses into the cooler, and the next week cut them into wholesale or retail cuts. In a later lab, we would bone out and roll fresh hams or rub pork bellies (destined for bacon) with a salt/sugar/sodium nitrate mix and pack them in rectangular salt cans for curing.

The first lab period, I asked four students to catch and hold down a 220-pound hog so I could do the bleeding. (This was also well before the concern for "humane slaughter" where, today, animals go to sleep as they are led through an oxygen-free channel or otherwise anesthetized before bleeding.)

In this case, because we yet lacked the electric hoist to lift the hog by a hind leg for bleeding, the hog would be on its back, with one student holding each leg. For the next three, the fifth student on a team, a volunteer, would do the bleeding.

We checked the scalding water temperature; it had to be 143 degrees to loosen the hair follicles. If under 143 degrees, I would open the valve on the steam line that extended down into the tank water. Those four students would then lift the lifeless animal into the tank.

When the hair was loose enough to scrape off, perhaps after two to three minutes in that 143-degree water, the carcass was lifted out, and with bell-shaped scrapers, the students would scrape off the hair. We would catch a whiff of sulfur in the air from the hot, soaked hair.

Eventually, we would have an electric hoist to lift the animal out of the tank, and after scraping, lift the carcass onto the rail. That hoist would also let us work with eight hundred-pound and heavier cattle, and we would also have a chute to hold cattle for stunning.

The kill floor had four stations for skinning (in the case of cattle or sheep) and eviscerating the animals. Bled animals would be lifted by the hoist and moved via overhead rails to the four stations. However, the mechanism for lowering the animals at the stations was better suited for a commercial operation than for teaching students. It was a brake drum, with the drum band released by a rope. In a commercial operation where skilled workers handled hundreds of animals each day, such would allow for rapid work. However, for inexperienced students, it was an injury waiting to happen. A light pull on the rope would slowly lower the animal. A hard pull could drop a thousand-pound beef carcass in the students' laps and perhaps the steel trolley wheel on a student's head.

There would be some close calls in those labs, but no fractured skulls or lost fingers. My demonstrations and lectures on safety may have helped. More likely, it was luck. Most of the "injury" in the lab was to some of the carcasses. It is not easy to split a pork carcass, hand sawing down through the center of successive vertebrae the full-carcass length. The dorsal processes of vertebrae are thin; the saw can easily slip to one side. More than once a student's saw slipped off that center line, and I would find it splicing the loin muscle on one side. What should have become pork chops would have to be ground pork.

*****

In late September, Shirley and I were at FarmHouse fraternity on Stillwater's North Washington, just around the corner from our rented bungalow, for an alumni card party.

Playing Hearts with the President

Jim and Luella Hillier had extended the invitation and mentioned something about bridge. We did not know the game, but Hillier assured us that some also played Hearts.

The group included three couples from animal husbandry, including the Hilliers, plus faculty couples from agronomy and dairy husbandry, assistant dean and Mrs. Fred LeCrone, president and Mrs. Willham, and the Merlyn Houcks. Houck was a New York Life Insurance agent who would, in time, sell me a term life insurance policy.

In introducing us to the group, the Hilliers mentioned that we did not play bridge. Mrs. Willham spoke up, "We'd rather play Hearts!" While the others competed in bridge, Shirley and I played many hands of Hearts with the Willhams and, in the process, began to realize that a college president and wife could be "ordinary people."

* * * * *

Most of my fellow graduate students at both Iowa State and A&M were aiming for research positions, either in the feed industry or in universities. My goal had been, and probably still was, the feed industry, but I had found in my first year at A&M that I enjoyed presenting concepts, explaining new technology, and watching students' facial expressions and body language to see when they understood. Perhaps I should reconsider that feed industry goal.

Do You Really like Teaching?

That question from the A&M's testing center counselor bothered me. But I would come up with an answer.

Many of my students were undecided about what they wanted to do after graduation. They would stop to visit after class or in my office seeking suggestions and advice. My first suggestion was usually to consider which courses and course topics they most enjoyed. We would then talk about careers to which those topics and their interests might lead. My summer jobs as a 4-H agent, at the radio station, KJAN, and at the Walnut Grove research farm had helped me, and so I would suggest they find a different job each summer.

I also suggested they take advantage of A&M's testing center. "Take some interest and aptitude tests. Results may give you some clues, either reinforce or bring into question your current plans."

It struck me one day that I had never taken such tests. Agriculture was clearly my interest, and my considerations had changed over time from farming to teaching vocational agriculture to, for a short time, veterinary medicine. It was in Catron's animal nutrition course that graduate study and the feed industry had come into view for me. Maybe I should follow the advice I had given those students.

I scheduled a full morning at the testing center and was first given a series of aptitude tests that involved matching numbers, words, and word and number sequences. Next was the Kuder Preference Test, a series of questions about what one likes to do versus activities one would avoid.

A week later my counselor, a thoughtful and thorough young member of the psychology faculty, shared with me my test results. In word skills, such as spelling, word recognition, and use of words, he said I was in the ninety-seventh percentile compared to employed stenographers. (I had no desire to be a steno, but I did flaunt my test results to a couple of our department secretaries.)

My numerical skills score put me in the ninety-fifth percentile compared to employed accountants. That seemed more reasonable; in high school algebra and geometry classes, Arnold Christ would challenge us each day with rapid-fire oral mathematics and I relished that. But accounting, per se, triggered no excitement for me.

In our initial visit the counselor had asked why I had come to the testing center. My response, given with apparent enthusiasm, was that I was teaching full time while pursuing a doctorate and was following the advice I had given some of my students. I wanted some confirmation or questioning of my career interests.

My Kuder test profile showed highest preference for scientific, literary, outdoor, and persuasion sectors. It showed a low preference for others sectors, especially social service.

That last item bothered the counselor, "Do you really like teaching? Teachers usually rank high in social service." I recalled a Kuder question, "Which would you prefer to do this afternoon? (a) Go hunting (b) Visit a sick friend (c) Do a crossword puzzle. (d) Study your history lesson. Had I chosen *b*, my social service score would likely have been higher." I had my answer.

"Look," I said, "teaching college students is not about helping them put on their overshoes or wiping their noses. For me, it is selling them on the animal industry's importance and that the information and principles I convey are needed for success in the industry!"

Perhaps most of his testing had been with students considering elementary or secondary teaching, where social service should be higher on the interest scale. Or, perhaps, he was just challenging me in order to see what my reaction would be. Regardless, his question was valuable; it forced me to articulate a response, which may have done as much to strengthen my interest in college teaching as did the test itself.

* * * * *

Though I had several students of Native American (then referred to as American Indian) ancestry in the courses I taught on the A&M campus, I knew little about the culture and traditions of this sector of the America's citizenry, especially prominent in Oklahoma and the other Great Plains states where I would later work.

A Day at Chilocco Indian School

The seventh grader across the small table was both bashful and afraid, his head down. I was his one-person audience, but his words would not come. We were in a little feed room on the edge of the Chilocco Indian School campus, on the west side of US 77 and just inside the Oklahoma State line from Arkansas City, Kansas. I was the official judge at a livestock and poultry judging event, arranged to climax the year's work in a junior-high livestock and poultry production course, and was listening to each student's reasons for how they had placed a class of four layer hens.

Fifteen students had judged classes of steers, lambs, pigs, and laying hens, with four animals in each class. I had made the official placing for each class and assigned points for scoring, zero to fifty. Each student was then scheduled to give me a three-minute oral statement of the reasons for their placings in the layer hen class. For the validity of their reasons, as well as clarity of presentation, I would record another score, also between zero and fifty.

I felt for this shy young man. He and his schoolmates had been placed by the Bureau of Indian Affairs system at this boarding school, miles from their families and tribal environment. Alone in that feed room, he was supposed to convince some college professor in three minutes that his placing of four layer hens was correct, and why.

He had apparently learned the preferred qualities of layer hens, such as width of pelvic space for ease of laying an egg. He had ranked the birds as I had—1, 4, 2, 3—and so had earned a fifty for his placing. He just could not tell me why.

After my greeting, I waited. No words. I waited more. No words. I moved my chair from behind the table, leaned forward and asked, "Which bird was the widest between the pelvic bones?"

I could barely hear, "Number one."

"Which was the most narrow?"

A bit louder. "Number three."

His three minutes were up; the door opened for another seventh grader to be ushered in. I smiled, thanked the young man, and wrote down a forty-five for his oral reasons.

I gave a lot of forty-fives that afternoon. For me it was a day of both learning and questioning, my first exposure to the bureau's boarding-school system. Perhaps I should make no judgment as to the system's purpose, to break the low-income, low-education, and societal isolation of tribal life for these young people. I could defend the school's emphasis on agriculture, one of Oklahoma's major industries. The students were familiar with open land and there should be opportunity for them in agriculture. The school's superintendent was an A&M animal husbandry graduate, sincere, enthusiastic, and interested in his students. I admired his giving his professional life to these young people.

However, it seemed to me there had to be a better way.

Postcript: Thirty-five years later, on our return drive from a commencement address at now Oklahoma State University, Shirley and I drove into the Chilocco campus. We found the school long closed, with building windows boarded up and roofs and walls crumbling. A better way had been found; Native American students were attending public schools in their home communities.

*****

For a doctorate in the sciences, in addition to course work and related comprehensive exams, one must write a thesis about one's "original research" on a topic of consequence. In most universities, there was another hurdle, the foreign language requirement.

Vitamins and the Language Hurdle

To earn a graduate degree in the sciences, it had long been the US tradition that students needed to demonstrate competence in reading at least one foreign language. The historic rationale was that much of the research was being done in German, French, or other European universities and US graduate students must be able to read published research papers in at least one of those languages.

For my master's degree at Iowa State, I had audited two courses in French and managed to pass what was considered a qualifying translation exam. For the doctorate at A&M, the requirement was a "reading knowledge" of two foreign languages or a "comprehensive knowledge" of one. I asked around and discovered the only difference between "reading" and "comprehensive" was that for comprehensive, there could be *no errors* in translating a page-long passage the testing professor selected from a book that the candidate chose.

I searched the A&M library for the right book in the French language and found *The Chemistry of Water Soluble Vitamins.* Perfect! Only the B vitamins and vitamin C are water soluble, so I had a narrow field on which to focus my translation effort, and technical terms are easiest to translate. Perhaps as important, I had just completed MacVicar's graduate biochemistry course on vitamins, so felt I knew rather well the chemistry and functions of vitamin C and all the B vitamins. They should be the same in French as in English!

Every spare minute for a month I was at my assigned desk in the A&M library, practicing translation from that little thin book. By the end of the month I had it virtually memorized, in both French and English, and scheduled my exam with a foreign language faculty member.

He leafed through the book and marked a page. I sat down at a table in his office, worked through the translation, and handed him my paper. I watched as he read my translation, constantly referring back to the printed page.

"I'm sorry," he said, and showed me three errors. Assuming I would want to study more, he added, "When would you like to schedule the next exam?"

Why wait? I thought. I had almost memorized the book. "How about this afternoon?"

He was reticent but agreed. The page he chose this time was on riboflavin; I breezed through my translation and handed him my paper. He moved rather rapidly through the first several paragraphs and then hesitated on "oxidation of fatty acids." It could have been translated as "metabolism of fatty acids," but I had used the more specific term, oxidation. It was unlikely that a professor of French had studied much biochemistry, so I quickly explained that MacVicar (also the graduate school dean, by the way) had used the more specific terms, oxidation.

After he finished reading, I could tell he was still reticent. I pressed a bit, and finally he said, "Well, if your major professor will concur on that translation, I'll certify that you passed."

I was in Pope's office within five minutes, got his okay and signature on my translation paper, and carried it back to the professor. I had cleared the hurdle.

*****

For part of my thesis research, on the value of stilbestrol in lamb rations, I wanted to use twins. Why twins? There is considerable genetic variation among animals in growth rate, feed efficiency, and, especially, carcass traits. With twins, one of each pair assigned to a stilbestrol-containing ration, the other to an identical ration but without stilbestrol, I would have higher confidence that any measured difference would be due to the stilbestrol, not to genetic difference in the animals.

Searching for Twins

I was driving the country roads between Medford and Pond Creek in north central Oklahoma near the Kansas line, searching for twin lambs. Most land not in wheat was then in permanent pasture, and many farmers had a small flock of Hampshire or Suffolk ewes.

If I could find and purchase the seven pairs I needed, farm superintendent Andy Kincaid and I would pick them up with the department truck the following Saturday. When I came upon a flock of sheep, I would stop the college station wagon and watch. (State regulations did not allow college-owned sedans, only "commercial vehicles," and station wagons qualified as such under A&M's interpretation.) If two lambs "mothered up" to nurse one ewe and were of the same sex, I would pull into the farmstead and engage the flock owner. "I noted your good flock of ewes and that you had some pairs of twins. I'm looking for twins." I would explain my research and that, because twins were more "efficient" for my feeding comparisons, I could pay well for his ready-to-wean twins. I enjoyed these visits with the flock owners and had stories to share from my youth.

By late afternoon I was able to find and buy only three pairs of twins, two of ewes and one of wethers (castrated males). To complement these three pairs, I had also purchased eight wethers that were not twins, but all from a single Hampshire flock and all sired by the same ram; their mothers were likely sisters or half-sisters. I would pair those wethers by weight; genetic variation among them should be minimal.

What did I learn from the research? Stilbestrol improved feeding efficiency. Those with stilbestrol in their rations ate slightly more, drank 10 percent more water, and gained 6.5 percent more per day on one-tenth pound less feed per pound of gain. I also learned some unexpected effects of stilbestrol. The pelts of stilbestrol-fed lambs were far more difficulty to remove (a score of 2.5 versus 1.86, with 1.0 for easy and 4.0 very difficult).

This illustrates the fascination of research; one discovers the unexpected and is tempted to check it out. I then wanted to find out if the pelt removal difficulty was a chance event and if other hormones might have the same effect. I followed up with a lamb-feeding trial at our El Reno station the following year, using both stilbestrol and another hormone. Both increased the density and volume of subcutaneous (just below the skin) connective tissue. In fact, while processing some of those later El Reno lambs in meat lab class, my students had to work in pairs for the strength to pull off the tightly held pelts. The "fell," the thin protective membrane that usually remains intact on the lamb carcass, was often torn in fragments during the process.

Though what I describe was new and important knowledge at the time and a requirement of doctoral research, stilbestrol for livestock feeding would be outlawed by the Delaney amendment to FDA legislation in the late 1960s.

* * * * *

A&M's animal husbandry department was, in essence, the research/education arm of the state's livestock industry; however we could help the industry, we should. Here is an example.

Three Meals from a Porterhouse Steak

We were in a hotel meeting room in Muskogee, Oklahoma, on a Tuesday evening. Facing me were a dozen butchers and grocery store meat cutters plus several area cattle producers. My job was to demonstrate how a homemaker could get three meat dishes from a single porterhouse steak, a small fillet, a cup of lean stew meat, and soup stock of the trim and removed bone. In front of me on a paper-covered table were two sixteen-ounce porterhouse steaks on a large cutting board, a smaller board I could hold in my hand, and two sharp knives.

The porterhouse is from the rear section of the loin and contains portions of two bones, a vertebrae and the pelvic bone. It also includes loin and leg muscles, the more tender loin muscle showing as a cross section and the less tender leg muscle running more longitudinally.

The purpose of my demonstration was to increase beef product sales. Twelve such sessions were scheduled across Oklahoma, cosponsored by the meat industry's National Livestock and Meat Board (NLMB), which had arranged the talent, and the Oklahoma Cattlemen's Association, which provided the meeting room and invited local retailers. Walters and I were part of the "talent." NLMB's Augie Ring had called Walters and outlined what was needed, and Ring had kicked off the series on a Monday night in Oklahoma City, with Walters and me watching.

Tuesday morning, Walters headed west; I drove east to Muskogee. Wednesday night I would be in Bartlesville and Thursday night in Enid. Ring and his NLMB partner would cover the southern half of the state.

Everything needed for the demonstration was ready, except for my comfort with the coming task. However, the retailers were respectful listeners, asked a few questions, and left with some charts and brochures. The cattlemen expressed appreciation and invited me out for coffee and a visit about their cattle business.

I hope that more beef sales resulted. I know that I gained some friends among the cattlemen, as well as more confidence and some ideas for my meat lab classes the following fall.

*****

I looked up with surprise from work on my lecture notes for fall classes. A fellow who had given us a problem in my meat lab section spring semester had just walked in.

Elk Steak for a Stolen Ham?

"I have a package of steaks for you," he said. This was the fellow who had tried to walk out of the meat lab last spring with a boned-out fresh ham under his arm, and now he was giving me a package of steaks?

That day in meat lab, we had boned, rolled, and wrapped sixty fresh hams to be stored in a basement freezer. I had demonstrated how to bone and roll a ham: I first peeled off the skin from the outer ham surface, slipped a slim boning knife under the pelvic bone, severed the ligaments holding it to the femur, and removed the pelvic bone. I then sliced through the inner body of the ham to remove the femur. The last step was to arrange that boneless mass into a roll about six inches in diameter, and tie it with white string. If done with some practiced skill and artistry, the tied boneless ham would be symmetrical, perhaps twelve inches long and an even six inches in diameter from end to end.

Among the twenty students, some had trouble finding those ligaments that held the pelvic bone. A few cut too deeply toward the femur, almost severing the ham into two portions. After such missteps, they might need a cloth bag instead of a string. Most, however, could make a decent looking roll with some squeezing and shaping as the string went on.

The fun part for me was demonstrating the tying; rapid and successive ties were part of the secret. First I showed how to tie a butcher's knot: With the left hand, pull the end of the string away from you under the shaped meat and back over the meat toward you. Then roll the lead end of the string over and around the remaining ball string (the latter held in the right hand) and form a loose knot. Hold that loose knot with the left hand, pull the remaining uncut string through the knot, do a "half-hitch" around the exposed string stub, and pull tight with the right hand. The knot tightens and grips. Cut the string from the ball with your knife; then move and inch or two down the roll for the next tie. An experienced worker can tie the needed six to eight loops in a minute or less.

The hams were then wrapped in butcher paper, string applied in a cross design, and tied with the same butcher's knot.

By four o'clock we had the sixty hams boned, rolled, and packaged, and I was in the freezer watching several students place packages on the shelf. Ancel Swader, my lab assistant, was headed toward the freezer with another cartload of wrapped hams and spotted this young man running up the stairs, a wrapped ham under his arm. Swader caught him in the parking lot.

Under university rules, the case had to be reported to the college discipline committee, and I do not recall the eventual punishment. His appearance in my doorway confirmed he had not been permanently dismissed from A&M, only reprimanded or perhaps put on probation. What about the package of steaks?

"I spent the summer on a Montana ranch and had a chance to go elk hunting," he said, "and I just thought *Mr. Acker might enjoy some elk steaks.*"

Was his gift of steaks to convey thanks for whatever I might have done that let him stay in school? Or were the steaks and the brief visit an acknowledgement to both himself and me that he had screwed up and would thereby bring the incident to a permanent close? Perhaps it was both.

I told him I was glad to see him back and thanked him for the steaks. We shook hands and I wished him well in fall classes.

* * * * *

It seemed hot as I worked, but I did not realize how hot. The evening news reported that Stillwater had reached 114 degrees that afternoon.

The Stork Arrives in Record Heat

Our second daughter, LuAnn, was born by Caesarean section early morning on September 14. Shirley's mother had come down to take care of Diane, the house, and me, and to help for a few days after Shirley's return from the hospital with LuAnn. After seeing that all was well and calling her mother and my parents, I headed out to mix lamb rations. I would get acquainted with LuAnn and see Shirley after she emerged from the surgery anesthetic.

Fifteen years later, as dean at SDSU, I would sometimes encounter difficulty recruiting faculty because of their perception of the South Dakota climate, too much wind, and winters that were too cold and lasted too long. However, their perceptions seemed to me more severe than reality; Brookings had less snow most years than we had experienced in Iowa, and we had not been bothered by the wind.

I knew that NOAA, the National Oceanic and Atmospheric Administration, had staff stationed at several land-grant universities from which we often recruited faculty and that the agency published brief climate summaries for those and other cities. I sent request letters for perhaps a dozen land-grant university cities; I hoped the data would counter those negative perceptions. As I signed the request letters, I predicted to my secretary, "When the Stillwater summary sheet arrives, it will show September 14, 1954, as having the city's all-time record high temperature."

It did; the stork had arrived in record heat!

The left photo shows Diane and LuAnn about December 1954 in our small living room. The right photo is of LuAnn and Shirley on the front steps of our Stillwater home.

* * * * *

Another role for animal husbandry faculty is to judge 4-H and FFA livestock shows across the state. Though I had been on and coached 4-H judging teams and had taken courses in judging, before joining the A&M faculty I had not judged a county show. Nor had I had experience in a racially segregated activity. The Civil Rights Act was yet to come and in most of Oklahoma, the primary and secondary schools, the extension service, 4-H and FFA, were separated by race. In Okmulgee County, the 4-H and FFA fair was a single event, but the ring competition remained separate.

A Judge in Panic, and I'm the Judge

"Show your hog!" The calls from mothers on the sideline echoed through the large brick barn as twenty Yorkshire market barrows (castrated males) raced back and forth in the makeshift ring of straw bales. The barn, which had served as a livery stable in earlier days, was alongside US 75 on the north edge of the town of Okmulgee, and large enough to hold both the black and white youth's animals, plus the show ring in the northeast corner.

Before the day was over, I would judge classes of hogs, sheep, beef cattle, dairy heifers, goats, and even some rabbits. For each species and age or weight group, I would first judge animals belonging to the black youth. After they left the ring, the white youth would parade in their animals. The climax would come about eight o'clock that evening; I would choose the grand champion black-owned steer, then the grand champion white-owned steer.

Oklahomans strongly supported their youth and their livestock shows. The fair book showed ribbons and premium money for nine in each class, so dozens of boys and girls would carry home one or more ribbons and some premium money.

This was my first experience in judging a county fair show on my own. I had worked several shows with other A&M faculty and had been confident I could handle this show. However, it would not be an easy day. To judge all the classes listed in the fair book, I would have to average a class every fifteen minutes.

Those twenty pigs were the first class of the show, their owners and I had been in the ring fifteen minutes, and I had made no progress. The pigs were like peas in a pod. I would later learn the pigs in the ring were all full brothers or half-brothers and cousins, born of five littermate females all mated to the same boar. Local leaders of the black clubs had purchased the five bred females from A&M. They had been managed and the pigs born at one location, and the pigs allotted to the FFA and 4-H members.

Twice I had the top two pigs identified, but when I turned to find the third, those two disappeared in the frenzy. I even suspected some of the boys or girls had lost their own pig and were chasing another. There was no way I could choose and keep track of nine pigs until my ring man, one of the black agriculture teachers, could hand out the ribbons. Perspiration dripped from my chin. For a moment, I was in a panic.

I grabbed the ring man, his fist full of ribbons and already a bit impatient. "When I point to the top pig, you hand his owner the blue ribbon and get both the pig and his owner out of the ring. Then I'll pick number two."

It worked. In rather short order, I had picked the top nine (though the pigs were so similar, any other judge could have placed them differently), the owners had their ribbons and the pairs had left the ring. I sat down on a straw bale and wiped my brow, waiting for the remaining pigs to leave the ring and the next class to come in.

But the ring did not empty. Eleven pigs and their owners were still in the ring and the black teachers and county agent were in a huddle on the far side.

Soon the ring man came over. "Mr. Judge, all the kids' York barrows were in that heavyweight class and there are no entries in the lightweight class. But we have the ribbons, and the fair board has put up prize money for nine placings for a lightweight class. These kids have all worked so hard. Would you be willing to judge the rest of these pigs as the lightweight class?"

There was only one logical response, "I'm just the judge. You folks decide what goes in the ring. If you call these remaining pigs the lightweight class, I'll judge them." In short order, I peeled off nine more pigs, and the ring man handed out nine more ribbons.

* * * * *

On p. 325 of the first edition of my text *Animal Science and Industry* (Prentice-Hall, 1963) are nine photos, showing live animal views and cross sections of meat type, "meatless" type, and fat type hogs, courtesy of George A. Hormel & Co. and the National Swine Growers Council. These and comparable photos deserve much credit for moving the US pork industry in the late 1950s and early '60s toward what consumers wanted, consistently lean pork. Here is the story of what I believe was the first step in the eventual production of those nine photos.

Taxidermy in the Freezer

The photos in my book show dramatic differences in size of the loin muscle (pork chop muscle) and the relative proportion of lean in the bellies (which become bacon) from animals of the three types, as well as side and rear views of the live animals before processing. Appearing nation-wide in industry publications and shown by extension specialists in their work with the swine industry, those photos helped convince thousands of pork producers and swine breeders that they simply had to move aggressively to the meat type. The live animal shots provided visual models for breeders as bases in selecting breeding stock (before use of the live backfat probe became common).

I do not know which of my several acquaintances deserve primary credit for the idea to position a dressed pork carcass as if it were standing on four legs, then to cut and photograph its cross sections. However, I am sure the soft carcass I watched A&M Professor Jim Hillier and his students pull up into a standing position on a two-foot by five-foot platform in the forty-degree meat lab cooler was the first test of the idea.

I am also confident that one or all of Hillier's three brothers-in-law, Carroll and Russell Plager, both with major meat processors, and Wilbur Plager, secretary of the Iowa Pork Producers' Association, deserve considerable credit for the idea. Hillier had led the A&M meats program for many years before shifting to swine research and teaching. Walters, then leading the meats program, was also likely involved.

To get the 155-pound limp carcass into a natural-appearing, standing position required a series of wires from a pipe frame superstructure threaded under the backbone, plus strategically placed braces and shims to hold the carcass sides and legs apart. For any carcass firmness at all, the crew had to work in the cooler. Even there, repeated loosening and tightening of suspension wires was needed, plus a bit of pushing and tugging on portions of the carcass. When more flesh firmness was needed, the project shifted to a walk-in freezer, held at ten degrees.

Once the pig's natural standing posture was achieved, the platform and carcass remained in the freezer. A day later, the fully frozen carcass was released from the frame, wires removed, the carcass cross-sectioned with a band saw, and the cross sections photographed.

Rarely does a single industry have such an effective team of relatives in leadership positions as the US pork industry had in Hillier and his brothers-in-law. When these four fellows got their heads together, good ideas emerged. In this case, an industry's needed change was markedly accelerated.

It was a privilege to watch such a teaching and learning device as it developed, to later use that set of photos in my classes and textbook, and, especially, to know the people behind it all. Russell Plager had often hosted our Iowa State meats judging team for practice sessions at Morrell's Ottumwa plant. Early in my Iowa State faculty years, Carroll would host our livestock team and me, as substitute coach, in his home after the Hormel-sponsored National Barrow Show contest. Wilbur would often be on the Iowa State campus and I would have his son, Paul, as a student.

*****

Feeders Day brought hundreds of Oklahoma livestock producers to the department's arena for faculty reports on the year's swine, beef cattle, and sheep research. At noon the attendees had lined up outside the west arena door to pick up a bun, a sizzling steak, baked beans, and potato salad, all supervised by Clay Potts. Though Potts' official title was director of short courses for the Division of Agriculture, his reputation was the guy that did the steaks for Feeders' Day and other of A&M's agricultural events across the state.

Later that evening, department faculty and spouses gathered for a dinner at the meat lab (three inch fillets pounded flat with a cleaver and then boiled a few minutes before grilling) and the man who had been recognized at Feeders Day was an invited guest.

Let's Start Over

The day's honoree was a beef buyer for a major meat processor at the Oklahoma City terminal market and a big help to the department's research. He always insured that individual research animals' identities were retained as they were processed in their plant, and helped us obtain carcass weight, USDA grade, and other data on each carcass. I do not recall his name, but as he expressed thanks and briefly described his career, he included an instructive anecdote.

After graduating from A&M he had entered the company's cattle-buyer training program. He had followed and watched experienced buyers and then tracked pens of purchased cattle through the plant to see how they had graded and yielded. He had also learned how to calculate cautious bids and how to negotiate. He was ready.

This was the first day he would represent the company, bidding on pens of cattle on his own. He had negotiated hard with a commission salesman, who represented the cattle owner, on three pens. He had lost one pen but purchased the other two at what he thought was a good price. He inspected a fourth load, estimated their weight, dressing percentage (carcass weight relative to live weight, influenced by how much feed and water they might be carrying), and carcass grade, made his calculation on a pocket card and then offered a cautious bid to the salesman, a man many years his senior. Some negotiation would follow.

However, the salesman quickly responded, "Sold," marked his card with the price and the buyer, and turned to walk away.

"Something must be wrong!" He checked his figures. He checked them again. Oh boy. A mistake. A bad mistake; he had overbid. And it was a large pen of heavy cattle. It would cost his company plenty. He had just blown it, and perhaps his job and the career he had trained for.

The salesman glanced back, noticed his discomfort and his going through his calculations. "Got a problem?"

"I sure have. I made a terrible mistake." He showed the salesman his card.

Almost choking back his emotions and referring to that seasoned salesman, our honoree continued, "He pulled his card for that load of cattle out of his pocket, tore it up, let it blow to the wind, and said, 'Let's start over.'"

One might ask, "What about the cattle's owner, who lost a generous premium in this process? Was he not cheated?"

Perhaps. However, if I know Oklahoma cattle producers or their counterparts in other states, had they, as owner, learned of the event, including all the details, the young buyer's first day, his thirst for the career, and the innocence of the mistake, the response would have been, "So I missed a premium. I still got a fair price, and a young man still had a career ahead of him."

* * * * *

A few months later I received a call from Dr. Leslie Johnson, who had just finished his first year as head of Iowa State's animal husbandry department. I did not know Johnson but knew he had come to the job from a USDA position, though headquartered at the University of Nebraska.

The Only Reason

"Would you consider talking to us about a teaching position at Iowa State?" Johnson asked.

We had been at A&M for only two years. Though five hundred miles from home territory and familiar corn belt agriculture, Shirley and I had adapted to Oklahoma and were living comfortably. We liked the modest home we had purchased, Shirley was involved in and enjoyed a child development group, and I was serving as a faculty adviser to the A&M FarmHouse chapter. We had been treated most generously by faculty colleagues and their spouses; we could not list all the gracious gestures that had made us feel welcome and appreciated. I fully enjoyed teaching, especially the open and friendly Oklahoma students, and had many rewarding off-campus experiences.

However, I was thrilled by Johnson's call and his question. Here was a chance to go back to my alma mater, closer to our parents, grandparents to our two daughters.

Johnson elaborated, said the job was largely to teach sections of the freshman courses, and to "kind of take the leadership of those courses over time."

I was definitely interested. Though it might be considered unwise to leave A&M before completing my doctorate, I had accumulated the minimum number of "resident credits" required by graduate school rules. I could take some courses and continue my research at Iowa State, and transfer the credits back to A&M, where both could count toward my degree.

However, my response to Johnson was less than tactful, perhaps even brash. I told him I appreciated the call, but in regard to teaching Iowa State's freshman courses (a two-course sequence), "The only reason I would want to come back to Iowa State is to change those courses; they were not worth much when I took them as a student."

Johnson laughed; it was a hearty laugh to which I would become accustomed. "Just come on up and let's talk," he said.

We drove to Iowa a week later. Shirley and I spent a day in Ames, the town and the Iowa State campus so familiar and inviting. Johnson's enthusiasm was infectious, and it was clear he would give me the freedom and support I would need on those freshman courses. He also assured me there would be no problem in continuing my thesis research in department facilities. The salary would be little higher than at A&M and I would remain at the instructor rank, at least for the immediate next year. However, with several of my former professors approaching retirement, I could not pass up the opportunity.

My return from Ames to Stillwater and my A&M department colleagues was not easy. Little more than a month before fall semester would begin I was telling acting department head Jim Whatley (Bratcher had suffered a heart attack in May, the night after Feeders' Day), senior meats professor Walters, and my thesis adviser Pope that we would be heading back to Iowa State. However, they were generous in their understanding, and Pope assured me his support in working out the balance of my degree work at Iowa State.

* * * * *

We carried many satisfactions from our time at A&M, including high respect for the university and many friendships that have endured. I am especially thankful for the freedom and support given me by Bratcher, Pope, and Walters. Hillier had even devoted a Saturday afternoon to go with Shirley and me as we looked for a house to buy, insisting that we ask to see the past year's utility bills, so we would know those costs.

Each decade has brought one or more opportunities to return to what is now Oklahoma State University for scientific society meetings, faculty seminars, university ceremonies, or alumni/faculty reunions.

I have also called on OSU for help. I once took several Kansas regents to see OSU's then new statewide communications facility, to stir their interest and support for a parallel unit at Kansas State, that unit now long in operation. We continue to feel a proud part of Oklahoma A&M/OSU.

Chapter VI

On the Faculty at Iowa State

Shirley and I were back home, in some respects, at Ames and the Iowa State campus. In the next seven years, Iowa State College would become Iowa State University, the Division of Agriculture would become the College of Agriculture, and my department would change its name from animal husbandry to animal science. I would work alongside former teachers, challenge some traditions in the department's curriculum and introductory courses, and travel the state for extension programs, student recruitment, class field trips, and to judge a few county fair livestock shows.

* * * * *

A half-century later, I still feel the excitement of being back in the classroom where Damon Catron had fostered my interest in nutrition and graduate study, but now as one of the faculty.

Back in Curtiss Hall

Among those in the room were my undergraduate adviser, Bill LaGrange, freshman course lecturer Art Anderson, meats judging team coach Ed Kline, and my favorite crops instructor, Darrel Metcalfe, plus other faculty I had known. Associate dean Roy Kottman, an instructor and Block and Bridle faculty adviser my freshman year, had gathered those faculty who serve as advisers to students, in order to give us the schedule and instructions for fall registration. Department secretary Lucinda Foster had handed me that morning a list of sixty-five freshmen who would be my advisees. Files for each would come later.

Registration would be a two-day affair in the old men's gymnasium. As advisers to new students, we would be there to answer their questions, help find a replacement for a closed course, or modify a schedule to accommodate a part-time job.

After Kottman's presentation, we walked as a group to the Union for the academic year's opening faculty convocation. The Union's Great Hall brought back more memories, from Religion in Life Week morning matins to dancing with Shirley to Louis Armstrong at the 1950 Homecoming. I spotted a few more of my instructors, including Leonard Feinberg, freshman English; "Wild Bill" Schrampfer, business law; and Bob Getty and Loyal Payne, veterinary anatomy and physiology, respectively.

We would hear a welcome by President James Hilton, but the first person onstage was as familiar as the room itself. It was Tolbert MacRae, the "grand old man of the music department" who had taught us the Alma Mater as freshmen and would lead us in it today.

We had arrived from Stillwater the previous week and unloaded our furnishings at a rented two-bedroom bungalow on a small farm west of Ontario, two miles from campus. In that week, Shirley had put the house in excellent living shape, we had sub-leased basement space to four graduate students, and had found bunk beds, chests, table, and chairs for them.

I had received my teaching schedule, including four lab sections of AH (animal husbandry) 111, the beef and sheep portion of a two-quarter freshman course sequence (the dairy and swine portion would be spring quarter), with likely forty to fifty students in each section. Anderson would give a weekly lecture to all students in the course; the labs were for discussing issues from his lectures and the book he had written for the course, plus judging a class of cattle or sheep. I would also handle the weekly animal husbandry orientation class for nearly one hundred new freshmen and transfer students.

I had not yet investigated what research I could do under the leader of beef and sheep nutrition research, Dr. Wise Burroughs, for part of my A&M doctoral thesis. I was not worried about that; I knew Burroughs would be totally accommodating. I had enrolled in a graduate human nutrition course in the College of Home Economics and would also audit Dr. Jay Lush's first course in population genetics. I had completed that course at A&M under Dr. Jim Whatley, one of Lush's former students, but it would be worthwhile to hear it under "the master." It would also better equip me for Lush's second course in the sequence, in which I would enroll for credit.

* * * * *

Shirley and other FarmHouse fiancés had stayed at the Ralph Anderson home south of the campus for their weekends in Ames for fraternity events. We had both become well acquainted with the Andersons and they had driven out one evening to welcome us back to Ames.

Be Willing to Pack Your Bags

"If you want to advance in university work, be willing to pack your bags!" That advice came from Anderson, associate professor of mathematics, as he and his wife sat in our living room. Anderson would retire at the end of the year and the couple would move back to their native state of Ohio. That might have been a second reason for their visit; their attractive home would be on the market and we would be looking for a house to buy.

Anderson expressed his regret that he had spent his entire teaching career at Iowa State, especially that he had not earned his PhD and reached the full professor academic rank. He commended us for our move to Oklahoma A&M to pursue the doctorate and to gain a new experience, and our move back to Iowa State.

I thought of my faculty colleagues and leaders. In the years since my department head, Leslie Johnson, had earned his degrees from Iowa State, he had served at both South Dakota State and the University of Nebraska. Dean Floyd Andre, also an Iowa State grad, had come just a few years earlier from the University of Wisconsin. The animal husbandry faculty that I considered most effective had also spent time at other universities, including Purdue, Ohio State, Kansas State, and Texas A&M.

Spending time at multiple universities (or companies and communities) exposes one to a variety of philosophies and circumstances. It also increases one's professional and personal acquaintances and more people may think of you when an opportunity develops.

*****

Several department faculty at Iowa State were recognized leaders in animal nutrition or genetics research and taught the junior or senior level courses in their specialties. The freshman course sequence had been left largely to Anderson, who was no longer involved in research, and there was little mention in the course outline of the more recently developed concepts and technologies with which I had become familiar as a graduate student.

Ask Permission or Forgiveness?

Anderson provided a weekly lecture to those 300 students enrolled in the introductory course, two sections of about 150 each. The laboratories, each section meeting twice a week for two hours, were handled by instructors and graduate assistants, with 40 to 50 students in each lab section. Though good at teaching what they were assigned, the lab instructors' main focus was their own graduate program, and they had no time or authority to challenge the course outline and content.

Every prescribed laboratory activity fall quarter had been visual judging classes of four animals. However, it was well-known that the correlation between visual judging and proportion of lean meat was far from perfect. Research had disclosed more accurate ways to assess or predict muscling, including the "backfat probe."

Those pork carcass cross sections Jim Hillier had created at A&M had made it even more clear to me that there were larger differences among animals than could be seen from the outside.

This first half of the spring course covered swine, and I suggested to Anderson that we should be using the probe in lab. Anderson did not hesitate with his response: "Oh, no, that idea is new; we need to stick to the basics, teach the strength of the pig's topline and fullness of the ham." (His colleagues' research documenting the accuracy of the probe in measuring leanness had been published in the *Journal of Animal Science* five years earlier, in 1950.)

I had not asked permission; I had only suggested. For the next lab, where visual judging of four pigs was scheduled, I took along a probe and a small scalpel and found a restrainer (a small cable to place around a pig's snout to hold the animal in place) in the small arena used for lab. I first described to my students what to look for in judging for leanness, a smooth topline, wide hams and shoulders, and absence of rolls of fat as the animal walked.

After the students had judged the class, ranking them in their order of believed leanness, I handed the restrainer to a strapping young man and asked him to get in the ring, grab, and hold pig number one. I used the probe to measure the pig's backfat thickness at three locations. A student recorded the measurements on the blackboard. We did the same with the other three pigs. Each student could see how closely his or her visual ranking compared to the measurements.

Anderson was not happy when he learned I had demonstrated the probe. However, my students had now seen precision in assessing leanness and had also learned that visual appraisal has its limits.

My next supplement to the course outline for my lab sections would be the performance records from the then new swine testing station that our extension specialists had helped establish west Ames, just a half mile from our rented home. My students would see the tremendous range in growth, feed efficiency, and meatiness among animals from herds that were then supplying breeding stock to the state's industry.

* * * * *

I emphasize that I respect and support live animal judging, both show-ring competition and FFA, 4-H, and college judging teams. County fairs and livestock shows motivate young people to manage and prepare their animals well and give them experience in presenting their animals to a judge. Judging teams help young people develop and refine their observational skills and, especially, training and experience in defending their decisions in written and oral form.

My focus in Iowa State's introductory course was to use what scientists had learned about the probe and other measurement or education devices, such as the pork carcass cross sections, to *aid* in selection decisions. My next effort was to teach that they needed performance data to assess growth rate and feed efficiency of breeding stock.

* * * * *

In looking for an Ames home to buy, we had been cautious. My annual salary was $5,400, and lenders suggested a price limit of 2.5 times income, so we had been looking in the $13,000 to $15,000 range.

We'll Leave That for You

After looking at many Ames homes on the market, in early March we purchased a three-bedroom Cape Cod south of the campus, at 2329 Storm Street, from the J. B. Davidsons and would move in during August. Dr. Davidson was considered the "father of agricultural engineering" in the United States and had been the first faculty member and then long-time head of Iowa State's agricultural engineering department. He was in failing health, so we dealt only with Mrs. Davidson, and our dealing was a lesson in generosity.

The Davidsons had their home priced at $16,500, above our range, but the location was just right, two blocks from a grade school and easy walking distance from the campus. It would fit our family perfectly. In our second visit we had told Mrs. Davidson we would stretch ourselves and would like to buy it, but we had only about $1,500 for a down-payment, likely not enough to satisfy a lender.

Her immediate response was, "Don't you worry about that; we'll see that it gets taken care of." Knowing Dr. Davidson had been a long-time director of the Ames Trust and Savings Bank, we accepted her response as having sold us the house and that financing would, in fact, "be taken care of."

As we were leaving, she retrieved my hat from a two-hat wire frame inside the front closet door. I commented that it was a novel hat rack. Her immediate response: "You like that? We'll leave it for you." We would see more of that generosity.

Owners of an adjacent vacant lot, a retired engineering professor and his wife, had urged we plant a garden on that lot so we would have vegetables after we moved into the Davidson house. During several of our summer evening or weekend visits to the garden, Mrs. Davidson took time to show us some additional feature of the house. One evening she wanted to show me the fuse boxes in the basement, and I noticed and commented about a new dehumidifier. There had been an older one in the basement the day we purchased the house; I assumed it had ceased to function and they had bought a new one for the summer.

"Oh, yes," Mrs. Davidson said. "Basements can be rather damp. We're leaving that for you."

"Now, Mrs. Davidson, you needn't do that."

"Oh, yes," she insisted. "The basement was dry when you bought the house last spring. We know you'll be renting it to some students. It needs to be dry when you move in and for those students."

I learned later that their old dehumidifier had not expired. The Davidsons had brought a displaced Latvian widow and her two sons to Ames and their home, and had put the two boys through college. Because the Davidsons were moving to be near family in Denver, they had purchased for the widow a small cottage just around the corner. They had sent that old dehumidifier to her basement and bought a new one to stay with this house.

I do not recall that we signed any agreement in March. Our next "business" discussion would be a few days before the Davidsons were to leave Ames. We went with them to the bank president's office, signed a contract purchase agreement, made our down payment, and signed a note for the balance.

* * * * *

Though I had spent five student years in Ames and had met a few business people in my role as fraternity business manager, I had essentially been a transient. I was certainly not considered, nor did I consider myself, a part of the community. Now we had a home and a job in Ames. How, and at what point, does one *become* part of a community?

It was a Saturday night, and I was on a table at Mary Greeley Hospital as my blood was flowing into a small bag. With universal donor blood type I had been called to donate; a newborn needed blood. The giving of blood was not a new experience; I had done that before. What I had not expected was an overpowering feeling that came to me as I walked out of Mary Greeley Hospital and drove home. Now I *was* part of the community; I had made a contribution.

* * * * *

It was haircut time, in those days of short trim about every ten days, and I had walked over to the Union barber shop after a morning class. I greeted Les Hegland, who had been at the first chair since before I was a freshman, nodded to one of my students in the second chair, and found a seat along the wall to wait my turn. My student's face had shown some surprise as I had nodded to him; perhaps he thought faculty had some special shop for their haircuts.

In a few moments, the third chair was open, and when I stepped up, my student looked up and asked, "What are you doing in town?"

Did he not know who I was? Had I left so little an impression in four weeks, three lectures a week? I could think of only one response. "I work here. In fact, I teach your animal husbandry course, in Room 109 of Curtiss Hall, and you sit in the second row."

His face reddened, "Oh, yeah!" Then he recovered fully. "I just confused you with our veterinarian back home."

It does one good to realize that your intellect and classroom presence may not leave a lasting impression on every student.

*****

Apparently one of my faculty colleagues had given department head Leslie Johnson an ultimatum. I did not know which colleague or the ultimatum. But I did know it had raised Johnson's ire.

Do This, or Else

It was near adjournment of the state legislature, and there would be money for at least modest pay raises. The last part of the academic year was also decision time for promotions and granting of tenure. It was also faculty recruitment time. Other universities respected Iowa State's strength in animal husbandry, and when there was a senior vacancy at another school, it was not uncommon for one in the department to get a "feeler" for their interest in the vacancy.

Apparently, one of my colleagues had a feeler, or even an offer, and thought this a good time to press for a large raise or a promotion. Or he may have thought it a good time to press for some new and costly laboratory equipment. Whatever it was, he had apparently gone about it the wrong way.

I had fallen in step with Johnson on the way to LaGrange's office for ten o'clock coffee. I drank little coffee but had noticed Johnson made it a point to join the teaching group every week or so for coffee. He did the same with other department faculty groups, such as dairy, genetics, or nutrition. It kept him in touch with all his staff and the issues and let all know he was interested in them and their work.

Though I was often reluctant to interrupt my work for the coffee visit, I usually learned a bit of department history or philosophy. This morning I had grabbed my cup to join the others, usually Jim Kiser, judging team coach and equitation instructor; Bruce Taylor, lead nutrition instructor; Anderson;

and Don Warner, with whom I shared a hole-in-the-wall telephone and, sometimes, his drifting cigar smoke.

This morning Johnson was moving with a bit more determination and resolve; something was bothering him. His short comment as we walked told me what: "When someone says to you, 'You must do this, or else,' they had better be prepared for 'or else'!"

*****

Fear of change, or undue caution about making change, is not limited to older people. In this case, it was a long-retired dean who told several of us younger faculty it was time for change.

It Is Time!

Johnson had called Bud Ewing, who taught beef production, Kiser, and me into his office to meet with him and retired dean of agriculture H. H. Kildee. The topic was how the department should react to a proposal before management of Chicago's International Livestock Show to add carcass competition to the show. Animals that placed high in the show ring would be processed and their carcasses judged for muscling and other qualities. This would be a significant change for the International Show and for most long-time show competitors.

Carcass competition had already been added to a few county and state fair shows. County and state extension staff, as well as local industry leaders, had been eager to demonstrate that carcasses disclose features that are not so apparent in live animals. After all, the purpose of raising and feeding meat animals is to produce more and higher quality meat. One can tell more with the hide off.

Kildee was a well-known livestock judge. He had not only judged the International Show beef competition several times, he had judged state and regional shows across the country, as well as major shows in other countries. Though he was in his mid-seventies and had retired from the deanship eight years earlier, he continued to be sought as a judge for major shows. He was scheduled to attend a meeting of International Show management and wanted to know the position of his home department on the issue of carcass competition.

Not only was our department respected for its solid science, calves from its purebred beef herd had brought a good many blue ribbons back to Iowa State. Both Kildee and Johnson wanted input from the department's younger staff; Kiser was in his mid-thirties; Ewing and I were yet in our mid-twenties.

My experiences had told me the correlation between live animal judging and desired carcass traits needed to be increased, and carcass competition would make that fact more clear. However, I wondered, *Would carcass competition be accepted by the International's patrons?* Was there yet enough precision in carcass evaluation techniques to convince show participants that it was a valid basis for awarding blue ribbons? Would it diminish the drama of the live animal show ring?

From questions and comments, it appeared Ewing and Kiser had similar concerns. "Is the industry ready for this? Has there been enough research?"

Kildee mostly listened, but both he and Johnson prodded a bit. "How much research is needed?" "What yet needs to be demonstrated?"

Discussion continued, including pros and cons, for perhaps thirty minutes.

Finally, Kildee leaned forward and laid out his own thoughts. "Consumers are asking for leaner beef. USDA is revising its grade standards to reflect that and to give more credit to evidence of muscling and leanness. If the International is to be a leading force in the livestock industry, it needs to change. *It is time*!"

This was a valuable meeting for me. I saw the forward vision and conviction in a man forty years our senior versus the caution in my younger colleagues and me. I also saw why an earlier university administration had named Kildee dean—and before that, head of the animal husbandry department.

Postscript: Decades later, as I spoke to county Farm Bureau annual meetings across western Iowa, I would often describe this meeting with Dean Kildee. A large part of my audience would be retired farmers and their spouses, many in their seventies; their younger family members were too busy running the farm and attending school events. I would urge my audience to "play the Kildee role," to prod their next generations to adapt to changing times.

* * * * *

Two years teaching at A&M had convinced me that college teaching was the right choice for me, and I had come to Iowa State intent on improving the freshman animal husbandry courses. I had also hoped I could teach some junior level nutrition courses.

I had taught one section of principles of nutrition the previous summer, and had taught a condensed freshman course, the way I wanted to teach the subject matter, for the winter quarter program students both years. However, Dr. Bruce Taylor, perhaps twenty years my senior, who had joined the faculty as an associate professor two months before I had arrived, had first "dibs" on both nutrition courses, the latter called applied animal nutrition and covering feed evaluation and ration formulation. Even more frustrating, I had seemed to hit a roadblock on making changes in the freshman sequence, AH 111 and 112. Anderson, in charge of those courses as well as leader of the department's teaching program, was not interested in change.

Revisiting the Decision

A trip to Story City and Roland with Wayne Rodgers, executive vice president and general manager of Foxbilt Feeds, would tell me if I should stay in academia or depart for the feed industry. This trip was midway in my second year back at Iowa State. I had just returned from a two-week interval at Oklahoma A&M where I had passed my "prelims," individual written tests in my two minors, and my final exam for the doctorate, including approval of my doctoral thesis.

Foxbilt Feeds had advertised for a nutritionist with a doctorate. I had made contact and spent a Saturday morning with Rodgers and his colleagues in their downtown Des Moines office. Rodgers had introduced me to Ed Fox, chairman of the Foxbilt board, and sales manager Ken Lepley. I had been impressed, especially with the enthusiasm of Rodgers and Lepley. They had outlined what seemed a great opportunity and made it clear I would be the third person of a three-person leadership team, with Rodgers the manager, Lepley handling sales, and me responsible for formulation, developing feeding systems, and salesman/customer education. Salary was about the same as my Iowa State salary. We had finished the morning at the Foxbilt research facility in northeastern Des Moines, a small but adequate version of the swine nutrition research facilities at Iowa State.

The trip to Roland and Story City was the follow-up. We would visit the company's poultry genetics business, Ames In-Cross, in both communities. It seemed to me that poultry genetics was a company sideline, managed separately from the feed business, and reporting only to Rodgers. Thus my time with him would be the main value of the trip. If I was sold on Foxbilt and Rodgers by the end of the day, and Rodgers was still sold on me, I could be the Foxbilt nutritionist. I had been essentially offered the job during the Des Moines visit.

We drove to Story City and Roland, walked through the company facilities, and ate lunch. Rodgers was more open than I could expect him to be, providing details of the Fox family, such as who was valuable to the company and who was less so, explaining to me problems and opportunities. Were I to join Foxbilt, I was convinced nothing would be hidden. I would experience what I had seen and been told, and I was sold on both Rogers and Lepley. If I wanted to be in the feed business, and especially be part of the company management team, I need not look further.

However, throughout the day, I had a steady, deep-down feeling of discomfort. *What am I doing here?* I felt ill at ease. Could I chart a course within Foxbilt that would give me the daily satisfactions I was enjoying? Would Shirley and our young daughters find the life related to the feed business and Des Moines as satisfying as life in a university community? Shirley had fit so well in the university setting, having students in our home at both Stillwater and Ames and helping chaperone fraternity, sorority, and other student events.

A day later Dean Floyd Andre helped me close the door on the feed business. Associate Dean Roy Kottman, whom I had known from my first weeks as a freshman, had asked me to come to his office to visit. As we visited, Andre stepped in. He said he just wanted me to know I had a good future in the university and I would have a lot of support for that future. Nothing specific was mentioned, but from that visit, I knew the university was our place.

My interest in the feed industry had not disappeared; it would be evident and valuable in my teaching of animal nutrition, as well as the freshman course, and I would do a bit of nutrition consulting.

Postscript: Bruce Taylor would leave at the end of that year to head the animal husbandry department at the University of Arizona, and I would inherit "first dibs" on the two junior level nutrition courses, principles and applied. And with help from the chair of the college curriculum committee, Louis Thompson, I would gain approval for a new, "experimental" freshman animal science course, described in the next section.

What happened to Foxbilt? John Morrell and Company, a major meat processor at Ottumwa, Iowa, purchased both Foxbilt and Golden Sun, a feed company at Estherville, and blended Foxbilt into Golden Sun. Wayne Rodgers joined Walnut Grove in Atlantic and, in time, became general manager, while Ken Lepley and the nutritionist that had been hired formed Triple F Feeds. Ed Fox joined the predecessor of US AID and went to a foreign post.

OMAHA DAILY JOURNAL-STOCKMAN

Iowa State's Hold "Class" at Yards

(Omaha Daily Journal-Stockman Photo)

Earlier this week the Omaha stockyards became a "classroom" for these 24 Iowa State College students from Ames and their instructor, Dr. Duane Acker (front row left, with glasses and light jacket). Members of Dr. Acker's class in livestock markets and grades, the boys were put through a rigorous but thorough one-day marketing school as guests of Omaha livestock market interests. Between sun-up and sundown they studied virtually every phase of handling, buying and selling livestock on a big terminal market. As they entrained for Ames they said the day had been an eye-opener in efficiency of market operation and competitive trading.

Spring quarter of my second year I also taught a senior course, Livestock Marketing. Because so many of Iowa's market animals were sold directly to processors, most of my students knew little about terminal markets, where a commission salesman represented the seller. I felt my students should get exposed to a terminal market and arranged a class field trip to the Omaha Stockyards. (Reprinted with permission from Drovers/Cattle Network.)

* * * * *

Except for using the probe to measure a pig's fatness, discussing performance records, and presenting current nutrition and genetics concepts in the discussion part of my lab sections, the introductory animal husbandry courses remained little changed from those of my own freshman year. Nutrition, genetics, animal selection, and marketing concepts applied to all species; it was a waste of student time to repeat them for each of the four species, but that was how the courses were organized. If I could not change the courses, perhaps they could be replaced. Two circumstances would help bring that about.

A New Course

The first circumstance was the three-credit AH 114 that I taught the winter quarter farm operation students. Instead of segments for sheep, swine, and beef cattle, I focused my lectures on the concepts and principles common to all species. I used labs for probing pigs, calculating selection indexes for breeding stock of all species, some live animal judging, field trips, and what some would call "outside the box" demonstrations. For example, to show that an animal's intestine had an immense surface area for nutrient absorption, I retrieved a lamb's internal organs from the meat lab, tied one end of the small intestine to a post in the corner of the arena, and strung it to a post in the opposite corner and then nearly back to the first. The students got the point.

The second circumstance was growing concern about AH111 and 112 by faculty and students in other departments, both the six credits of a student's curriculum that the courses consumed and the emphasis on judging. They wanted basic nutrition, genetics, selection, and marketing concepts in less than six credits.

Two years earlier, the agricultural economics faculty had asked that the three-credit 114 for the winter quarter program students also be available to their ag business freshmen; their course section was called 114B and I also taught that. Soon agronomy was asking to make the same shift from 111 and 112.

Now was my chance. As chair of the department curriculum committee and member of the college committee, and with some encouragement from Johnson and from the college committee chair, Louis Thompson (also in charge of farm op and professor of agronomy), I proposed a four-credit "experimental" course, 114C, available to *any* major in agriculture, *including* animal husbandry majors. It would be three lectures and one two-hour lab each week. Labs would be the same as in 114 and 114B.

I had great support from my colleagues in the dairy section of animal husbandry and from the other departments, and 114C was quickly approved by the college committee and the college faculty. Dairy colleagues Fred

Foreman, John Sims, and Art Porter helped me write a lab manual, and we had it printed at the university print shop.

By 1960, AH 111 and 112 would no longer exist. The university catalog would show only the four-credit 114 and the three-credit version, now called 114A, for the winter quarter program.

* * * * *

My outline and material for the winter quarter program 114 course had become a basic skeleton for an introductory text that I wanted to write. This was delicate territory; Anderson's book had long been the text for 111 and 112.

Now, a New Textbook

Late in my first year back at Iowa State, I had quietly mentioned my interest in writing a book to several textbook salesmen who regularly stopped by my office, and they liked the book outline I described.

At the 1957 American Society of Animal Science meetings in Chicago, a publishing company editor got me together with H. H. Cole, head of animal science at the University of California, Davis campus. Cole had also put together a book outline, and it was almost identical to mine. If Cole and I would work together, this editor's company would publish the book. However, Cole wanted to have each chapter written by a specialist in their subject and proposed that he and I assemble and "edit" the chapters. That did not interest me. Continuity and efficient use of space would be difficult to achieve with multiple authors. I wanted to write the content, and if the book was successful, I wanted the royalties.

What really forced my proceeding to write the book would be accepting the leadership of the farm operation curriculum in 1958 (described in a later section), near the end of my third year at Iowa State. That job could well lead me into a career in administration. However, to be accepted by a faculty for an animal science department headship or a college of agriculture deanship, one needed to be well established in his academic discipline, most often by research papers published in scientific journals. Only ten percent of my faculty time had been budgeted for research, and my research publication record would be considered modest; my primary job was teaching and advising students. As leader of the farm operation curriculum and serving as adviser to many of its six hundred students, there would be little time for research. While there was no way that I could establish a strong animal science reputation via research papers, I could with a respected textbook.

The day I made the decision to accept the farm op job, I also made the decision to write the book. That fall, in addition to my farm op student advising work, I would teach a lecture section of 114 on Monday, Wednesday, and Friday, and with a lab assistant, handle one section of the two-hour lab. I wrote in the evenings, with a target of one chapter drafted for each lecture.

After dinner, I would play with our daughters until their eight o'clock bedtime, and from eight to ten I would be at my desk writing. Three mornings a week I would hand my secretary a handwritten chapter draft, which she would type and reproduce on ditto paper. I would then hand out copies in class as reading for the next day's lecture.

A year later, I was using my second draft, a spiral-bound version typed by my neighbor and reproduced and bound by the W. C. Brown Company of Dubuque, but under my copyright. With Johnson's approval, I had signed a commitment that over the next few years our students would purchase the two thousand copies that Brown would print. That gave me time to make more refinements, gather photos and other visuals (with Shirley sketching those I could not find), and pursue a contract with a publisher of hardcover books.

Prentice-Hall published the hard-cover book in the fall of 1962 (just after I had moved to Kansas State) and it carried a 1963 copyright. Because administrative work pulled me away from the industry, Animal science faculty at SDSU and Kansas State helped me revise the work for the second and third editions. Purdue Professor Merle Cunningham did most of the work for the next editions, and his Purdue colleague, Mickey Latour, took the lead for the seventh edition. By the mid 1990s, however, I was back on the farm, working closely with the animal industries and helping develop an egg production cooperative, so I updated or re-wrote several chapters for the later editions (and they still carried some of Shirley's hand-drawn illustrations).

Postscript: Advances in animal genetics and nutrition, structural changes in the animal industry, the rapid movement toward continually-revised e-books, and the ability of instructors to tap multiple electronic sources of material prompted a recent decision to revise the book no more. Just as the Wiota School had done its job by 1963 after forty years, my Animal Science and Industry book, after fifty years and seven editions, had done its job.

*****

It was Sunday night, and our bus driver, "Chick" Anderson, agronomy professor Frank Gardner (my farm crops lab instructor eight years earlier), and I were having dinner at a small Mexican café in Tucumcari, New Mexico. It was June, 1957, after my second year at Iowa State. We had completed the first week of Iowa State's agricultural travel course.

Food of the Region

Gardner and I had been at work since January, arranging a four-week travel agenda covering sixteen states and selecting the thirty student participants, mostly juniors and seniors. Each had enrolled for the eight credits, four in agronomy and four in animal husbandry.

Our first week out, we visited the Kansas City Board of Trade, Kansas State's Flour and Feed Milling Department, Ed Smith's beef cattle research at Kansas State, and the Dewey Ranch south of Manhattan, Kansas (managed by Orville Burtis and, during my Kansas State presidency, purchased by Nature Conservancy for use by Kansas State and renamed The Konza Prairie). We had also visited K-State research stations at Hays and Garden City, a large turkey growing business at Cheraw, Colorado, and a nearly century-old irrigation project at nearby Rocky Ford. Saturday night was spent in Las Vegas, New Mexico.

Before getting back to Ames, we would see the Carlsbad Caverns; goat ranches in Texas; rice farms in Louisiana and Mississippi; cattle operations in Alabama's "black belt"; tobacco production and marketing in North Carolina; our US senators' offices in DC; Amish farms in Pennsylvania's Lancaster County; and tractor manufacturing in South Bend, Indiana.

This day we had driven a tortuous and narrow highway from Las Vegas to Conchas Dam, where rancher George Ellis had met us and led our Greyhound bus eight or ten miles north over a dusty ranch lane to the Bell Ranch headquarters. Bell Ranch and Ellis were well known among both progressive cattlemen and academics for using performance records to select heifers and bulls for the next generation. Extension colleague Ralph Durham had told me about Ellis, so I had made contact and asked if we could visit his ranch. Using both his cattle and charts of data, Ellis had given our students a college course worth of information and inspiration on the value of performance records.

Photos from the 1957 Agriculture Travel Course. Upper left, at an alfalfa dehydrating plant near Lawrence, Kansas. Upper right, riding over the Dewey Ranch (now Kanza Prairie) south of Manhattan, Kansas. Lower left, Dewey Ranch manager Orville Burtis answering a student's question. Lower right, I help hold the chart while Bell Ranch manager George Ellis shows performance differences between Cow A and Cow B on his ranch.

Our hosts often provided noontime meals for the group. When we checked into a hotel or college dorm at the end of the day, the students would scatter, finding their own fare. Anderson, Gardner, and I would cruise in the Greyhound, usually to a restaurant Anderson knew. He had driven for the course many years, and it had generally followed the same route.

As we left Ames, Gardner had been on the speaker, giving instructions, rules of the road, and how all should represent the university. He finished with, "You will not only see diverse agriculture but will also experience diverse cultures. When in Kansas City, eat steak. When in Mississippi, eat grits. Eat food of the region!" He had repeated that admonition several times, in Kansas City and the night before in Las Vegas.

Anderson, Gardner, and I had certainly experienced "food of the region" in Las Vegas. It was a Mexican restaurant, we had all ordered the house special, and it had been hot! Never had my mouth experienced such fire.

This evening in Tucumcari, Anderson, Gardner, and I were at another Mexican restaurant, and Gardner was studying the menu. "You know," he said, "I think I'll order roast chicken."

I could not resist. "Frank, don't you dare order chicken. What if the students walked in here? You've been telling them since we left Ames to 'eat food of the region'! You would never live it down."

Gardner was caught. I emphasized with him, though; I could still feel the effects of those Las Vegas chili peppers. We all ordered the special but asked for the chili pepper sauce on the side.

* * * * *

It had been a long afternoon; Cliff Iverson and I were judging the last of more than a dozen classes of 4-H pigs at the Plymouth County Fair in LeMars.

The Crowd Let Us Know

Pork production is big business in Iowa, so pigs were a popular 4-H project, and the Plymouth County show was large. Since noon we had judged crossbred market pigs and both female breeding stock and market pigs in each of several breeds.

Livestock show judges are usually imported, for two reasons. They likely will not know the contestants, so if they or their parents, in the case of 4-H or FFA, are unhappy with their decisions, they can quickly leave town. I had come from the Iowa State Campus 175 miles away, and Iverson had driven another 100 miles from Iowa State's Ottumwa extension office.

With so many entries, the market pigs had been divided into weight classes, those above or below 210 pounds. From the top two in each weight class a breed champion and reserve champion would be chosen. The two classes made judging easier and, more important, more ribbons could be awarded. That is what a 4-H show is all about, letting young 4-H members show off their animals and, if they do especially well, the satisfaction of winning a blue or purple ribbon.

If a 4-H member had more than one entry in a class, a brother or friend would help, each using a light panel and stick to keep the animal in view of the judges. We studied each animal for muscling, thick hams and shoulders, and absence of any bulging rolls of fat as the animal walked.

We had finished placing the lightweight Chester White market pigs, and it was breed championship time, so the stands were packed. The top two heavyweight pigs were being guided back into the ring to join the first and second place lightweight pigs we had just chosen.

It had been obvious to Iverson and me that the two heavyweight pigs would be the breed champion and reserve; the top two lightweights did not measure up. No need to take a lot of time; with all four pigs in the ring, we took a couple steps forward, pointed and signaled "one" and "two," and the crowd gasped!

We had been careless. We had not noticed that the boys handling the two heavyweights had switched pigs. We quickly corrected ourselves, both embarrassed and wiser.

As soon as the show was over, we slipped out of town.

*****

Examinations are a good measure of student learning, and I consider them also a measure of my teaching effectiveness. From time to time, though, a rare student will try to beat the system. Here are a couple of cases, and though unfortunate, each became a chance for the student or students to "correct course," and each included an element of humor.

What Is under Your Foot?

It was the final exam for AH 216, feeds and feeding, a sophomore course for nonmajors, and we were in Room 19 in the southeast corner of Curtiss Hall. The room held ninety students, and every seat was taken. I was especially attentive; the temptation to glance at another's test paper is ever present. If the instructor is visibly attentive, there is less temptation.

About ten minutes into the exam, I noticed that a young man in the back row seemed to be spending more time watching me than working on the test. Something was amiss. I sauntered to the back of the room and stood for a moment behind and to his right. Though he appeared nervous and glanced over his shoulder toward me once, I could not put my finger on the problem.

As I started to move on, I noticed the corner of a card extending from under his shoe, and I hesitated. His foot moved slightly to the right, covering that corner. I moved to the left and spied momentarily an opposite corner of what appeared now to be a 3x5 index card. He quickly shifted his foot to the left. I moved back to the right; his foot shifted to the right.

I tapped him on the shoulder, apologized for interrupting, and said, "I'd like to see what that is under your foot."

He raised his foot and exposed a totally blank 3x5 card, at least blank on the exposed side. I picked it up, and on the other side, which had been facing the floor, was considerable information one might find useful for an exam.

"You finish the exam," I said quietly, "and then come up and let's visit."

He waited until most others had turned in their exams and left the room. Visibly distraught, he handed me his test with a shaking hand and blurted, "This is the first time I've every tried anything like this, and it's going to be the last! I'm sorry. I apologize. I shouldn't have. It's terrible!"

"But," I said, "the card was face down on the floor."

"Yes. I filled it out and put it up my shirt sleeve where it would be handy. When I sat down, it fell out and landed face down. I was afraid to reach down to pick it up or turn it over; I was sure you would see me. I'll never do it again. It isn't worth it!"

My response: "Okay. Here is what we'll do. I'll grade the test and record your score; I know you didn't use what was on the card. I'll then calculate your total course points for a letter grade, and then drop it one grade. I believe you. Case closed."

"Thank you! I appreciate that. I'll never do it again!" He left the room a relieved and wiser young man.

He Couldn't Even Whistle

Colleague and neighbor Walt Woods and I were walking from the east door of Curtiss Hall to his car in the lot across the street. It was just after five thirty on a Friday evening, and we had come from the weekly department seminar.

We met three students headed toward Curtiss, and after they passed, I commented to Woods, "I'm suspicious. Two of those fellows are in my animal nutrition class and have an exam scheduled tomorrow morning. They all belong to a fraternity, and most fraternities serve dinner at five thirty on Friday evenings." (Fraternities would often schedule a one-hour dance exchange with a sorority or women's dorm at seven o'clock on Friday evenings.)

As we got into Woods's car, I said, "Walt, if you aren't in a rush, let's drive around to the visitor's stall behind Curtiss; I want to see what's going on."

Woods parked, and I jumped out and hurried into the building. As I rounded the corner at the center of the ground floor, one of the three students was at the water fountain. The shocked look on his face was enough to confirm my suspicions. I'd failed to notice the second student of the trio as I passed the reading room. He was at the reading room window overlooking the visitor's parking stall but apparently had not made it there before Woods and I pulled in.

Woods, following behind me, later told me the boy at the water fountain had tried to sound a warning, but was so surprised "he couldn't even whistle."

Our office suite door at the south end of the hall was ajar. I walked in and around the secretary's desk to a storage room where reproduced tests were kept. That door was open, and student number three, the one not in my class, had several file drawers open.

"What are you doing here?" It was the obvious question.

"Well," he admitted, "you just as well know—looking for the nutrition exam."

"How did you get in here?"

He handed me a key, which I later learned fit most of the doors on the floor. "One of the graduate students keeps it above his lab door so his student helper can get in at any time. I knew where it was."

He had not yet reached the drawer that held the test. I closed the drawers, locked the door, and the two of us went into my office. I called the fraternity house, asked for the other two members of the trio, and left a message that they should call me at my office as soon as they returned. Within minutes, I got the call.

"I'll wait for you in my office. Your partner is here; we need to visit." I then called Professor Anderson and described the situation. Because the boy I had caught in the storage room was not in my class, so beyond my authority for any action, I needed Anderson's advice. Anderson came to my office to join in listening to the three boys' confessions. He and I then agreed to brief Johnson the next morning.

In my office Saturday morning, about eight thirty, I got a call from agronomy professor Bugs Firkins, adviser to the student who had been at the fountain. Firkins told me the boy came to see him and told him about the incident. He was sure the boy was an innocent victim of circumstances; he had simply been waiting at the water fountain and had not realized anything improper was going on.

I responded, "Bugs, I appreciate your defending and supporting one of your advisees, but he was square in the middle of the whole process." The boy had fully confessed to Anderson and me the evening before.

After the exam, Johnson, Anderson, and I were in Dean Andre's office. (Johnson and I knew that the father of Firkin's advisee was an influential banker in the state and also a personal friend of Andre. This was a perfect illustration of Murphy's Law in academics: a student in trouble is likely the son or daughter of a very influential alumnus, legislator, or regent.)

Andre listened to our description of the event, my phone call to Anderson, his joining me to visit with the students, and Woods's presence at the initial encounter. Andre's perceptions, logic, and basic integrity led him to stand squarely behind our judgments that all three students were fully involved.

My two students continued in my course. After grades were tabulated, I dropped each a letter grade. From my standpoint the case was closed, but the case went to a student/faculty discipline committee, and all three were placed on probation.

Student number one, perhaps near borderline in academic ability, was most remorseful. He apologized personally to me, wrote a lengthy letter declaring his guilt, and offered his example and his time if there was any way he could encourage other students to avoid getting involved in such an episode. In due time, he graduated (and I would have been pleased to recommend him to any employer).

Student number two, who had enlisted the aid of his adviser (and, we later learned, his father) remained resentful throughout the balance of his time on campus. The third boy, the one with the key and whom I had found looking for the tests, did not return the following year.

*****

Johnson caught me in the hall as I returned from the library, my briefcase crammed with nutrition test papers that I had just finished grading.

The Dean Wants to See You

"The dean wants to see you," Johnson said. He did not say what about; perhaps it involved that recent student test incident.

For the hundred students in applied animal nutrition, I gave essay tests of thirteen questions, each worth ten points, and a student could answer any ten. For grading, I would list the components I expected in each answer, and a point value for each component. After a test, I would head to a small room in the university library for uninterrupted grading (I had been assigned the room for work on my intended book). Essay questions are the best way to find out what students know and how well they can articulate what they know, but they take a lot of time to grade. I had spent most of two half-days in the library when I bumped into Johnson.

Five minutes later, Johnson and I were in Dean Andre's office, and he got right to the point. "Duane, would you be interested in taking over the farm operation curriculum?" (Farm operation was less specialized than animal husbandry or agronomy and included a four year degree program, a two-year certificate program, and a winter quarter program, all with college credit and designed for students who intended to operate farms. Enrollment totaled about six hundred students versus about four hundred undergraduates in animal husbandry.)

This was a shock. I knew the current curriculum head, Louis Thompson, was moving across the hall to become associate dean, with the current associate dean, Kottman, departing to become dean at West Virginia, but I had assumed Dr. Bob Collins, Thompson's senior assistant, would be his successor.

I do not recall my exact response, but it likely included appreciation for the question, and certainly, "I would need to think about that for a while."

"You think about it a day or two and stop in anytime with a question or to just visit about it," Andre said, and the meeting was over.

Back in my office I recorded the test scores in my grade book, told our secretary I would be out for the afternoon, and walked home for lunch and to tell Shirley the news.

I needed the afternoon to think. After lunch I drove down to Carr Hardware, bought a cheap rod and reel and a small fishing box, and spent the afternoon at Ledges State Park, doing more thinking than fishing.

Was I willing to give up most of the teaching I enjoyed, the introductory course and the two junior level nutrition courses? The farm operation job was 75 percent advising students, plus managing two staff positions and a secretary. As a result, I would be limited to teaching one course per quarter. Second question: Did I want to set my sights on administration? If so, this could be a good first step.

Andre was well-known as being cautious about exposing administrative moves; he did not like rumors or gossip. There were only three people other than Andre I could talk to for advice: Thompson, Kottman, and Johnson.

I told Johnson I was torn between the farm op job and what I thought might be a golden opportunity within my department, leading the teaching program (current leader Anderson was near retirement).

Johnson confirmed I could have that opportunity, but with his characteristic laugh. "You can't be in two places." Both opportunities were or would be open to me; I would just have to decide.

Kottman clearly enjoyed administration. His response: "You can't afford to pass up the farm op job!"

Rumors had begun to float among the faculty. Thompson's move to associate dean had been announced, but there had been no announcement of his replacement.

It was later that day or the next that Collins confronted me in the hallway and asked if I was going to be the new head of farm op. I had responded, "Bob, if I am, you know I can't say a thing; if I'm not, there is nothing to say."

Collins was intense. "If the dean names you, I'm going to fight it; I deserve that job!"

I now needed more advice from Kottman; he knew all the personalities. Further, he had no stake in the outcome; he was on his way to West Virginia. Kottman offered an idea. "How about asking Dean Andre to move Collins full time to agricultural education? His doctorate was in ag ed, and he now teaches a course there."

It was good advice, and Andre agreed to do it. However, I would be lacking that position until Andre found enough money to replace Collins in farm op.

Thompson had not been in the room when Andre had offered me the job. Yet the work related strictly to academic advising and curriculum issues, the purview of soon-to-be Associate Dean Thompson. I needed to ask Andre, "To whom do I report, you or Thompson?"

"To whom do you want to report?"

Most would want to report to the highest level, but I replied, "It seems logical that it be Thompson." That was the response Andre wanted.

Eight years later, early in my deanship at South Dakota State, I was invited to speak at one of the two-year agricultural technical colleges in western Minnesota. Bob Collins was my host. We spent several hours touring the college farm, talked curriculum issues, and had a thoroughly enjoyable visit. I was pleased to see him content and proud in his work there. Iowa State's farm operation program was not mentioned.

*****

When I had agreed to co-teach the agriculture travel course the second year, 1958, it had been on the condition that my new partner, agronomist Ot Burger, and I could plan a route different from what the course had followed for more than a decade. A new route would require more work, to identify new contacts and describe the group and our purpose. However, different farms, ranches, and industries would give me a broader perspective, as well as more illustrations for my animal science classes.

In the first several days of the course, we had visited the Omaha stockyards, toured Omaha's Kitty Clover potato chip plant, and visited irrigated farms and feedlots near Grand Island. Our next stops were a sheep ranch north of Cheyenne and another near Laramie; on a Friday afternoon we headed south to Walden, Colorado.

We're Holding Supper at the Church

We had just unloaded at a motel on the south end of the main street in Walden, a town of about six hundred people and county seat of Jackson County. Walden is the major town in Colorado's "North Park," a colorful ranching valley between the Rocky Mountains to the west and the Medicine Bow Mountains to the east. The streams in North Park flow generally north and combine to form the North Platte River, which continues into Wyoming before turning east into Nebraska.

Faculty colleague and Colorado native Bob Temple had told me about this beautiful ranch valley but could not give me the name of a contact. I had addressed a letter to "County Extension Agent, Walden, Colorado." The letter described our course and asked if he would arrange a couple of ranch visits for us. The response came from a Walden veterinarian. He had previously been the county agent but had resigned to devote full time to veterinary work, and the county agent post was vacant. He had taken my letter to the county cattlemen's association meeting, and that group would be delighted to host us. We would spend a morning visiting ranches and be the association's guests for a "mountain trout lunch up in high country."

My department's hotel/motel Redbook did not list any lodgings in Walden, so I had addressed a letter to "Hotel or Motel, Walden, Colorado." Soon I received a response, "Yes, we have sufficient rooms."

Our hungry students tumbled out of the bus at the Walden motel, and rather than stand in line to get their motel keys, most took off down the street to one of the cafés we had passed. I was just stepping into the motel lobby when a pickup came rolling in and screeched to a halt. A fellow jumped out, saying, "Sure glad to see you; we've been waiting supper for all of you up at the church!"

He explained that the local conservation club, a mix of ranchers and townspeople, had heard we were coming and "just wanted to host this bunch of Iowans." The tables were set and the food was ready.

Both surprised and impressed by such hospitality, I said, "But some of our boys have scattered." I jumped into the pickup with him. "We'll have to pull them out of the cafés before they order."

Within fifteen minutes we were all in the basement of the local church, amid the aroma of roasted lamb and beef, hot rolls, and casseroles, and friendly greetings.

Though we had a fantastic meal, the discussion following the meal was even more memorable to these Iowa farm boys. They knew only privately owned land devoted to corn, soybeans, fenced pastures, and confined livestock and poultry. Here we were in "public land" country; most of the land in the county was owned by the federal and state governments and managed by the US Forest Service, National Park Service, or the Department of Interior. Grazing rights were leased to adjacent ranchers.

An important issue was up for discussion: Were the grazing leases limiting or detrimental to hunting and fishing? Tomorrow we would be guests of the local cattlemen's association; tonight we were guests of the local Conservation Club, a mix of ranchers and nonranchers.

Some of the hunters wanted a portion of the public land excluded from the grazing leases and reserved exclusively for hunting. A grazing lease-holder responded, "I bought my ranch in part because of the grazing lease; it would lower the value of my ranch and I'd have to cut the size of my herd." Ranchers complained about hunters leaving open the gates. Discussion was intense and, to us, highly educational.

Saturday was just as memorable, with visits to two ranches with grazing and hay meadows irrigated from the North Platte and its tributaries and then to a picnic area high in the Routt National Forest. Several members of the cattlemen's association had spent a day catching Rocky Mountain trout for us and our ranch hosts. Large pans of cooking grease sizzled over a grate and blazing fire, and we feasted in crisp mountain air on trout fillets rolled in flour and cracker crumbs, plus bread and baked beans.

It always pays to take a different route!

North Park ranchers and our 1958 Ag Travel Course group gathered for trout fillets among the tall pines of the Routt National Forest.

* * * * *

For our wedding anniversary, we might have planned a dinner out in Ames or a candlelight dinner at home, but this anniversary day Shirley and I had driven to Sac City to hire Harold Crawford, whom I wanted to join me as a student adviser in the farm operation curriculum office.

Our Seventh Wedding Anniversary

Andre had found the money so I could fill the position left vacant by Collins's move to ag ed. Thompson and I had agreed that we should seek a top vo-ag teacher who also wanted to pursue graduate study. We also agreed that Crawford was that person.

Atlantic friend Tom Magill had introduced me to Crawford winter quarter of my freshman year. We were all in the same Horticulture lab section, wading through the snow pruning Concord grape vines. Magill and Crawford had both transferred to Iowa State from Tarkio College, and Crawford was then a senior.

The following fall, Crawford was teaching vo-ag at Story City High. I had enrolled in a one-credit agricultural education course to acquaint prospective vo-ag teachers with the field (an option I was considering), and we had taken a field trip to Story City. Though it was early in Crawford's first year of teaching, I was impressed with his program.

By 1958 Crawford was teaching at Sac City. His students were winning state and national recognition, and he had emerged as an Iowa leader in his profession.

When I called Crawford early in the week, he had shown some interest in the open position but said he needed to talk with his wife as well as learn more. So Shirley and I drove to Sac City, having arranged to meet at the Crawford's home after school was out.

We were well received, and it was apparent that Crawford badly wanted to come back to Iowa State for graduate study. It was equally apparent that both he and his wife, who also was teaching, were reticent to give up their good jobs and income, the home they had purchased, and the level of living their combined salaries provided. Their children were doing well in school and they were well known and respected citizens of the community. To give all that up for less income and multiple responsibilities, teaching, advising students, and graduate study, would not be easy.

After an hour and a half of lively conversation, Harold declined the position. He thanked us for our interest but felt he could not consider the job at this time. For us it was a disappointment, but it was still our wedding anniversary, so Shirley and I headed to Trealor's, a popular Fort Dodge steakhouse.

The following October at the national FFA convention, where again several of his students were being recognized, Crawford suffered a minor heart event. There was no permanent damage, and he recovered rapidly. In early December Shirley and I encountered Crawford at the Delta Sigma Phi fraternity house. It was a pre-agriculture banquet reception, and he and some of his students were to be recognized at the banquet. I asked Crawford how he was doing.

"You know, Duane, I sure wish I had accepted your offer last spring. I've given a lot of thought the last few weeks to what is really important in life." He followed up, "I really want to be on a university faculty. I really want to pursue graduate study; I just hope there will be another opportunity."

*****

A few years after we left Iowa State, Crawford was invited to a faculty position in the agricultural education department, where he would also earn his doctorate in the spring of 1968. In March of that year (I was dean at South Dakota State), I was invited to address the North Central Agricultural Education Conference in Chicago.

As I walked into the conference room, Crawford spotted me and made a beeline my way, smiling from ear to ear. "I've got some good news, and I want you to be one of the first to know it. Dean Thompson has asked me to head farm op." He added, "I turned down the chance to join farm op that you gave me nine years ago, but the good Lord gave me another chance, and I wasn't going to pass this one up."

Though I had failed in my effort to bring Crawford to Iowa State, perhaps our seventh wedding anniversary visit in Sac City had been a step in the process.

*****

In addition to managing our young daughters, the home and me, and hosting department club officers in our home for their monthly meetings, Shirley was an advisor or sponsor to two student wives' clubs, animal husbandry and farm operation.

The Wives' Clubs

It was nearly eleven, well past our bedtime, and they did not want to leave. Three young women, wives of our animal husbandry students, as well as Betty Kiser, who, along with Shirley, was an advisor to their animal husbandry "wives' club," were still visiting at our front door. The formal meeting had likely ended before ten; this extended visit was a reminder that the club was filling a need. (Though at this writing about seventy per cent of the animal science majors are women, through the 1960s nearly all animal science students were men.)

The GI Bill was now serving Korean War veterans, and many were married. Compared to my student years, more nonveteran students were also married, so there were a lot of student wives. Few were themselves students; most were secretaries, nurses, teachers, or had other jobs. These young women wanted a group to which they could belong; they needed a connection to their husbands' interest and also women friends with mutual interests. The wives' clubs also benefitted the students; the more a spouse knows about the other's work and the people with whom he works, the more interest and support they can provide.

Shirley had been asked by the animal husbandry group to join Betty Kiser as an adviser early in our time at Iowa State, and when I took over the farm operation curriculum in September, she was eager to work also with that group of student wives. She would give up her role with the animal husbandry wives' group at the end of the year and encourage another faculty spouse to get involved.

The farm op wives' group and Shirley would plan a spring commencement reception in our backyard. For the previous winter graduates and spouses, Shirley and I had hosted a Sunday afternoon reception in our home; the word got around as to how highly that had been appreciated. Spouses of the to-be spring graduates were looking forward to their reception and had volunteered to help. Planning and helping were part of the fun. The value Shirley saw in these two clubs would give her continued satisfaction, and have positive impact on other campuses in our years ahead.

There would be more late-night visits at our front door.

Iowa State's Professors of the Year, 1959. At the election of student body officers in the spring of 1959, voters in each division (college) were asked to name their most outstanding instructor. Back row, left to right: Clair Watson, professor of architectural engineering; Jean Hansen, associate professor of child development; William Monlux, professor of veterinary pathology. Front row: Duane Acker, associate professor of animal husbandry; and E. W. Peterson, assistant professor of history.

* * * * *

An early morning fire in October of 1958 gutted FarmHouse fraternity. With help from Dean Andre and President Hilton, most of the members were moved into a vacant home management house on the east side of the campus. Because there was not room for all members in that house, Shirley and I had accommodated four in the basement of our home. The fraternity house was owned by the FarmHouse Association, led by interested alumni, and the association leadership was faced with a decision, rebuild the old structure or try to build a new house. For the latter there was an unusual constraint.

For Two and One-Half Feet

FarmHouse had been at 311 Ash since 1937, after Lambda Chi Alpha had lost the house in bankruptcy. During my brief time as FarmHouse Association treasurer, while working on my masters degree, we had begun setting aside a portion of the monthly rent the chapter paid to the association for a building fund, and had purchased two frame houses immediately south of the fraternity as a future site.

I had noted on the real estate tax statement an interesting legal description of the fraternity house property: North 72.5 feet of Lot Y and South 2.5 feet of Lot X, Z addition to the City of Ames. The envelope had also contained a second statement, for the "South 2.5 feet of Lot Y, Z addition to the City of Ames," showing the owner as Lambda Chi Alpha. There seemed a likely explanation, that Lambda Chi Alpha had owned 77.5 frontage feet but their mortgage had covered only 75 feet and the FarmHouse association had purchased that 75 feet from bankruptcy.

I had asked, "Why should the FarmHouse association pay taxes on the 2.5 feet yet owned by Lambda Chi?" By the late 1940s Lambda Chi Alpha had reestablished its chapter in two frame structures a block north of FarmHouse, so I passed that second tax bill on to Lambda Chi.

It was important to get the chapter house back in operation as quickly as possible, but there was not enough money in the building fund for a new house, and the burned-out structure was hardly salable. If we rebuilt, we ought to increase the square footage.

The most practical option was to raze the adjacent frame house, rebuild the burned-out structure, and add a wing to the south. However, the association did not own that 2.5 foot strip between the two lots! Lambda Chi might have sold it to us in 1953 for a dollar just to avoid paying that tiny tax bill I had refused to pay. Now, in 1959, we paid Lambda Chi Alpha $2,500, $1,000 per frontage foot!

* * * * *

Thompson stepped into my office near the end of spring quarter with a thought. "After grades are all in, I'll be sending out probation and dismissal letters (to those students with grade averages below a set point). Some of those students, though, may have already decided they won't be coming back next fall."

Policy versus Wisdom

Thompson was correct. Several of my freshman advisees had passed up filling out schedules for fall quarter, and all but one had low fall and winter quarter grades. Just that morning one of the young men—I'll call him Bill—had told me that his dad needed his help with their large farming operation, so he would not be back in the fall.

Thompson continued. "Would you give me a list of your students having grade trouble and that you think don't plan to come back next fall? I'll not send them probation or dismissal letters; there is no need to tell a young man he is a failure."

I had gained much from Thompson. Before replacing him as head of the farm operation curriculum the previous fall, I had served with him on college committees and had had several interactions in my three years as the animal husbandry instructor for his winter quarter program students. He once told me he never told a student his ACT (American College Test) scores unless the scores were high and he needed to build the student's confidence or motivation. Otherwise, he just told each one, "You can achieve whatever you want to achieve." From both his military and teaching/advising experience, he knew no person should feel he or she had a lid on his or her potential.

Thompson elaborated on this thinking. "There may be a dozen students who don't receive the letters that college policy says they should. What if one or two do return next fall? That won't destroy the university. I'd rather take that risk than tell one that he has failed at Iowa State, and perhaps carry negative feelings toward Iowa State." Later that day I gave Thomson a list of twelve freshmen, including Bill.

More than twenty-five years later, Shirley and I were having dinner at a steakhouse as we drove across Iowa. Bill and his wife happened to be in that steakhouse and Bill spotted us. He stepped over to visit. His main topic: how proud he was that his kids were attending Iowa State.

* * * * *

The young man was glad I had come to visit at his farm home. He was both excited and worried about going to college. I was also worried; I had studied his high school transcript and ACT scores, and they were not good.

Get Ready for Freshman English

Iowa State policy at the time was to admit any graduate of an accredited Iowa high school. I believed that if a student was admitted, the university was obligated to give that student the *opportunity* to succeed. Some faculty and administrators feel differently, that every new student should be enrolled in a standard list of course and credit load, to "sort out" those who can succeed in college from those who cannot.

In presentations during later years, I would refer to this young man as Red Jones. Red was in the bottom third of his high school class. His ACT quantitative (mathematical skills) percentile was 30, meaning that if one hundred students took the test, seventy scored higher than Red. His ACT linguistic (word-related) percentile was 13. Not many with such percentiles would earn a degree at Iowa State, but Red wanted to try, and I felt obliged to help him.

Red was the oldest child in his family, and I had noted places for ten around their large kitchen table, including a high chair and two chairs with booster seats. Red might want to farm and was enrolling in the curriculum designed for that, but with so many younger brothers and sisters who could help on the farm, he might need to look toward a nonfarm job. Except for an uncle who had graduated from Iowa State, Red would be the first in his extended family to go to college.

Not far into our conversation at that kitchen table, after mentioning that he had a dorm room arranged and had asked what he would learn during "freshman days," he got to his major worry. "Do I have to take English?"

I was ready for that question. "Yes, you do, but not necessarily your first quarter." That was not only breaking with tradition, it was violating the first-quarter curriculum printed in the university catalog.

I continued. "Red, how important is it to you that you graduate in four years?"

He looked at me with surprise. "Never thought about that, just assumed you were supposed to."

"Not necessarily. In fact, nearly half of those who graduate from Iowa State have been enrolled more than four years. The important thing is that you graduate; how soon is not so important." He relaxed a bit.

I followed up. "I suggest that you limit yourself the first quarter to twelve credits, instead of the normal fifteen or sixteen. I know you had some difficulty in high school. We will choose the courses in which I think you will have the best chance to do well."

He relaxed some more, but came back with, "How about English?"

"Rather than include freshman English this first quarter, we've arranged a special tutor class to get you ready for college English."

A dozen or so of my to-be freshmen advisees had low ACT linguistic scores and high school English grades, so I had huddled with Thompson. What emerged was the idea of a tutoring arrangement, quickly approved by university dean of instruction Bob Parks (who would later become Iowa State's president). I wanted the students to pay for the tutoring; all I needed was a classroom and permission. I would find a former high school English teacher in the Ames community to join our effort.

Fred Lorch, head of the English department, was a backyard neighbor. He gave me several suggestions, and I located a woman who was not only interested but enthused about the idea. She looked at my students' files, and suggested that in two hours per week for a quarter she could make good progress, as long as there were not more than ten students in the class. We agreed the students would pay her directly, twenty dollars each, one dollar per class hour, or two dollars per week, for ten weeks.

I described the arrangement to Red. He relaxed and smiled. I was still worried, but at least Red would have a chance to succeed.

How did Red do? He got mostly Bs and Cs in his first three quarters; he was now on the road. It might take him five years to graduate, but I was confident he would.

However, in the middle of his sophomore year he stopped in for a visit. "I've decided I want to go to vet school." I swallowed hard. Red had earned a B and C in his first two general chemistry courses, but to become a veterinarian he would need more chemistry, including organic and biochemistry, and many biology courses. Doing well in the latter is highly dependent on linguistic skills. Vet school also involves a heavy course load every quarter; I had held Red to fifteen credits or fewer. Still, he was set on the idea.

I was not about to squelch Red's aspirations at this stage; that happens to too many young people. "Red, you will need another sequence of chemistry, so let's enroll you in organic chemistry spring quarter."

He needed to test his new aspiration. If a hill proves too steep, the human mind often rationalizes that it is better to not climb the hill.

Midway through spring quarter, Red stopped in again. "I'm not so sure I want to go to vet school." He dropped the organic chemistry course.

I regret I was not around when Red received his bachelor's degree from Iowa State.

Ten years later I learned of an opportunity that I thought was tailor-made for Red, one that needed his determination and positive personality. I tracked him down and told him about the job. His response: "Doc, I sure appreciate your thinking of me, but I'm making so much money now and enjoying it so much, I can't afford to consider a change."

More recently I happened into a conversation with one of Red's relatives and mentioned that I had known and admired him as an enthusiastic student. Her response was, "The whole family is very proud of Red and what he had achieved in his life; I hope my children will follow his model!"

Visiting with the Christensen family in their farm home south of Ogden, Iowa. Roger, on the right, was a sophomore; Rex was just entering his freshman year. Roger and Rex followed their parents as successful farm operators and community leaders. At this writing, the next generation of Christensens is leading the farm business.

*****

I was having lunch with a young man—I'll refer to him as Harvey—and his mother in Harvey's farm home in southernmost Iowa. Some Iowans would call it "Lapland," where Missouri's rough terrain "laps over" into Iowa. Except for creek bottoms, the land is hilly and quite erosive, and relative to most of Iowa's soils, less productive. Most farm boys in the area were looking elsewhere for their future; consequently, we had few students from that area enrolled in the farm operation curriculum.

Another Eighty Acres or College

Harvey was already in his twenties, but he would be a freshman and my advisee at Iowa State. I had called and arranged to stop about nine in the morning for a brief visit. He was eager to show me his crops and livestock on several tracts of land; his energy and enthusiasm were boundless.

Harvey was farming eighty acres before he graduated high school. He had married early, and he and his wife had two children. He had seen opportunities in farming that others could not see, and with long hours and hard work, he had succeeded. He had purchased the original eighty and had bought or rented an additional eighty acres or more each year.

However, Harvey had apparently worked too hard and too many hours; he returned to the house one evening to find his wife had run off with the hired man. His mother had stepped in to help look after the children and give him needed support.

Harvey had now reconsidered his future; he would go to college and start a new life. He would give up the land, sell his equipment and livestock, and enroll at Iowa State. (The reader might ask at this point, "Why, then, would he enroll in the farm operation curriculum?" Answer: It was more flexible than other curriculums, such as animal husbandry or agronomy, and over time had earned a reputation of adapting the curriculum to a student's individual needs.)

Though his decision had been a shock to his mother, it was apparent that she was internally thrilled at Harvey's plans. She would be the anchor for the children.

Harvey had many questions. Though he had done well in high school and in his farm business, could he "cut it" in college? Would his age be a handicap? He needed information, my judgments, and my reinforcement.

My visit had stretched until noon, his mother had fixed lunch, and they insisted I stay.

Regarding college, Harvey would exhibit the same "full bore" pattern that had characterized his farming. He would not wait for registration day to get started. Instead, he would participate in a pre-university orientation and seminar at a camp near Ames the week before registration, an option few students chose. He would live in the residence halls and have the total university experience. In a hurry to get that degree and move on to his new life, Harvey would take a rather heavy credit load and do well academically. He would also drive home many weekends to see his children.

Unfortunately for me, I would leave Iowa State before Harvey graduated and would lose touch.

Postscript: In 2002, I was in Des Moines for a presentation at the annual Farm Bureau Convention. As I finished my meal, and before the formal program began, the president of a central Iowa bank stepped to the table and introduced himself; it was Harvey. Part of our brief conversation I yet recall: "I've had a great career; you and Iowa State helped me change my life."

* * * * *

Several of these stories involve students with academic challenges. However, my task also included challenging those with high academic abilities to use those abilities to the fullest, to enroll in more challenging courses in math, chemistry, communications, or advanced courses in their agricultural interest. More than one eventually earned graduate degrees in what became their special interest, and ended up on a college faculty or as a scientist or manager in the private sector. As important, more than one of those returned to their family farm, and they were successful not only in their farm business but became state and national leaders in one or more agricultural organizations.

To better accommodate the range in both academic skills and career aspirations, and to add to the challenge for some, we had also opened up the animal husbandry (animal science) curriculum, traditionally focused on animal production. We established three options: production, business, and science options. The business option replaced some farm management or production courses with such courses as personnel management, psychology of salesmanship, or accounting. The science option included advanced courses in math, chemistry, and biological sciences.

* * * * *

Until I moved to lead the farm operation curriculum, my career and role was limited to teaching my subject matter and, in the process, guiding, encouraging, evaluating, and supporting students. My relationship to other faculty was as a colleague, to most a very junior colleague. Now I had a different role to play.

A Promise and a Hearing Aid

Being "associate professor in charge" of the farm operation curriculum was my first administrative position. I was responsible for about six hundred students each year, a winter quarter program, a two-year certificate program, and a four-year bachelor's degree program. I also supervised two academic advisers, a secretary, and the instructor of one course, Ag 450, which involved a two hundred-acre farm south of the campus. Senior students and the instructor, Jim Wallace, met regularly at the farm, considered operational and management issues, and made decisions to be carried out by the farm operator.

Wallace had been one of my former teachers, fall quarter of my senior year. He was the long-time manager of a series of tenant-operated farms owned by the Iowa State Agricultural Foundation and had taught a senior course in the agricultural economics department, managing tenant-operated farms. The class met Monday evenings and included several half-day or day-long field trips, mostly to those foundation farms that Wallace managed. Wallace now had an assistant, Jack Alexander, to help with the foundation farms, so Dean Andre has asked Wallace to teach Ag 450.

At twenty-eight, I felt a bit ill at ease having supervisory responsibility over a sixty-five-year-old former teacher. However, Wallace immediately put me at ease. "Duane," he said, "I want you to promise me one thing: if you ever get any complaint about my teaching, I want you to promise that you'll tell me."

I promised. Wallace had taken my attention off my discomfort and reminded me of my responsibility. He had made me promise to do my supervisory job.

Wallace's experience and his sensitivity to his students' inexperience were the right combination for Ag 450. I received good vibes from his students, most of them my advisees.

A year later, Alexander was handling even more of the foundation farms responsibilities, and Wallace was asked to also teach Ag Econ 130, the farm management course for our winter quarter students. Midway through that quarter, one of my winter advisees mentioned to me, "Mr. Wallace seems to ramble a bit." I quizzed him and others for details. One said, "He doesn't really address our questions. He'll sometimes respond on some other topic." One in the group commented, "You know, I don't think he hears very well." Others nodded in agreement.

I asked the students to observe Wallace carefully for another class session or two and then come back and see me. When they came back, they were unanimous in their assessment. "He tries so hard. We know he's not trying to avoid our questions. He just has difficulty hearing."

Later that day, Wallace came into our outer office to pick up his mail, and I heard him greet our secretary.

I stepped out. "Jim, do you recall the promise you extracted from me when you began teaching Ag 450?"

He said, "I sure do."

"Come on in. I have some information that might be helpful." I shared with Wallace my several conversations with the students, emphasizing, of course, my respect for him and the students' diagnosis that his hearing had diminished.

Jim thought about it for only a moment. "They're right. I knew I'd lost some hearing, but I probably didn't realize just how much."

Within a week, Wallace was wearing a hearing aid. All was well. Both our seniors and our winter short course students could continue to profit from his rich and wide farm-management experiences.

I still cherish a handwritten note Wallace gave me as I was leaving for the associate dean job at Kansas State a couple years later: "Good luck in the new job. I'll watch your smoke!"

* * * * *

As a land-grant college, Iowa State had the traditional divisions of agriculture, engineering, veterinary medicine, and home economics, plus a division for the basic sciences and other disciplines. The relatively conservative faculty (remember, this was 1960) expected and accepted institutional leadership to come from the president, deans, and department heads. A faculty senate, which would assume certain academic policy prerogatives, was yet to come.

The President Is Calling

It was early on a Sunday morning; we had not yet dressed for church. "President Hilton is on the phone!" Shirley called, her voice reflecting both surprise and wonderment. I too was surprised. But I was chair of the university's faculty council and would learn that was the reason for the call.

Hilton had felt the need for a faculty "sounding board" and a "two-way communication vehicle" between administration and faculty. He had encouraged formation of this faculty council, comprised of twenty faculty members, one of each rank from each of the five divisions. I had been elected by the agriculture faculty as the assistant professor member in late spring of 1958 and was elected council chair a year later. The council met monthly, heard and relayed faculty concerns, and reacted to issues from the president or provost.

President Hilton came right to the point. "Duane, can you get the council together for a brief meeting this morning at eleven in my conference room? I need some input from the council." He did not tell me the issue, but with the legislature still in session, there could be any number of items.

In contrast to Minnesota, Missouri, and Nebraska, each of which has one major university that includes law, the human health sciences, and liberal arts, as well as agriculture and engineering, Iowa and many other states have what I call the "dual-university" structure, with the University of Iowa as home to law and human health sciences, and a land-grant university, Iowa State, home to agriculture and engineering programs (UNI was then Iowa State Teachers College). As some of the land-grant colleges had grown and become more diverse, adding colleges of business or education and more curriculums in the liberal arts, they had sought the "university" designation. In fact, Oklahoma A&M had become Oklahoma State University between my time there and the awarding of my doctorate degree.

I knew that changing Iowa State's name to a university was under consideration by the legislature. Were University of Iowa alumni opposing the change? Was there some compromise required to get legislature approval?

In his conference room at eleven, Hilton quickly got to the point. "I think we can get the legislative votes to change Iowa State's name from college to university. The board of regents supports the change, but I would feel more comfortable if I had a resolution of support from the faculty council."

Members of the council discussed the issue. Iowa State College had earned high respect. However, "university" carries more prestige and would more accurately describe the existing Iowa State and what it was destined to become—a larger, stronger, and more diverse institution. If the institution became a university, the divisions would be renamed colleges, also a plus in the academic community.

There was more to the issue, however. Iowa State's full name was Iowa State College of Agriculture and Mechanic Arts. The proposed new name was Iowa State University of Science and Technology. Would that bother faculty in agriculture or engineering?

Here the discussion took a serious turn. There was no reservation about the phrase "science and technology." It well defined agriculture and engineering, as well as much of the balance of the institution. And it was understood by all in the room that such a qualifying phrase was no doubt a condition for acceptance by University of Iowa alumni or friends in the legislature.

Discussion, though serious and thoughtful, was brief. A resolution supporting the change was framed, presented as a motion, seconded, and passed. Hilton had formal faculty support, the Iowa legislature changed the name, and on July 1 we would be faculty of Iowa State University.

* * * * *

Though I resented his taking my time for a pitch about life insurance, I was trying to not show my irritation. First, I did not want more insurance; I already had the term insurance coverage I needed to protect my young family. Second, I felt personal sales contacts should be to one's home.

Show That You Are Proud!

However, the agent was pleasant and enthusiastic. He was already in the door, and courtesy required that I offer him a chair. He made a good pitch and I listened. When he got to what every good salesman gets to, "Just what do you feel your needs are?" I thought, *Here is where I bring this conversation to a close.*

We had just completed preregistration, a two-week period when students select their classes and make out their schedules for the next quarter. I had had productive visits with each advisee, often urging a journalism or speech course because I believed communication skills so important, and had signed their forms.

The last student with whom I had visited would graduate in March. He was bright, had taken heavy credit loads, and needed only thirteen credits to graduate. However, he had handed me a schedule showing twenty-one credits. He was a shy young man, did not say much, and did not radiate enthusiasm. He was from a large family, with several brothers and sisters still at home, and had told me he planned to find a job for a few years before going back to the family farm.

I had slid his schedule back across the desk. "Joe, I'm not willing to sign that."

He was surprised. "Why not?"

"You will be interviewing for jobs. You are bright; you've completed your major courses and plenty of others. What do you need most, in order to land a good job, more courses? I want you to go downtown and find a part-time job selling shoes." That got his attention.

I followed up. "I don't care what job you look for, but you need some experience where you have to show interest in your customer and enthusiasm about your product. That will do more for you than would two more college courses. These forms are not due for a couple of days; think about it."

Joe was on my mind in my answer to the salesman. "Here is what I need. I need some way to develop some personality skills among some of my students."

That was not the response he had expected. But he was listening, another good salesman's skill. I told him about Joe and that I had a dozen more like him, able young men, but who needed to develop some people skills.

That was when he mentioned that he also taught a Dale Carnegie course. That got *my* attention. I wondered aloud, "Wouldn't it be great if some of my students could get exposed to you and what you teach?"

Here came the third skill of a salesman: he asked, "Is there some way I can help?"

"There sure is!" I exclaimed. After all, he had come in and taken some of my time. It would be fair to ask for some of his time. "If I got some of these young men together some evening, would you be willing to spend an hour with them?"

He could not but agree and seemed pleased to do it. We agreed to an evening the following week.

I sent a short note to each of ten students, in essence, "Will you join me at seven next Thursday evening in Room 207 of the Union for a good discussion? I have a topic in which I think you will be interested." All ten showed up and took places around the table, with my guest and me at one end. They wondered what was up.

I welcomed them, mentioned they were among my best students (and they were, all with very good academic records), and that I had a friend with me. I gave his name, saying only that he would lead the discussion, and I thought they would be interested in what he had to say.

He introduced himself and then asked that they, around the table, introduce themselves. Each gave his name in a cautious, modest way. After the tenth, he slapped the table, gave his own name with more vigor, and said, "Let's do this again. Show me that you are proud of your name!"

The second time the self-introductions were different.

He then reintroduced himself and added, "My hometown is Ames. Tell me your name and your hometown." This time the names showed some pride, the hometowns less so.

Again there was a slap on the table. "Let's do it again—show your pride in your hometown!"

So it went, for most of an hour; the students gave their name, hometown, college major, why they chose it, and their life's goal. The young men soon realized why they had been invited.

I think we did some good. I should restate that: *He* did some good for those young men; I only provided the setting. My only regret is that I do not recall the salesman's name, so I can not give him credit in this writing. He had paid my students well for those thirty minutes in my office.

* * * * *

When I had accepted the farm operation curriculum job, Andre had agreed that I would not be judged by student enrollment; agriculture was then in a state of low morale, and there was concern that enrollment in the division of agriculture would decline. However, enrollment was still important to me; students will seek a course with a top teacher, and if a department's advising is effective, students will more likely enroll in or transfer to that department and those there will stay.

Dinner and a Show

Shirley and I were at Johnnie and Kay's restaurant across Fleur Drive from the Des Moines airport with my two student advisers and their spouses, Roger and Barbara Bruene, and Gerald and Mary Wagner. After dinner, we would head downtown to a movie. Roger, Gerald, and their spouses had picked the date and the show. Though the night would cost me more than sixty dollars, a princely sum in those days, I was thoroughly enjoying it.

Roger had joined me as an adviser almost two years earlier, Gerald the following fall. Roger was also teaching a course in rural sociology, Gerald one in animal husbandry, and each was pursuing a graduate degree.

My first winter in the farm operation job we had forty-seven enrollees in the winter quarter program. The second year, enrollment dropped to thirty-seven. That hurt my pride, and I issued a challenge to Bruene and Wagner. "If we double enrollment next winter, I will treat you and your wives to a dinner and a show in Des Moines."

Farm operation staff had traditionally traveled the state during the summer, visiting new fall enrollees on their home farms. It was helpful to both the students and their parents, often both understandably apprehensive about college. We could respond to their concerns and we saw each student's farming opportunity, or lack thereof. We also saw the degree of parent support and enthusiasm for the college experience. As a result, we could be more constructive advisers.

The following summer we would also recruit winter quarter program students. For each county where we had a fall enrollee to visit, we would call ahead to county extension staff and vocational agriculture instructors and ask them to identify prospective students for the winter program. All were eager to help and often accompanied us to call on the prospects.

After those visits, we followed up with letters. We also tracked some in the livestock barns at the state fair. A few prospective students would be exhibiting at the fall Aksarben livestock show in Omaha, so Roger and I accompanied Iowa State's Aksarben scholarship recipients on their bus trip to Omaha. We walked the barns, reinforcing our personal interest in them.

In November and December we sent letters of welcome to those who had enrolled. To prospects who had not yet enrolled, we sent a note of encouragement and included the names of nearby youth who had enrolled.

By mid-December we had more than sixty applications and made arrangements for agronomy, ag engineering, ag econ, and animal husbandry to provide two sections of each course. When classes began the first week of January we had seventy-four students, thirty-seven in each of the departments' two course sections.

Though this evening would cost me more than sixty dollars, I would not often spend money with more satisfaction. And the next winter's enrollment would increase even more, requiring three sections of each course.

(After Iowa's community college system was established by the legislature in the late 1960s, the community colleges developed a number of quality agricultural programs which appeared to fill the state's need for less than B.S. degree programs. Iowa State's winter quarter program no longer exists.)

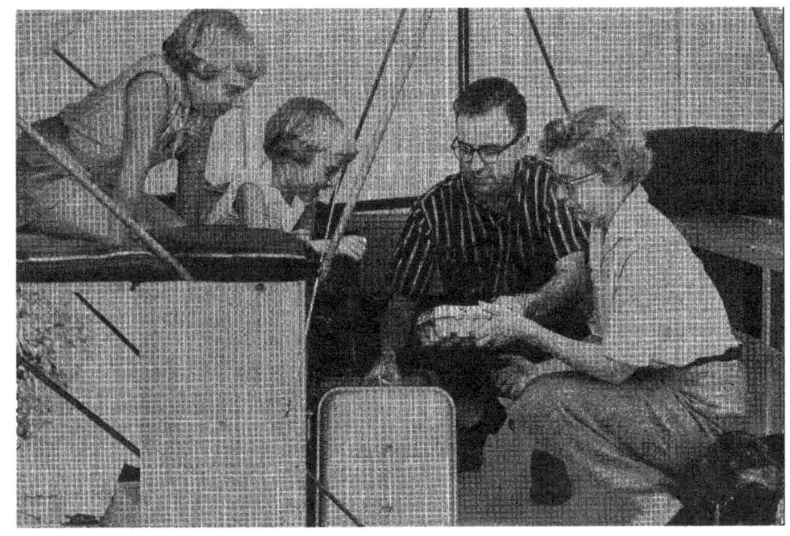

This photo of our family preparing for a camping trip appeared in the July 1961 issue of News of Iowa State*, a publication for alumni and parents of students. The photo and some text was part of a series, "These Are the Teachers."*

* * * * *

Iowa State had been asked by the International Cooperation Administration, the predecessor agency to the current Agency for International Development, to assist Argentina in developing their agricultural research and education programs. I became the junior member of a three-person team for a month in that country. This not only introduced me to the global potential for agricultural development, it gave me "quality time" with two gifted administrators, Dean Andre and department head Johnson.

Why Is He Telling Me All This?

Andre and I were in the back seat of a little French Citroen riding across the Pampas (grassland plains of Argentina). Johnson was up front, conversing in a mix of English and Spanish with our driver, an assistant minister of agriculture. We were in Argentina as curriculum advisers for a dozen agricultural high schools, some run by the Ministry of Agriculture and some by a Catholic order, the Silesian Fathers. It was late at night, and we were driving from one school to the next.

Andre spent most of that three-hour ride telling me about personnel problems he had dealt with at both the University of Wisconsin and Iowa State. The cases varied widely: A faculty spouse had asked him to intervene in a case of infidelity. A staff member had billed a university account for fertilizer applied on his personal farm. A former president had once given him oral instruction to fire a department head. He also described a staff problem in his own office.

I listened, but wondered, *Why is he telling me all this?* I was just a young associate professor, and some of the cases involved senior colleagues whose offices were just down the hall from mine.

We returned to Ames late on a Friday. In my office mailbox Saturday morning was a letter from the dean of agriculture at Kansas State University, Glenn Beck, inviting me to consider a position there as associate dean of agriculture for instruction and student advising.

Andre knew, though I didn't, that I was going to receive that letter. He was coaching me for that job.

*****

While I was having coffee with Colorado cattle feeder Ken Monfort and a Kansas State animal husbandry professor, Don Good, at a beef improvement meeting on the Colorado State campus in July of 1961, Good mention that Kansas State was seeking a new associate dean for instruction and that Bill Pope, my major adviser at Oklahoma State, had declined being considered for the position. I thought, *That would be the right job for me!* Also, what better place for me than a university similar to Iowa State?

What should I do to get myself considered at Kansas State? Both naïve and cautious, I made but one move. Bob Skinner, my first quarter FarmHouse roommate was by then executive director of the Iowa Feed and Grain Dealers Association and would have some contacts in the feed manufacturing program at Kansas State. I confided in him my interest, and he had passed my name along to Kansas State friends.

Unbeknown to me, Iowa State's associate dean, Thompson, had spoken at Kansas State's Alpha Zeta (agricultural honorary) banquet, had been asked by Beck for suggestions for their associate dean position, and had recommended me. (I learned that only during a visit with Thompson at his retirement home in February 2002.)

Shirley and I drove to Manhattan to interview at Kansas State just before Christmas 1961. My impression of Beck matched the impression I held of other K-State faculty I had known: he was a gentleman in all respects. Beyond that, he was a respected scientist and teacher and had clear goals in mind for the instruction program.

A round of visits with department heads told me there were definite needs to be addressed. The major problem was that a recent college-wide curriculum revision had deleted most of the traditional freshman courses, such as animal husbandry, horticulture, and farm crops and soils, and replaced them with two new interdepartmental sophomore level courses, animal science and plant science. The change had apparently passed the college faculty by a narrow vote, and only after intense (and, perhaps, acrimonious) debate, and a residue of unhappiness remained.

At both Oklahoma A&M and Iowa State, the wisdom of offering freshman courses in the applied disciplines had been questioned by a few faculty, especially those who devoted most of their time to research. They urged that students first get grounding in math, chemistry, biology, genetics, and physics, and delay all applied courses until the junior and senior years. For time efficiency, that was a logical argument. However, at both universities I had worked largely with new agriculture students and knew that both they and typical engineering freshmen (I had learned from friend John Lagerstrom, Iowa State's assistant dean of engineering) had come to the university with occupational goals. They wanted to become a county agent, a vo-ag teacher, a horticulturist, a farm lender, a forester, an engineer, or whatever. A freshman course in their applied discipline gave them a taste of what they enrolled for. Their motivation contrasted with that of typical arts and sciences freshmen, who likely came to college to "get an education." I was worried about the curriculum change, but that battle was history. My options would be either to help make it work or help refine it.

The second problem was the college's declining enrollment. I knew I could lead a turnaround there, though the curriculum change might handicap my efforts.

After two days visiting at Kansas State, it was apparent the job was right for me, and Beck's comments led me to believe he thought I was the right person for the job. However, a problem arose. President James McCain was ill, and my scheduled interview with him was cancelled. Beck was soon leaving for Nigeria after Christmas, and it would be some time before both he and the president would be in town on the same day; he would need to get back in touch with me later. I told Beck that was no problem; I had plenty of work to do in the weeks ahead, especially with what turned out to be 134 winter quarter students. Shirley and I left Manhattan impressed and feeling good.

It was not until early March that Beck and McCain were on campus at the same time. Roads were ice-covered, so I took the train from Des Moines to Manhattan for a one-day visit.

We would be moving to Manhattan, and over the Easter weekend, our family would drive down to look for housing.

* * * * *

When we had purchased our house on Storm Street from the Davidsons, we learned it had been built by a Mr. and Mrs. Beatty, who, during my college years, had operated a small store, soda fountain, and short-order business in a frame structure on Knapp Street. I planned to wall off the toilet and shower in the basement for student renters and called Mr. Beatty, then retired and living in downtown Ames, to learn if the cement floor was thick enough to support the wall. Beatty was complimented by my call; he drove out that evening and assured us the floor was thick enough and gave us other details of the house's construction. Beatty also shared with us that he and his wife had moved to Ames in the late 1930s to build houses on then vacant lots south of the campus. Our house had been their first and last. After putting their money and labor into the work, they hardly got back their cost of material, so they quit the house-building business and purchased the shop on Knapp.

Don't Sell until My Husband Gets Back!

That appeal in a phone call to Shirley was from Mrs. Beatty. We were leaving Ames at the end of the month for our new job at Kansas State, and selling our story-and-a-half Cape Cod at 2329 Storm Street, south of the campus, was proving to be an interesting experience.

We first offered the house to close neighbors, who were renting, and quickly agreed on a price, a bit more than our purchase price plus some built-in bookcases and basement improvements. However, they could not meet the down payment their lender required, so we placed an ad in the *Ames Tribune* and told other friends.

Now open to a wider market, we gave more thought to how we should price the house. We approached it two ways: (a) our purchase price plus a few improvements, as I recall, $17,200; and (b) a recent property appraisal by the City of Ames, which was, I believe, $19,600.

We quickly had several enquiries. When asked the price, we responded with the two figures and their bases, and said we would listen to any bids within the range. That yielded two bids, one above the middle of the range.

Mrs. Beatty had spotted our ad the third day it had appeared and called. She reminded Shirley that they had built that house and wanted to get back in their old neighborhood. "I'd sure like for us to buy that house, but my husband is out of town, so *please* don't sell it until he gets back." He was due back the next day.

By the next afternoon we had what we thought an excellent offer and told the party we needed to visit that evening with another who had expressed interest.

The Beattys came by about seven; they wanted to buy the house, and Mr. Beatty asked, "What are you asking?"

I told him the price range, how we had arrived at the figures, and our willingness to listen to any bids.

"That's a heck of a way to sell a house," he said. After selling the shop on Knapp Street, Beatty had worked part time in the real estate business with his son.

"It may be," I said, "but we have had several good bids."

Though he obviously did not like our system, he made a bid, a bit higher than the one we had received that afternoon.

The phone rang. It was the party who had placed that afternoon bid. "Have we bought a house?"

I had to respond, "No, not yet at least. Another party is here now, and they just gave us a better bid."

There was a short pause on the line, and then a higher bid close to that $19,600, and he said, "We'd sure like to have the house, but this is as far as we can go."

I thanked him, put down the phone, and told the Beattys the party on the phone still wanted the house. Mr. Beatty offered another bid, but not enough. (I remind the reader that a bid raise might be $100 or $250. In 1962, $100 was real money.)

Beatty persisted. “We want the house. What will you take?” Mrs. Beatty was watching the process, visibly holding her breath.

Shirley and I looked at each other, and I said, “Well, your question is fair. You have made two good bids; we should respond with a price. Give us a few minutes.”

Shirley and I headed to the kitchen and asked each other, “How high can we go?”

We settled on $21,000, stepped back into the living room, and gave our figure. Beatty said, “Okay,” pulled out his checkbook, and wrote us a check for $1,000 to seal the deal. Tears streamed down Mrs. Beatty’s face.

*****

Though a professor’s role is to teach, I felt I learned more lessons in my seven years at Iowa State than I had taught others. As was true when we moved from Oklahoma A&M, we left with many satisfactions and much appreciation, especially for the leadership, the encouragement, and the freedom to try things that Johnson, Thompson, Andre, and others had provided.

Chapter VII

Associate Dean, Kansas State University

In contrast to colleges of business, education, or liberal arts, colleges of agriculture in land-grant universities have long had relatively large research and extension programs financed by state and federal funds. The total agriculture program is commonly led by a dean and three associate deans, each of the associates carrying an additional title, director of resident instruction, director of the agricultural experiment station, or director of extension. As associate dean for resident instruction, I could make good use of my teaching, curriculum, and student-advising experiences and the philosophies I had developed.

Kansas State University agriculture leadership, fall 1962. Dean Glenn Beck in the center; associate dean and director of the agricultural experiment station, C. Peairs Wilson, upper left; extension director Harold Jones, upper right; and associate dean and director of resident instruction Duane Acker, lower.

Most agriculture faculty carry a "joint appointment," with portions of their salary coming from both instruction and experiment station funds, experiment station and extension funds, or, in a few cases, all three. Department heads are responsible for all three functions within their department, and though they personally report to the dean, I would be working with each one on matters relating to curriculum, instruction, and student advising.

* * * * *

Saturday, May 26, my last day at Iowa State, had been busy, with spring commencement followed by a reception for graduates and their parents. Early Sunday morning Shirley and I loaded the car and departed for Manhattan and Kansas State. We dropped off our daughters at my parents' home on the way.

A New Dean with no Suit

It was Sunday afternoon, and we were within sixty miles of Manhattan when it hit me: my suits were still in our front hall closet in Ames. I had packed the trunk with my books and personal items for my new office, plus some clothes to last me for ten days (our household goods and complete family move would then occur), but I had forgotten to put in my suit bag.

I would call our neighbor and ask her to pack and mail my suits. But I had no suit for my first day in the dean's office and a 10:30 meeting with an accreditation team reviewing K-State's new landscape architecture curriculum. An associate dean in jeans would hardly be appropriate.

We recalled that a former student, Larry Anton, was stationed at nearby Ft. Riley, and he and his wife, Judy, had a Manhattan apartment. Perhaps he would lend me a suit. Though sympathetic, Anton could be of no help; his total wardrobe was army fatigues and a dress uniform. "But Sears opens at nine in the morning," Judy offered. Sears it had to be.

Monday morning I was in the office early. I explained to my new secretarial staff that I was still arranging my books and would be in a suit by the time the accreditation team arrived. I met Shirley behind Waters Hall at eight forty-five. She had a Sears charge card, and I found a suit on the Sears rack that fit.

Landscape architecture was granted accreditation because the curriculum was solid; my suit was inconsequential.

* * * * *

Kansas State's spring graduation had also been on Saturday, so one of my first duties was to follow up on any issues from its academic year just completed.

Ninety-Two Dismissal Letters

My first major responsibility as associate dean was to send dismissal letter to ninety-two of the 720 undergraduates in the college of agriculture. Most had just completed their freshman year, and their grade averages were below the minimum required by university policy for continuation.

The large number of dismissals surprised me. My clerk responsible for student records was already typing the dismissal letters and had some ready for my signature, but I told her, "Before I sign and send those letters, I want to look at each student's file."

She gave me a questioning look and then explained that there were no individual student files; all high school transcripts were in one file drawer, computer cards with ACT test scores were in another drawer, and semester grade slips for all students were held in separate semester notebooks.

Her focus had been on having each data set on file; my focus was the student. I wanted to have all relevant data on each student in that student's file. She had some rearranging to do.

It took her a full day to get those ninety-two files prepared, and when the job was done, I studied each student's file. I then sorted the files into three piles. In one were those students who, based on my interpretation and judgment of their data, did not have a decent chance of succeeding at a university like Iowa State or Kansas State.

In the second pile were students I believed could have succeeded at Iowa State or Kansas State if careful attention was paid to credit load and course selection. Had each taken a lighter credit load and/or their courses limited in accord with their skills, their performance may have been satisfactory. More careful scheduling would not have guaranteed academic success but would have increased the odds.

It was the third stack of files that bothered me the most. These students' high school transcripts and test scores suggested they should have earned As and Bs at Kansas State. Some had good high school grades in math and ACT quantitative scores but modest linguistic skills, and success in English and biology courses depend heavily on those linguistic skills. Meanwhile, some with good linguistic skills but modest quantitative skills had done well in English but failed math and chemistry. The mismatches here, in course selection or credit load, were especially costly. These were able students. Yet they were to be dismissed.

On the job less than a week, I had no basis or credibility to challenge longstanding university policy; I signed the letters. At the same time, I set my course to work with department heads to strengthen the college's academic advising system; we could lower the dismissal rate and elevate the success rate. We could also contribute to an enrollment increase just by saving more students who had chosen to come. Even more important, we could enhance the self-esteem and future opportunities for more students.

*****

The morning after our furniture and total family arrived in Manhattan, daughters Diane and LuAnn would make a neighborhood acquaintance, and it was fascinating to watch the process. It illustrated the personalities of the two, with LuAnn more eager to make a contact and Diane more cautious.

The Girls Get Acquainted

It was a Sunday morning, our family's first day in our rented house just west of the campus, where we would live until our new house under construction on Oregon Lane was finished. Though apprehensive about the move, leaving their third grade and second grade classmates in Ames, our daughters seemed to be handling it well. They knew they would need to make new friends, but school, the best opportunity, was still three months away.

The girls were on the front steps playing with their Barbie dolls when a boy close in age tricycled down the walk, glancing at the girls as he pedaled by. He turned around at the end of block and rode by again. LuAnn picked up her doll and doll clothes and moved about halfway down our front walk toward the street.

A few minutes later, the boy came by again, glanced at our girls, and pedaled on to the end of the street. When he returned this time, LuAnn had her doll and doll clothes in his path. He stopped and they talked. Diane had remained on the front steps working with her dolls and watching the process. After LuAnn and the boy had visited for a while, Diane picked up her dolls and doll clothes and moved down to the front walk to join the conversation.

Having observed a batch of new freshmen each fall, I saw a clear parallel. As our daughters had moved to a new community, so do new college students. As our daughters needed new friends, so do new college students. As our daughters needed to "make a move" to achieve that new friendship, so do new college students.

Regardless of age, only when one reaches out and makes contacts is there a chance to become part of a new community and achieve some comfort in it. It doesn't "just happen." It takes initiative, sometimes repeated initiative.

*****

I had looked forward to the evening in Emporia, in the heart of the Kansas flint hills. If all flint hills cattlemen were as generous and friendly as Orville Burtis, who had hosted our Iowa State ag travel course a few years earlier, I would enjoy every conversation.

A Flint Hills Connection

I was at the annual cattlemen's stag at the Chase County fairgrounds in Emporia. It was important that I be there; I would meet flint hills cattlemen, and they could meet K-State's new associate dean. A bonus was that the evening's speaker would be Earl Butz, Purdue University's dean of agriculture (and later a popular US secretary of agriculture). Though Butz's humor was a bit earthy, his talks were informative, and he always left an agricultural audience feeling good and important.

As I worked my way through the group during the social hour, I noticed the name tag, Wayne Rogler, on a short, stocky, and friendly faced fellow about sixty years of age. I introduced myself, with the comment that I had been raised near a Rogler family. He asked where, and when I told him Atlantic, Iowa, he smiled and replied, "They're cousins of mine." He then told me about several visits to the Iowa Roglers, all the way back to his childhood.

I would learn that Rogler's ranch was headquartered in a beautiful creek valley just north of Matfield Green and extended along both sides of Highway 177. Rogler also had a second business, arranging the leasing of others' flint hills grassland to cattlemen from Nebraska and other states who wanted to summer graze their yearlings on the area's highly nutritious grass.

I would often encounter Rogler during the next several years. He was a K-State graduate, former state legislator, and very close to the university. His daughter, then in the ranching operation with her dad, would enroll in the winter short course for young farmers and ranchers that we would initiate. He was also part of a group of ranchers who called on our college to do more research and extension work on the impact of the state tax load on farm and ranch viability. He never missed K-State cattle feeders' day and, in my last month at Kansas State before departing for South Dakota, he was on hand when I spoke at the Chase County soil conservation banquet in Cottonwood Falls.

Postscript: When Shirley and I returned to Kansas State nine years later, Rogler was among the first to greet us with a handwritten note of welcome. He and others with whom I had gained acquaintance as associate dean would be valuable friends and supporters during my presidency, especially when I was dealing with some contentious issues.

*****

An early challenge at Kansas State was to cause my department heads to focus more on the student-advising responsibility within their departments.

Department Heads and the "Barnwarmer"

While department heads had interest in their students, other duties often demanded their time and attention. Research administration involves a plethora of responsibilities, including renovation of facilities, purchase of equipment, and administering research grants and contracts. For most department heads, there are industry meetings where their presence is a high priority. Such multiple duties, in most cases, precluded a department head from teaching an undergraduate class and having direct student contact. Further, once teachers are assigned to their classes, not much administrative oversight by department heads is required.

To increase student success and retention, we needed more-effective academic advising. Specific faculty needed to be identified and trained (for example, how to use high school grades and ACT scores in designing a student schedule), and their advising time budgeted for. In order for that to happen, I needed department heads' attention and involvement.

Shirley and I had hosted a series of evening receptions for student advisers and their spouses. I had also organized a series of workshops for department heads and advisers, in which we built, with their input, a total academic advising system, with the goal being, of course, student success. Among the workshop outcomes were a base figure for the amount of faculty time to be budgeted for the advising function and the respective responsibilities of the adviser, the department head, and my office. (The department heads, as well as Beck, had been concerned about the enrollment decrease in the college; they would lose faculty positions if it continued. After I shared with them the data on those students to whom we had sent dismissal and probation letters in June, they were ready for the workshops.)

I felt we needed one more thing—involvement by department heads in a major college student function. The annual student dance, the "Barnwarmer," was to take place in Nichols Gym, and I asked the Barnwarmer committee, mostly juniors or seniors, if department heads had ever attended.

"Not that I can recall," one answered. "I think we sent invitations to all one year, but I don't think any came, just the ag council faculty advisers."

Shirley agreed this was a good opportunity. We invited all the department heads and their spouses, plus Dean Beck, and my associate dean counterparts for research and extension and their spouses to a seven o'clock "pre-Barnwarmer reception" in our home. We included information about the dance, scheduled for eight.

The reception accomplished two things. Because they were a group when they left our home, the department heads and spouses felt more comfortable going into Nichols and this student event than each would have as a lone couple, and it made the department heads and dean's office people visible to the students.

*****

It was not easy to hide the eggs this Easter morning, our first egg hunt in the backyard of our new home on the northwest edge of Manhattan. We had seeded the lawn only in September, so there was no tall grass from the previous season, and we had only a newly planted moraine locust, a redbud, a three-foot blue spruce, and a row of very small lilacs along the back lot line.

The Easter Bunny

I had forgotten to hide the eggs the night before and had rushed out with a basket of candy eggs this morning before daughters LuAnn and Diane were awake. I placed one by the base of the locust, two behind the blue spruce, several under those little lilacs, and had even used the utility pole cable anchor to protect one.

It was then that I spotted a small pair of eyes watching me through the wooden fence that separated the Allinghams' backyard from ours. Their son, Kent, about four, was up early and looking for evidence of the Easter Bunny.

I felt bad; he had seen me placing those eggs, and I had likely destroyed his perception of the Easter Bunny. I put the basket out of view, retreated to the house, and confessed to Shirley what had happened.

Later that morning, Kent's mother stopped over to borrow some sugar. Shirley apologized to her for me placing the candy eggs in Kent's view.

"Don't worry about that," she responded. "It was probably about the time I spotted Kent outside. I told him to come back in because I didn't think the Easter Bunny had gotten to our neighborhood." Her husband, Larry, had also forgotten to put out the eggs and was still in bed.

Kent disagreed. "Yes he has! Mr. Acker is out picking up his eggs."

At every age, we believe what we believe.

* * * * *

President McCain devoted considerable time to dealing with the state regents and legislators, as well as the public, and several college deans felt they needed a top person more available to their daily needs.

Two Bosses?

In early 1963, a year after I had arrived on campus, McCain established a vice presidency for academic affairs and named arts and sciences dean Bill Bevan to the position. In announcing Bevan's appointment, McCain made it clear the position was largely related to instruction, curriculum, and graduation requirements and was not a line officer for extension or the agricultural experiment station. Beck would continue to report directly to McCain, while other deans would report to Bevan.

Bevan would chair a "dean's council" that would include me, not Beck. That created a potentially awkward situation for me. Would I now have two bosses? I was not unduly concerned; I had been hired by Beck and would remain loyal to him. At the same time, I respected Bevan and felt I could work well with him and the other members of the dean's council.

There was another potential problem to address, however. With most teaching faculty in the college of agriculture paid in part by experiment station funds, who would sign off for the president on their appointments and promotions, Beck or Bevan? As this was unfolding, McCain had suggested Beck write his own job description (which should obviously address that issue). While Beck did not seek undue authority, he did want to confirm the authority and responsibility he currently held. Beck had written that he would have full responsibility for the agricultural experiment station and the cooperative extension service, and asked me, "What should I write for the college of agriculture (the resident instruction program)?"

I suggested he be responsible for the budget and staffing of the college of agriculture. "Glenn," I said, "if you have the budget and the staff, you have responsibility for the college."

Beck wrote that into the description, and McCain approved it.

The following two-and-a-half years were as enjoyable as the first. I functioned as Beck's associate dean for instruction, worked easily and productively with other deans as a member of Bevan's dean's council, and kept Beck fully informed on intercollege issues. Beck and I annually reviewed salary and rank promotions with McCain.

However, a structure works only as well as the relationship among people in it. In time, this structure at Kansas State would have problems (a subject I cover in detail in my book *Two at a Time*, 2010, iUniverse).

*****

Beck wanted K-State to provide something similar to Iowa State's winter quarter program for young farmers and had asked Jones and me to get it organized. We had chosen extension farm management specialist Wilton Thomas to lead the effort; he and staff in animal science, agronomy, and economics had developed course outlines and related details. The next step was attracting students.

Wait until We Get to Pittsburg

Extension director Harold Jones and I had just left Topeka, where we had described to northeastern Kansas county extension staff this new short course we would be offering the following January. We were driving toward Pittsburg, Kansas, where, the next day, we would tell our story to southeastern county staff. The reaction by our Topeka audience had been disappointing. Instead of enthusiasm for the new program, we had heard mostly reservations and worries.

Awareness and endorsement by county extension staff would be critical to the new program's enrollment. They could publicize the course and encourage likely students to enroll. The five extension district summer conferences in

June were an opportunity for Jones and me to present the program, seek county staff reaction, and find out how many young people they thought might be interested. Our first session had been in Colby, in northwestern Kansas. We made our presentation and asked for responses. There was evident enthusiasm: "It's about time K-State offered such a program." "Good idea." "I can think of two in my county this is tailor-made for." "There is one I'll talk to when I get home." And so it went.

The next day found us in southwestern Kansas, at Dodge City. Though I had been in the state less than a year, I knew a number of local county staff. Extension ag engineer Russ Herpich had taken me out to speak to several county "high yield" dinners the previous winter, where producers of two hundred bushels of corn per acre were recognized. Western Kansas was "positive thinking" territory; I expected we would receive as positive and enthusiastic reaction as at Colby, and we did.

Our third day was in Salina, with county staff from central Kansas. Though the response was not as enthusiastic as in Colby or Dodge City, many expressed eagerness to alert some of their clientele. K-State would see some of their young farmers on campus the following winter.

Topeka and Pittsburg were scheduled for a week later. The northeastern Extension district extended from Riley County, the home of Kansas State, east to Kansas City, and north to Maryville. Much of this area would be considered part of the corn belt, with farming operations more diversified, with more livestock and less acreage per unit. Jones and I made our Topeka presentation, the same as in Colby, Dodge City, and Salina, and asked for responses. The room was quiet, a few questioning expressions evident. Eventually, one agricultural agent asked, "What did you say the cost would be?" Next, "Will they be in the dorm with other students?" Finally, "Sounds like a good idea, but I don't know if our people can get away for that long."

Jones and I then pressed a bit. "Do you think there will be some from your counties interested? Are we on the right track?" In time, we got some positive, though cautious, responses, including "I've got a couple I'll talk to about it." Several suggested they might have one or more for which the course would be worthwhile, and they would let them know about it. No enrollment predictions were volunteered.

As we headed south from Topeka on Highway 75, I turned to Jones and asked, "Did we screw up in our presentation? Didn't we say the same thing we said in those three meetings last week?"

Jones just laughed. "If you think these guys were cautious, just wait until we get to Pittsburg!" He continued, "Eastern Kansans are different. Those agents were reacting to us in the same way the people they talk to back home are going to react." Jones was a native Kansan and knew the state and the people. He had been a long-time extension soils specialist before being named director.

I had also seen differences among Kansas's regions. The western Kansans I had met were, on the average, much more aggressive, more forward looking, and quicker to accept new ideas or technologies. The limited rainfall, the Dust Bowl and its consequences, and the Great Depression had made farming especially difficult in western Kansas, and a higher proportion of the population had left. Only those who were especially creative and adaptive had survived; they and their offspring were now making things happen.

Those I had met in the northeastern part of the state, though friendly and hospitable, were more reserved and cautious. I had not yet spent much time in southeastern Kansas. Perhaps in eastern Kansas there had been enough rainfall and enterprise diversity for more farmers to survive the problems of the 1930s, without change or with significantly less change than in western Kansas. The eastern Kansans and their descendants might be more dedicated to tradition and less welcoming of change or new concepts.

Jones's warning, "Just wait until we get to Pittsburg," was right on target. The reaction to our presentation there was even more reserved and cautious than at Topeka. However, in January we had a mix of students from all sections of the state, including northeastern and southeastern Kansas.

It was a good lesson for me. Most people make good judgments; some just take longer, are more cautious, and take into account more factors. They don't "show their hand" so quickly. It depends on their heritage, their culture, and their environment.

*****

It was clear we could increase success and retention of new students by selecting courses and a credit load their first semester or two in accord with their demonstrated academic skills, high school transcripts, and ACT scores. But I had also learned there are other influencing factors. New students sometimes get homesick. They fail to establish friendships or otherwise get involved in this new "community." Some feel they are just a number, only a face in the crowd.

Why Students Persist

Experiment station editor Lowell Brandner, whose office was near mine, showed a lot of interest in our student recruitment and retention effort, and I would ask him for advice on brochures, newsletters, and other communication efforts. Brandner also happened to be faculty adviser to a graduate student in journalism, Joannie Sistrunk, and suggested that Sistrunk interview one hundred of our College of Agriculture students to find out what they believed caused them to persist.

The most consistent response was "being called by name by one or more of my instructors or my academic adviser." It did not appear important that the instructor be in their college or major, only that he or she demonstrated enough interest to address the student by name.

Most good college teachers work at knowing students' names; for large classes they develop seating charts to help. Sistrunk's finding reinforced one of the adviser responsibilities established in that advisers' and department heads' workshop: know every advisee by name.

* * * * *

I had just finished an evening presentation about career opportunities in agriculture to parents and students at the high school in Council Grove. The evening had been arranged by loyal K-Staters, Don and Lucille McNeal, in concert with the school superintendent and guidance counselor.

All These Degrees?

To illustrate my message, I had used both an overhead projector and a shopping bag. From the latter I pulled a box of cereal, a bouquet of flowers, a package of meat, a large plastic insect, and other items, each related to one of the curriculums in our college and an industry for which a student might prepare.

One woman was especially excited and impressed; she told me she was so sorry that her son could not be there to hear the program and to meet me. I told her I would like to meet her son and handed her my business card, suggesting he come to campus for a visit.

The front of the card was standard, my name, title, address, and phone. However, on the back was printed all of the college's curriculums and the degrees offered in each—for example, agronomy, BS, MS, PhD; animal science, BS, MS, PhD; food science, MS, PhD; horticulture, BS, MS; etc. The list was long; I was promoting the total college of agriculture.

As I responded to others' questions, I noted this woman turn the card over, look at me, and then look back at the card. She did this several times and finally interrupted, saying, "You look so young; have you earned all these degrees?" It was a reminder: communication can never be considered complete. Or, if a message can be misunderstood, it will be.

* * * * *

Frank Carpenter had joined the college resident instruction office as assistant dean a year before I arrived. He was a K-State graduate, a successful vocational agriculture teacher, and then a state agricultural education supervisor before returning to the campus. He had the background and positive attitude I needed for a close colleague.

No Time for a Rocking Chair

One of the first things I noticed in Carpenter's office was a rocking chair. Though only forty-two, he was a new grandfather, so a rocking chair might be appropriate. However, the rocking chair was largely ornamental; Carpenter had so many good ideas, worked so hard, and traveled so much recruiting students that he had little time to sit in it.

We needed to increase enrollment and student retention, and Carpenter had good thoughts on both. He arranged for himself, Bob Bohannon (assistant to Dean Beck), or me to be at each of the district vocational agriculture teacher meetings, as well as meetings of high school guidance counselors. We told them about our curriculums, provided information on graduates' jobs and salaries, and generally kept them acquainted with the college.

One of our most effective programs, and valuable to Kansas State over the long term, was our work with junior colleges (now called community colleges) and some four-year church-related colleges where students might attend one or two years before transferring to our college of agriculture.

Credit transfer is often a problem. Some course credits may be "accepted for transfer" by the destination institution but not count toward graduation in the curriculum chosen. A university department may change a curriculum requirement. If a student reads those K-State requirements before entering the junior college, and the rules change before he or she arrives at K-State, some credits earned might not count.

We felt that most of those problems could be avoided, at least for those whose career goals remained on one track. We began by working on two-year curriculums with several junior colleges from which we had a number of students. Our goal: if a student transferred within three years of entry at the junior college and with a C average or better, all credits would transfer intact.

Considerable negotiating was needed, both with the junior colleges and with our K-State departments. Department by department, Carpenter and I were the negotiating intermediaries with the deans and faculty leadership at the junior colleges. For example, one of our curriculums might require eight semester credits of chemistry and three semester credits of algebra. The community college chemistry sequence might be one four-credit course and one three-credit course; algebra might be a five-credit course. By the end of the second year, we had a number of junior colleges printing in their catalogs a specific "Kansas State University Pre-Agriculture Curriculum." It showed the courses students should take and a statement that the package would be accepted intact for college of agriculture curriculums if the student entered Kansas State within three years of entering the junior college.

Carpenter took a leave for the 1964–65 academic year to pursue his doctorate at the University of Missouri. When he left, that rocking chair still had its initial coat of wax.

* * * * *

A freshman in our flour milling curriculum was in my office to tell me about the displays his student organization was planning for Ag Science Day. Busloads of high school students would arrive on a Saturday morning to get acquainted with the college. Each department's faculty and students had arranged displays and demonstrations to show what really goes on in their field of study.

So Enthusiastic, There Must Be Something There!

I had noticed the young man's high school transcript showed only his last two years of high school at Salina, so I asked him where he had lived earlier. He had lived largely in metropolitan areas far from the midwest; his father was career military and was eventually transferred to the air force base at Salina. The young man's only apparent exposure to agriculture was enrollment in vocational agriculture his senior year at Salina.

"With the background you've described, what prompted you to enroll in vocational agriculture?" I asked.

"I didn't know a thing about agriculture," he said, "but I had a friend in vo-ag, and through him I met the teacher, Mr. Mugler. You know, he was so enthusiastic, I figured there must be something there." He then added, "I am glad I enrolled. Otherwise, I wouldn't be here at K-State."

This conversation and his comment came at the right time. I was looking for the right person to replace Carpenter for the year he would be away. I wanted the best young vo-ag teacher or county extension worker interested in earning a doctorate, one proven effective with students and who also foresaw a career in higher education.

Two names kept coming to me from a variety of sources, Mugler and Nelson Galle, the vo-ag teacher at Moundridge. By the time I had studied the files and notes I had on each, I learned Galle had just accepted a new job with Hesston Manufacturing. I recalled the freshman milling student's comment, "He was so enthusiastic, I figured there must be something there!"

I hired Mugler.

Postscript: Mugler started work on a doctorate in poultry science, and after the year in my office, he moved to an instructor position in that department. As the undergraduate adviser in that department and instructor in the beginning poultry course, he steadily built enrollment in both the course and the poultry science major. He later moved up the academic ranks, became chair of the university's faculty senate, moved back to the dean's office as assistant dean, and served many years as an adviser to the senior men's honorary, Blue Key. He finished his career with an outstanding record in my former job, associate dean of agriculture and director of resident instruction.

Behind a banquet lectern at the International Gamma Sigma Delta (agricultural scientific honorary) convention held on the K-State campus, June 1964. To the right is President McCain. From the time I became associate dean at Kansas State until I would return to our farm after service in Washington, DC, a high proportion of my time would be behind a lectern or on the road headed to some gathering, selling or representing the programs for which I was responsible.

*****

One of my significant victories as associate dean at K-State was promotion of Walt Smith, an associate professor of animal science who lacked the PhD degree, to the top academic rank of professor.

An Intellectual without a Doctorate?

For more than twenty years, the professor rank in most university disciplines had virtually required successful completion of the PhD degree. This had been especially true in the biological, physical, and social sciences, including colleges of agriculture, engineering, and home economics. There were exceptions: in veterinary medicine, the doctor of veterinary medicine degree (four years in the professional school plus now two or more of pre-professional course work), plus a master's degree sometimes allowed promotion to full professor.

Other exceptions were in law, architecture, or the visual or performing arts, where professional experience and demonstrated expertise was more often considered as qualifying one for the top rank.

Though respecting and appreciating the intense training and learning involved in earning a PhD, I had always been averse to the premise that one had to have a doctorate to be an intellectual, to do credible research, or to be an outstanding teacher. Walt Smith was an embodiment of my belief; not only had I been impressed by his research in beef cattle genetics, I was impressed by his ability to explain the research purpose and design to producers. His undergraduate course in genetics, a difficult subject for most students, consistently received high praise from students who had taken the course. I considered Smith one of our most outstanding classroom teachers, and student evaluations confirmed that. In addition, he was a respected undergraduate and graduate student adviser.

I believed it was time to recognize a basic truth, that a doctorate does not guarantee intellectualism. Any of us might name several PhDs where the word intellectual would not come quickly as a description. Intellectualism is defined as showing intelligence, needing or using intelligence; an intellectual is a person who is well informed and intelligent. Smith characterized those definitions in spades.

I knew that convincing McCain of a promotion for Smith would not be easy; he had pressed for the doctorate as the university-wide standard for promotion to full professor. Making an exception, granting the full professorship to a person without a doctorate, would raise eyebrows. Someone might suggest the university was "lowering its standards," and believe me, *no one* in a university wants to be accused of lowering standards.

Beck was supporting my recommendation, and I had documentation, including research publications, course enrollment, student evaluations, and supporting comments from respected faculty colleagues. My oral comments to McCain were largely focused on course enrollment and student evaluations. After all, teaching students is the basic purpose of a university. Though Smith's research publications and faculty colleague recommendations were solid, I wanted this promotion to be approved primarily on the basis of teaching effectiveness.

McCain's approval of the promotion was one of my most rewarding moments.

* * * * *

Shirley and I were having dinner at Keck's Steak House, east of Manhattan on Highway 24, with South Dakota State University president Hilton Briggs and Oscar Olsen, a biochemist and SDSU's interim dean of agriculture and biological sciences. South Dakota State needed a new dean, and Briggs and Olsen had driven to Manhattan that morning to interview all three of Beck's associates, experiment station director Floyd Smith (Wilson had gone to the University of Hawaii as dean), Jones, and me.

He's Eating My Steak!

Should I say something? Shirley wondered. The fillet she had ordered had just been served to Briggs, and his knife and fork were already at work.

I had met Briggs before. He was an Iowa State animal husbandry graduate and had been the dean of agriculture at the U of Wyoming, Laramie, in 1951, when a carload of my Iowa State fraternity brothers and I drove out to help install a new FarmHouse chapter. When Briggs moved on to South Dakota State as president in 1958, I had sent him a note of congratulations. Coincidentally, I had taught two of Briggs's nephews at Iowa State, and, I would later learn, the father of the Wedemeyer kids I had hauled on the Wiota school bus had been Briggs's coworker and roommate at Iowa State's sheep barn during their college years.

Keck's was known for steaks. Shirley and I had ordered the small fillet (tenderloin); Briggs and Olsen had ordered the New York strip. Briggs had said he did not care for fillets. "The New York strip," he said, "has more flavor." This fit with what I knew about Briggs; he had strong convictions on any issue.

Briggs was so intent on telling us about South Dakota State and what he saw ahead for a new dean that he had paid no attention to the shape of the steak placed before him or, apparently, its flavor. Shirley had been served Briggs's order and eventually decided she just as well enjoy the flavor of a New York strip.

We would spend eight years with Briggs at South Dakota State, and although we laughed many time about this incident, Shirley never found the occasion to ask Briggs if he enjoyed her fillet at our first dinner together.

* * * * *

Before Briggs and Olsen left town the next morning, they stopped to see me in the Weber Hall lecture room where I had just finished teaching my orientation class for freshmen, agriculture in our society.

To Be a Complete Dean

Briggs was direct. "We would like to invite you and your wife to Brookings to visit about the dean position as soon as it can be arranged."

I quickly agreed; I felt ready to lead total agricultural programs, including teaching, research, and extension.

Early the next week, before our trip to Brookings, McCain asked me to stop by. McCain had often commented that K-State's dean of agriculture position could as well be a vice presidency; it was on a few other campuses. I was therefore not surprised by his approach. "We know you are the likely person for the SDSU job, and you probably would like to be a dean. Why don't you just stay here, keep on doing the good job you are doing? We'll make Beck a vice president and you the dean of the college."

I thanked McCain for his compliment and his confidence and told him I would be thinking about options over the next week or so. However, as I left his office I said to myself, "If I'm ever to be a dean of agriculture, I'm going to be a *complete* dean of agriculture, responsible for teaching, research, and extension."

By no means do I suggest that dean of K-State's college of agriculture (the instruction leadership position) would not be appropriate and descriptive of the duties. My successor, Carroll Hess, would hold the dean title, and counterparts at Minnesota, Louisiana, Florida, Nebraska, and California, then or now, have carried that title. Each has given the title its deserved respect.

For me, however, it was the new experience and responsibility that I sought, not the title.

* * * * *

Shirley and I drove to Brookings two weeks later for a two-day visit. While I visited each department in the college and the men who would be my key leadership colleagues in instruction, research, and extension programs, Shirley was visiting the school our daughters might attend and getting acquainted with the community. The evening of our first day was a reception in Olsen's home for us to meet all the department heads and other key people and their spouses. The next afternoon, Briggs offered me the job as dean. With the total program smaller than at Iowa State or Kansas State, I would also carry the title of director of the experiment station and be the "program leader" for research.

My to-be key colleague for extension, John Stone, had both a director and dean title. In addition to leading the cooperative extension service, he was dean of extension for a developing program of off-campus courses offered by any unit of the university. I wondered, *Could one with the title of dean be comfortable reporting to another with the title of dean?* I told Briggs I was very interested but wanted to think about that extension relationship a few days.

Back in Manhattan, I called Orville Bentley, the former SDSU dean who had become dean at Illinois. I knew Bentley well, from the time my ag travel course had visited his beef cattle nutrition work nine years earlier at Ohio State's Wooster research station, and had worked with him on several regional projects. He assured me that Stone was a team player and that the titles were of no consequence.

I called Briggs to accept the job; we would be moving to Brookings for a February 1 starting date.

* * * * *

The dollars one earns are spent or invested; it is the experiences and satisfactions that endure for a lifetime. As in earlier jobs, most of my Kansas State salary had been spent on consumption items such as food, clothing, books, vacations, or gifts. The rest had paid the loan interest and increased the equity in our Manhattan house. Because SDSU provided a campus home for the dean and we had sold the Manhattan house, we were using that now released equity for a down payment on some Iowa land. What we would carry from Manhattan was not money, but experiences and satisfactions.

On the Road Again

We celebrated Shirley's thirty-fourth birthday on the road to Brookings and SDSU. In place of a birthday cake, it was sandwiches from a fast food outlet on Highway 77 in Fremont, Nebraska. Our conversation centered on the many friendships, in Manhattan and statewide in Kansas, that we would retain and the satisfactions that were locked in for our lifetime. Shirley had been "homeroom mother" for both daughters' classes and helped establish a new 4-H club, in addition to her student and faculty hosting.

One of my early mentors had told me that one should stay in a leadership position long enough to have positive and lasting impact. On that issue, I felt good. With the help of Carpenter, Mugler, and the department heads, we had established an effective student-advising system in the college. Undergraduate enrollment had increased from seven hundred to eleven hundred. There was a new graduate program in food science, a new undergraduate curriculum in natural resource conservation and use, and a bakery management curriculum that had relocated to Kansas State from a Florida university.

Chapter VIII

Dean, South Dakota State University

The name of the college at South Dakota State, Agriculture and Biological Sciences, reflected that it included the botany, bacteriology, and zoology/entomology departments. On some campuses, these departments are in a college of arts and sciences. The college also included the economics and sociology departments, those too, usually, in a college of arts and sciences (sometimes with separate agricultural economics and rural sociology departments in a college of agriculture). The economics department even included accounting and business law.

I reported directly to President Briggs (SDSU had no vice presidents, only a newly named dean of academic affairs). Briggs reported to a seven-member state board of regents, which established policy for SDSU and six other institutions, the University of South Dakota at Vermillion, South Dakota School of Mines at Rapid City, Northern State College at Aberdeen, Black Hills State College at Spearfish, General Beadle State College at Madison, and Southern State College at Springfield. All of these institutions in a state of fewer than seven hundred thousand people meant state money for higher education was spread rather thin.

I had much to learn about the state, the college, and the job, and the learning had begun before our physical move.

Some Things We Didn't Tell You

"We need to talk." That had been Al Musson's greeting when I had arrived at the November 1965 convention of state and land-grant universities in Chicago, a few weeks after I had accepted the SDSU job. Musson's title was assistant director of the SDSU experiment station, suggesting he would handle the operating mechanics of the research program.

Though Musson and I had had desks in the same "graduate student bullpen" at Iowa State thirteen years earlier, we had hardly been acquainted. He had been finishing up his doctorate and working full time on a genetics research project, and I was usually at the nutrition farm or in class. During my October interview on the SDSU campus, he had been most helpful, direct, and informative, and it was clear he would be a valuable coworker.

Surprises always appear in a new job, and I had wondered what they would be. I soon found out. At our first opportunity, after a convention session, Musson had laid it out. "There were some things we didn't tell you during your interview. To finish the current fiscal year, we will be short about three hundred thousand dollars in the experiment station budget and about the same amount in the college budget. You will be facing some decisions."

This was more than a surprise; it was a shock, "Why the shortage; what happened?" I had studied the budget; $600,000 was close to 10 percent of the total budget for the college and station. It was a lot of money, especially when faculty salaries ranged from $6,000 for instructors to $12,000 for the highest paid department heads. With shortages of that magnitude, I knew there would have to be drastic cuts.

"We gambled and lost," Musson said, and then explained. State policy had long allowed the university to keep its income from tuition or from livestock and crop sales in revolving accounts, and the board of regents set a limit on how much could be spent from each account for the fiscal year. The 1965 legislature had changed the state policy; henceforth, tuition and livestock and crop sales income would be deposited in the state treasury, and all money to be spent (for seed and fertilizer, for example, as well as for faculty salaries) would have to be formally appropriated by the legislature. As part of this new policy, on June 30, 1965 (the end of the 1965 fiscal year), all balances in revolving accounts would revert to the state treasury.

Musson continued, "We had some major equipment needs and could not see our large revolving fund balances going back to the state treasury on June 30. We took a chance the board of regents would feel the same, so we ordered about six hundred thousand dollars of needed equipment. The equipment was delivered, but the regents balked on raising the FY 1965 spending limit. We had to pay for the equipment with the new fiscal year appropriations."

Yes, I would have some decisions to make—leave vacant positions unfilled, cut travel and supply budgets, and/or approve no equipment purchases. It was a great way to become popular as the new dean and director.

* * * * *

The first Monday in February, having arrived from Kansas on Sunday evening, we took care of several family priorities.

Book Covers and an Engine Block Heater

A South Dakota native had suggested, "You'll want to have an engine block heater installed." He had called it a "soft plug" heater; the engine block had a soft plug on one side that could be removed for a heating element to be installed, its cord extended through the car's front grill. In time, I would also install a small electric heater under the dashboard of the car, and a time clock at our garage front wall outlet, so the car's interior, as well as the engine, would be warm when Shirley drove our daughters to school. Though two school buses went by our campus home, it was just inside the city limits, so the girls were not eligible to ride.

The second need was getting Diane and LuAnn comfortably in their new schools. Shirley had driven them to the school in the morning, Diane to junior high and LuAnn to the middle school, both on the same campus near downtown. The principal welcomed them and assigned each a classmate to help them get oriented. Shirley was still unpacking in the afternoon, so I picked the girls up at school about three thirty.

"How did it go?" I asked.

"Fine, but we need to go to the bookstore on Main Street." That surprised me; the school furnished all the books, and each girl was carrying several.

So I asked, "Why the bookstore?"

They wanted book covers, with Brookings School colors, for each book. They would then belong!

* * * * *

My secretary, Marcella Hoffman, was scheduling individual visits with department heads my first week in order for me to learn the issues they and their departments were facing. But Lloyd Glover, head of the economics department, beat me to the punch; he had already called earlier in the week and asked for a meeting.

Ten Needs of the Economics Department

Glover welcomed me to the job and wished me well. He told me he was proud of his department but wanted me to be aware of some needs. That was exactly what I wanted to know. Glover's list included several personnel problems, his need for additional faculty for the department's university-wide service teaching load, and a new building. His twenty-five-plus faculty members were housed in a U-Shaped WWII barracks structure between the meat lab and the dean's home.

We had discussed each item briefly before we got to Glover's item number ten, "a new department head." Though the department was large and a big management job, Glover also taught a large section of the introductory economics course. Having been alerted by Briggs that Glover was one of the campus's most popular teachers and also that he did not enjoy administration, I had a ready response. "Lloyd, I respect your wishes and will help bring about the change. Just give me a few weeks to get my feet on the ground."

Two weeks later I suggested Glover call a department faculty meeting to announce his plans. In that meeting, I asked for written suggestions of persons I should consider for interim head, so Glover could prepare for fall semester and I could start the search for his permanent replacement. Rex Helfinstine, a steady and long-time faculty member was suggested by most. I asked him to serve and he agreed.

When a department head steps back to a faculty position, there is usually a salary reduction to that of the highest paid professor. In this case, I felt that was inappropriate. Glover was an outstanding teacher and would teach several sections, each with large enrollment. I also wanted everyone to know that I respected teaching. Not only did I leave Glover's salary unchanged for the next fiscal year, there was an increase. For the balance of his time at SDSU, he remained one of two highest paid professors in the college and probably in the entire university.

* * * * *

The first week of March, a month after I had arrived, the entire state of South Dakota was hammered with one of the most severe snowstorms in recent years. SDSU shut down on Friday; students and faculty were told to not try to get to class. I appreciated the free day; it let me catch up on correspondence and read budget and other documents in the warmth of our living room. But it was not so cozy out in the country.

Probing the Snow for Sheep

Starting in Montana and Wyoming, and sweeping on into Minnesota and Iowa, strong winds and heavy snow had enveloped the northern plains, leaving many vehicles stranded on highways and causing a few deaths, including one of my former Ames friends who succumbed in his car, snowbound for three days on an open stretch of highway near Fremont, Nebraska. To South Dakota cattle herds and sheep flocks, the consequences of that intense snow storm had been deadly. Cattle had drifted ahead of the storm into the southeast corners of their range pastures where they packed together, their coats and nostrils coated with wet snow and ice, and had simply suffocated.

At our Antelope Research Station in the northwestern corner of the state, the losses had been modest, a credit to superintendent Ralph Trevelyan and his staff, who had brought most of the cattle and sheep in close to headquarters as the storm approached. The topography of the ranch also helped. Those cattle more distant from headquarters and which Trevelyan could not reach had drifted ahead of the storm but found sufficient shelter in the ravines or "breaks" in the landscape. Within those ravines, they moved enough to avoid getting buried.

Sheep, however, behave differently. In rough weather, they stand nose to nose, heads down, and rarely move. The sheep that Trevelyan and crew could not get to headquarters found shelter in the breaks but let themselves get buried in the drifting snow.

As soon as the three-day blizzard abated and snowplows moved out to clear the highways, Trevelyan called the county agent, Roger Moul, in Buffalo. "Roger, drive down to the lumberyard and get four of the longest 1x2s they have, tie them on the roof of your car, and come out. We need to probe for sheep."

Trevelyan, Moul, and the ranch crew probed those drifts for three days. They would wade into the drift and probe with a 1x2 until they hit what felt like an animal body. They would then dig, with shovels and by hand. A sheep standing alone would be alive. If two were nose to nose, both that were found through the first day of digging were still alive. If three were nose-to-nose, most were dead; they could not get enough oxygen through the dense snow to survive. The work was exhausting, but after a night of rest, the men were back out the next morning with their 1x2s. Until near the end of the third day, the crew was still finding a few live sheep. By that night, when most of the "shelter breaks" had been checked, the men were bone tired, but they had saved more than two hundred sheep.

At our Highmore station, on a flat and open plain fifty miles east of Pierre, our superintendent remained in his house two full days during the blizzard; it was simply not safe to go outside. Though cattle were confined in the headquarters lot and barn, he became concerned for them and watched for a lull in the blizzard. He put on heavy clothes and headed for the barn, a mere three hundred feet northeast of the house.

The lull did not last; he was soon enveloped in intense, swirling snow, became disoriented, and lost his bearings. In time, he stumbled on something and fell down. He groped around to find what he had stumbled on. It turned out to be the tip of a hayrack standard (the ladder-type structure on the front of a hayrack).

"But," he told me later, "that hayrack was northwest of the house; the barn was northeast!" Fortunately, the hayrack was parked on the leeward side of an east-west shelterbelt. He used that shelterbelt, kept it on his left, and waded east through snow toward the barn. In doing so, he walked over and tumbled down off the end of a stack of bales, almost falling into the barn door. Had he not tripped on that hayrack standard, he could have walked through an opening in that shelterbelt to his death in the blizzard.

*****

It was a week after that blizzard that the head of the animal science department, Rick Wahlstrom, Musson, and I headed west and north from Brookings. I had seen the campus and near-campus operations and wanted to visit all of our out-state research facilities; only by seeing the facilities and talking with each superintendent and some industry leaders in the area could I adequately understand the programs, their significance to the area, and the opportunities and needs that lay ahead.

Tall Grass, Federal Money, and Selenium

Our first stop was an irrigation research farm near Redfield. South Dakotans had dreamed for years that water could be lifted out of the Missouri River's Oahe Reservoir near Pierre and channeled eighty-five miles overland to irrigate thousands of level and fertile acres in the James River Valley, especially the wider portion between Aberdeen and Huron. SDSU was doing research ahead of the need. This farm, with water pumped from wells, was to show the benefit of irrigation, as well as compare irrigation systems and determine how much water should be applied.

We continued northwest through Faulkton to Norbeck, not much more than a grain elevator and not even shown on state maps, to visit a new grass research project. Dr. Ray Moore, a top young scientist in agronomy, had won a large USDA research grant to study how to increase grass productivity in this limited-rainfall, "short-grass" country. The university had obtained a long-term lease on a two hundred-acre farm for the research, and Moore had seeded several grass varieties in pastures separated by a variety of fencing systems. His major focus was comparing rotation grazing systems. I was so impressed with the volume and height of Moore's growing forage that I would later tell audiences this research was paying off; in this "short-grass" country we nearly lost our 1965 Chevy in the tall grass.

We crossed the Oahe reservoir on US 212, and the next eighty miles was through the Cheyenne Indian Reservation. Eighty miles more took us to Newell, a town of fewer than six hundred people a few miles north of the Black Hills. We checked into Newell's finest hotel, a frame house with sparkling-clean rooms and a shared bathroom for six dollars a night. The next morning we would visit a USDA research station a mile northwest of Newell where three of our university research and extension staff were headquartered. The facility had gotten the attention of South Dakota's senior US senator, Karl Mundt, a few years earlier, when USDA had announced plans to close it. The local community protested the closing, appealing directly to Mundt. Soon, a senate committee demanded the facility remain open, and, in addition, recommended an appropriation to improve the facility. Mundt had senate seniority; additional money was even provided to pave the road from Newell to the station.

It was soon clear to me that the original USDA decision to close the facility was correct. Though established to determine the best irrigation practices for several thousand acres in the area, the soils on the site were varied and did not represent the soils of the area so research results were hardly useful. Further, it was difficult to get research or extension faculty to live in Newell; most commuted from Spearfish or Belle Fouche.

Though I had not yet visited Rapid City, the business center of South Dakota's west river country, I wondered, *Why not find office space for our faculty in Rapid City and do applied research on cooperators' farms?*

After visiting the USDA facility, we headed north for lunch in Buffalo and then east to the Antelope Range cattle and sheep research station. It was on state-owned land, formerly managed by the state agency Game, Fish, and Parks, but recently assigned to the experiment station. There we learned firsthand from Superintendent Trevelyan what it was like to probe for sheep after a blizzard.

We backtracked south, to Rapid City and brief visits to the Pennington County Extension Office and the headquarters of the South Dakota Stockgrowers Association. Heading back east, we spent an hour at a crops and grazing research station near Cottonwood. Then we headed to a small ranch south of Pierre where soils, and the grass that grew in those soils, was high in selenium. Cattle research at the ranch had focused on measuring the economic consequences of selenium toxicity as well as how to minimize the toxic effects on animal performance. Useful research findings had been published, and the findings were in use on ranches in that soil-type area.

On return to Brookings, I had several items on my to-do list. Within weeks, the selenium operation would be closed down; it had done its job. Not long after that we established a West River Agricultural Research and Extension Center in Rapid City and moved our Newell staff to that center.

*****

I was having lunch with Roger Blobaum, a college classmate and FarmHouse brother, across the street from the Russell senate office building in Washington, DC. Blobaum was an aide to Democratic Senator Gaylord Nelson of Wisconsin, and I wanted his advice on how I could make the most use of South Dakota's two senators and its lone congressman.

Don't Bother with the Senator

I had come to Washington for a four-day USDA orientation for new agricultural experiment station directors. Though I had been involved previously in research, most of my administrative work had focused on instruction and student advising, financed almost exclusively with state appropriations. I knew little about rules and regulations for handling USDA funds that came to state experiment stations and extension services on a formula basis (number of farms and rural population). A power shift from state legislatures to Congress and Washington agencies was also underway; more research funds were going to experiment stations as grants or contracts, some from USDA and others from the National Institutes of Health, National Science Foundation (we had obtained an NSF grant at Kansas State to provide a Saturday morning science seminar for high school students), and other federal agencies. Universities, as well as the private sector, were directing more lobbying effort to Washington.

Depending on seniority and committee assignments, individual senators and representatives can influence agency grant decisions and, in some cases, earmark appropriations. (Dr. Cecil Wadleigh, leader of soil and water conservation research in USDA's Agricultural Research Service once told me his administrator called him to say, "There will be a new USDA soils research facility in House Speaker Carl Albert's hometown. You have thirty minutes to decide what it is going to work on.") South Dakota's two senators, Republican Mundt and Democrat George McGovern, as well as Representative Ben Reifel, all had considerable seniority.

"Roger, how do I make most effective use of these people?" I asked. Since Blobaum was working for a Democratic senator, I suggested, "Let's start with McGovern."

"First," he said, "don't try to get time with the senator. Get acquainted and spend time with his agricultural aide. He knows the territory, he'll tell the senator what needs to be done, and after the senator concurs, he'll get it done!"

"Okay," I said. "Who is McGovern's ag man?"

"Ben Stong. He's the guy you need to know. I've worked with Ben; he's tops. Get to know Ben."

The name, Stong, rang a loud bell with me. "Roger, is Ben Stong any relation to Duffy?" "Duffy" was Norma Stong, married to our FarmHouse brother and my pledge father, Joe Lyon. She had been one of the few Iowa

State women majoring in animal husbandry (and the one who had enticed me as a freshman to pucker up for a wet hog lung). I recalled that she had spent much of her youth with a grandmother at Keosauqua, Iowa, and that her uncle, Phil Stong, had written *State Fair*, on which the subsequent musical and films were based. However, I knew nothing of her parents.

"Never thought about it," Blobaum said.

We headed across the street to McGovern's office, and Blobaum asked the receptionist for Stong. She said he would soon be back from lunch and led us to his desk area, a corner of a large senatorial staff office. Above Ben's desk was a picture of Duffy.

Ben soon arrived, and we learned he had just spent the weekend with Duffy, Joe, and his grandkids on the Lyon's Jersey farm near Toledo, Iowa.

It was an auspicious meeting; Ben Stong would be a great help to SDSU and me during the next eight years.

* * * * *

Most problems in management are personnel problems, and I was briefing Briggs on one at our Southeast Experiment farm near Beresford. The cause and solution seemed obvious to me, but I wanted to test my analysis with my more experienced boss. I also wanted him briefed in case he heard about it from some other source. No university president (or dean or department head) wants to be surprised.

They're Also Testing You

The experiment farm was small, with 320 acres for crops and livestock research and two professional staff, an agronomist, and an animal scientist, the latter also superintendent. Among our off campus research locations, this one had the most followers, and with good reason: area farmers had formed an association to buy the land so the university would do crops and livestock research in the corn belt part of the state. The association's board functioned as an advisory committee to the farm superintendent, as well as to Brookings-based research leaders, on the research needed.

The agronomy research leaders thought their plot work was not getting enough attention; their farm agronomist did not have enough control over equipment or budget for part-time workers. Their concerns had spilled over to nearby association board members, and a delegation of the board, mostly representing the agronomic interests, called on me.

The delegation suggested we separate the two areas, with a crops superintendent and a livestock superintendent. But there was only one set of equipment, and only one full-time support worker. I told the delegation I would spend some time on the issue and get things straightened out. (I suspected the superintendent/animal scientist was so busy with the swine and cattle projects he was not communicating with his advisory board members and his own staff).

Briggs agreed with my analysis, and he also added, "The association board and your staff are also testing you, the new dean." He suggested, "Spend some time with members of the association board, especially one or two you feel are the most solid."

My first step was a session with my animal science and agronomy department heads, Rick Wahlstrom and Larry Fine. Both agreed the Southeast farm professionals were good people that we should try to keep, and that the conflict needed to cease.

My next call was to Leonard Dailey, a board member and farmer near Jefferson. Daily had impressed me as steady and very supportive of both the experimental farm and the university. Among board members, he lived far enough away from the station that he had not been involved in the recent flare-ups.

I drove down on a Saturday morning to visit. He introduced me to two of his three sons, all involved in his operation, and explained that one led on the crops enterprises, the second dealt with equipment, and the third focused on the farm's livestock.

We talked about the Southeast Farm; he had been one of the organizers. I then shared with him the current problem as it had been described to me and asked, "Any advice?"

His response was direct. "You've got to have one boss at the site." He continued, "It's like our operation. I have three sons in the business, and sometimes there are disagreements. But we have one set of equipment and one business. That is where I come in. There has to be one who settles the issues." It was a perfect illustration, and helpful.

My next stop was the board chairman, a near neighbor to the station who had been too much involved in station personnel and operations issues. I acknowledged his desire for a solution and also emphasized that he should not have to worry about university personnel problems; I would handle those. I emphasized there had to be one boss at the station, that my two key department heads and I would see that the two professional staff would do their major jobs, whether that be superintendent, animal scientist, and/or agronomist.

The final step was a session with the superintendent/animal scientist, agronomist, and the two department heads as a group. I had four agenda items: (1) past problems are history; (2) there is one superintendent, whose responsibility is onsite supervision and communication with department heads and the advisory board; (3) the agronomist reports to the superintendent; and (4) any disagreements or appeals are brought to me or my associate director, not to people outside the organization.

The issue was settled. I briefed President Briggs and felt that, at least on this issue, I had passed the test.

* * * * *

SDSU did not train veterinarians; its veterinary science department only conducted research on animal health, provided diagnostic service for the state's practicing veterinarians, and advised preveterinary students who would seek admission to veterinary colleges in neighboring states.

In February, my first month on the job as dean, $600,000 had been appropriated by the state legislature to build a new animal disease research and diagnostic laboratory at SDSU. Over several preceding years, livestock industry leaders had convinced the governor and legislators of the need. An architect was now designing the building, and the industry leaders had high expectations. But, at their May meeting, our board of regents had taken disturbing action.

The Governor Decides

Governor Nils Boe called all seven members of the board of regents, Briggs, and me into his office; he had been told by some of the state's livestock leaders that the animal disease research and diagnostic lab he had recommended and for which the legislature had appropriated money was about to be interfered with, and he wanted some answers.

A Washington lobbyist, hired by the board of regents to "get federal grant money for the state universities," had reported at the May regents' meeting that he could get atomic energy commission money to double the size of the animal disease lab building and that more "atomic energy money" would follow.

Neither Briggs nor I had been contacted by the lobbyist. Briggs and one board member had raised concern in the meeting. "But this lab is for livestock research and diagnostic work, not research in atomic energy."

The lobbyist had the answer: this federal agency's mission is so broad, the lab could use radioisotopes for disease research, and Senator Mundt would ensure that commission staff allocated research money to the lab. Despite Briggs's and the one board member's objections, enough board members were convinced, and a resolution was quickly passed to "seek the atomic energy commission money for the veterinary lab."

I had been stunned by Briggs's report of the regents' action. The lobbyist had not done his homework; there was no way atomic energy money could be used to finance the research needed by the state's livestock industry. I had been to DC to visit several agencies, including the commission, to learn what parts of my college could tap federal funds, and for what purposes.

My first step after the regent action had been a phone call to the lobbyist. "What is going on? Why was there no contact with Briggs or me?" He gave me the same story he had given the regents.

My next call was to the atomic energy staff I had visited weeks before. I wanted to be sure of my facts, the types of projects on which their grant funds could be used.

Next I briefed livestock industry leaders on the regents' resolution and the facts regarding atomic energy funds. It was not long before the governor was alerted by livestock industry leaders. With only seven hundred thousand people in South Dakota, most everyone has a direct or indirect link to a legislator or the governor.

Soon I got a call from Briggs. "We are to meet in the governor's office at one p.m. Tuesday, *along with the board of regents,* to talk about the animal disease lab. We'll fly out in the college plane; be prepared to tell him about plans for the lab, and how the federal atomic energy funds might impact the lab's job." Briggs's phone conversations were always short and to the point.

The meeting did not last long. The governor said he had recommended the disease lab appropriation to the legislature and had signed the resulting bill. He had made a commitment to the livestock industry, and now he had received a few phone calls from livestock-industry leaders worried the lab was going to be diverted to atomic energy research due to the regents' action. He wanted some answers!

Briggs volunteered me to brief Boe and the group. I opened a large easel tablet to the building design. I reviewed the name and purpose of each lab room, flipped the sheet to a list of specific commitments Briggs and my predecessor had made to the industry, and finished with constraints the atomic energy funds would impose.

Boe asked several board members if they had known all the constraints. They had not. He announced a decision. "Planning for the diagnostic lab as envisioned by the legislature should proceed." Addressing the board, he said, "Your Washington representative should look for other funds for other purposes." The meeting ended.

The following September, Regent Hilbert Bogue, who had opposed the May regents' resolution, invited me to stop by their home for supper after a field day at our Southeast Farm. He was especially interested in the lab's construction progress and my efforts to hire a new veterinary science department head.

Over peas and pork chops, I questioned Bogue about the meeting in the governor's office. "I know the governor appoints the board members, but since the board is an independent body, it seemed to me he might have urged the members to reverse their action. Instead, he simply made and announced the decision. How come?"

Bogue leaned forward. "I'll let you in on a secret. When the governor appointed us to the board, he got from each one a signed and undated letter of resignation."

Welcome, academic, to the world of politics.

* * * * *

Musson had warned me about many things, including that Cletus Nagel, head of the plant pathology department, would consistently plan more research than his budget could handle, run out of money late in the fiscal year, and come to the dean and director's office for a bailout.

I'm out of Money

Nagel struggled into my office on his one crutch. (I had never asked the history of his walking difficulty. With that one crutch he was not slowed in getting where he wanted to go, and I had learned to never offer to open the door for him.) He told me he needed $13,000 to finish the fiscal year; his budget for student labor and supplies was exhausted.

Nagel understandably believed that plant diseases were important and more research was always needed. However, priorities and budget allocations for the current fiscal year had been set by my predecessor; I respected his judgments and would adhere to them to the best of my ability.

A dean or director always tries to maintain a "rainy-day" fund for unforeseen research needs, major equipment breakdown, or emergencies. However, according to Musson, Nagel had systematically dipped into that rainy-day fund to expand his program at the expense of other college and experiment station priorities.

I quizzed Nagel. "Any equipment breakdowns or critical replacements? Have there been new disease problems during the year that you have had to address?" There had been none.

The legislature had completed its work in February, the university had its appropriation, and I had allocated the next fiscal years' instruction and research money to departments in April. Nagel and his fellow department heads knew what money they would have for the next fiscal year.

I told Nagel I would come to his rescue. I would transfer $13,000 from the station reserve account so he could pay his student labor and buy necessary supplies — and that I would reduce his next year's budget allocation by $13,000. "I'll initiate the transfer; you go back and redo your department's research budget for the coming fiscal year."

Though in coming years I would allocate reserve funds to Nagel or others for unforeseen needs, this day I needed to break Nagel's habit. I also knew "word would get around" that Acker expected department heads to manage their budgets.

* * * * *

My office visitor this day was one of many South Dakota farmers and ranchers who stopped in during my early months as dean or I had encountered across the state. Agriculture was the state's major industry, and the SDSU campus was "agriculture's headquarters." They wanted to meet the new dean, "size him up," and, if they decided he was up to the job, be a friend and supporter.

Have You Moved Irrigation Pipe?

After a brief greeting and shaking hands, Harold Frizzel asked, "Have you ever moved irrigation pipe?"

"No," I responded.

"If you are going to be dean of agriculture in South Dakota, you'd better know how to move irrigation pipe!"

Frizzel told me he lived on the west edge of DeSmet, *Little House on the Prairie* country. His question to me made a point: South Dakota has low rainfall, twenty-six inches or less a year, and crop production could increase markedly with irrigation. Furthermore, it is a good idea for a dean to know what your clientele do and how they do it.

I was not about to shy away from a challenge. "Next time I'm on my way to Pierre, Harold, I'll stop by and you can show me how." I think I surprised him with my response. I had an afternoon commitment in Pierre the following Monday, so we set the time; I would be at his place at eight thirty.

Frizzel had a "towline" system, with a water-supply pipe extending down the middle of a pasture. Connected to it, at a right angle, was a four-hundred-foot line of pipe, supported by a series of triangular frames that also kept the working sprinkler nozzles vertical. Frizzel turned off the pump, and we drove his tractor down alongside the supply pipe. He disconnected the four-hundred-foot sprinkler line, I chained the near end to the tractor drawbar, and he towed it to the opposite side of the field. We then drove back for Frizzel to reconnect it to the supply line, and he then turned on the pump.

After coffee at the Frizzells kitchen table and a thirty-minute drive with Frizzell past his country school and some nearby farms, I headed on to Pierre. By evening, or at least within a week, I'm guessing that several in Frizzell's circle of agricultural friends and his neighbors had learned that the new dean was credible; he had helped move irrigation pipe.

* * * * *

"Governor Boe is on the phone," my secretary, Marcella Hoffman, said as she stepped to the door.

The Pheasant Population Is Down

Boe got right to the point. "Dean Acker, we have a problem. Our pheasant population is down, and that will hurt business all across the state this fall. Some conservation people are blaming the fertilizers and chemicals that our farmers are using. Is that the problem? I want you to get to the bottom of it."

No doubt some staff in the state agency, Game, Fish, and Parks, had raised the concern. Perhaps Boe had also heard concerns from some motel and restaurant owners, whose businesses would suffer with fewer hunters coming into the state. A good governor keeps in touch with a lot of people.

I could only respond, "Governor, I'll see what I can do."

"Let me know what you find out." The conversation was over.

I needed some advice, and walked downstairs to see Oscar Olsen, head of biochemistry and who had been interim dean before my arrival. A native South Dakotan and SDSU graduate, Olsen had served in many roles, including dean of the graduate school. Most important, he had a lot of common sense.

"What you need to do," Olsen said, "is get together all the scientists related to the issue, agronomists, entomologists, wildlife, and others, and have them lay out their data." If data exist, they should tell you the answer. You'll want to involve some of the Game, Fish, and Parks staff, so it would be better to have your meeting at a neutral location."

Fortunately, I had a good working relationship with the Game, Fish, and Parks director, Bob Hodgins. SDSU was the site of US Department of Commerce-financed wildlife and fisheries research units, both housed with our three-person wildlife management department. Hodgins and I served on the policy board for each of the units.

I called Hodgins, told him of the governor's call, and proposed he join me in getting the key people together. A few days later we had a dozen scientists, from both his staff and mine, in the meeting room of a Sioux Falls motel. Hodgins's staff had many years' data on bird counts at numerous locations in the spring, summer, and fall. Data showed the good and bad years in spring hatch and numbers harvested. They also showed relationships to individual years' rainfall, temperature, or major weather events. Our wildlife and fisheries faculty, especially those in the wildlife research unit, added their data.

Our agronomists and pesticide researchers, including a biochemist who had studied pesticide and nutrient fate in streams, also had plenty of data, showing trends in fertilizer and pesticide use, as well as the impact of a season's weather on fertilizer utilization or pesticide breakdown and disappearance.

Early in the session there was some finger-pointing by some wildlife specialists, and evident defensiveness by entomologists and agronomists. However, as the data were presented and discussed, the finger-pointing and defensiveness disappeared, and we moved to interpreting and openly discussing the data's significance.

By four in the afternoon, there was a consensus: The low 1966 bird count was simply part of a population cycle, normal in undomesticated animal species. As bird population increases, incidence of disease increases and predator population increases in response to their food supply, the birds. The birds compete for limited cover and their own food supply, so bird population reaches a peak and then declines. As bird population decreases, predators search elsewhere for food, incidence of disease declines, and bird population again begins to grow.

Hodgins and I cosigned a summary letter to the governor. Our half-day conference did not increase South Dakota's pheasant population that fall, and coffee shop debate on the problem would continue. But the governor had his answer, and our staff in related disciplines had a better understanding of relevant factors. The low pheasant count was just part of a normal cycle.

*****

Congress had appropriated several million dollars to the USDA to be allocated to state experiment stations for facility construction in the same way that annual operating funds were allocated, a formula based on number of farms and rural population. Our station was receiving $100,000 of that money, and I had committed it to the new animal disease lab. Among the many sources of federal construction funds, this money through the USDA was an exception, in that there was no requirement that federal architects review construction plans or that contractors pay federal minimum wage rates on the projects. However, our state architect did not believe that.

What Opinion Do You Want?

Construction plans had been completed by our architect, but before contractor bids could be solicited, the state architect in Pierre had to approve the plans and bid specifications. When he saw that the specifications did not state that contractors had to follow federal minimum wage rates, he withheld approval.

He had dealt with many construction projects that used federal funds, from schools to Missouri River dams to hospitals. All had required federal plan approval and federal wage rates. I quoted USDA fund transmittal documents (faxing documents was yet to come), but he was unyielding. "If I violate federal regulations, the state will risk repaying money to the federal government."

Finally, on a Friday afternoon, I reminded him of the state's livestock industry involvement and told him of the meeting a couple of months earlier in Governor Boe's office. The governor would not be pleased to see this project held up. That got his attention, and he changed his approach. "I'll need an attorney general's ruling on those USDA guidelines you have."

The attorney general was Frank Farrar, completing his second term and campaigning for governor. Saturday morning I tracked down Farrar on the campaign trail by phone; he was at a livestock auction barn at Pukwana, just east of Chamberlain. After I described the situation, he said, "It sounds simple; just tell me what opinion you want."

By Tuesday, I had a letter from Attorney General Farrar that satisfied the state architect.

Postscript: Farrar was elected governor but served only one term. He got crosswise with the rural electric cooperatives on service territory boundaries, and that is costly in South Dakota politics. I would see him from time to time in Pierre, and he accepted my invitation to come to the campus a couple of years later for the dedication of new plant science greenhouses that he had recommended during his administration.

* * * * *

Shirley and I were at the home of director and dean of extension, John Stone, and his wife, Bea, who had invited all the deans and spouses over for dinner and bridge. This was the first time we would be with the entire group.

The Dress Came out Clean

After dinner, Shirley and I found ourselves at a bridge table with Vivian Volstorff, the university's long-time dean of women. Volstorff had just returned from a meeting in Dallas and was sporting an especially attractive white dress from that city's famous Niemen Marcus department store. Shirley was on my left, partner to Volstorff, who was on my right and wedged rather tightly into a corner. As we sat at the bridge table, Bea had given each of us a tall glass of red punch. On the third hand, my partner and I bid a small slam, I was playing it, and as the play unfolded, it appeared I would go down one trick. On a high-risk finesse, the face card I was missing dropped.

"I can make it!" I shouted. My right hand shot out in the excitement and knocked that glass of red punch into Volstorff's lap, right on her new white dress.

We grabbed the napkins but had to move the chairs and table to get at Volstorff's lap. I felt terrible and very embarrassed, apologizing, of course. Volstorff took it in beautiful stride; a dean of women has encountered trauma far worse than red punch.

A few days later, returning to my office from across campus, I encountered Volstorff coming out of my building, Agricultural Hall. She said she had come over to my office to tell me to not worry; she had sent her dress to the cleaners and it had come out clean.

She continued, "When I found you were not in, I started to leave that message with your secretary. Then I thought, 'No, that would not be the right message to leave with a man's secretary'!"

The Ackers' 1966 Christmas photo, in front of "The Dean's Home" on the north edge of the SDSU campus and fronting on US 77. LuAnn in front of Shirley, Diane on the left.

* * * * *

How we were fortunate enough to be included in the next experience, I never learned. But I had an idea.

The Marshall Plan and East Berlin

It was well after dark on a Sunday night when Shirley and I, along with another couple, boarded the subway for the twenty-minute ride to East Berlin. Should we have made this trip to the other side of the Berlin Wall? Our host, a West German junior finance minister, had warned us not to. "But if you should go," he added, "don't take any pictures; don't even take a camera!"

The temptation had been too great, especially when "Cousin Brucie," a New York City radio host who wanted to describe the place to his radio audience, declared he and his wife were going.

We had spent the morning looking at the wall, the cement block barrier topped with rolls of barbed wire and constructed a decade earlier. In the open space between where we had stood and the wall were dozens of heavy iron bars sticking out of the concrete pavement, placed to stop any vehicles that might crash through the wall.

East German soldiers occupied elevated shelters atop the wall. During the previous decade, dozens of East Germans, nearly free after scaling the wall, had been gunned down and left to die in that open space.

Our concerns were heightened at the first East German subway station we had zipped by, seeing teenage soldiers holding machine guns, and noting that Cousin Brucie had brought along his camera.

This adventure began six weeks earlier as I scanned a stack of opened mail that my secretary, Marcella Hoffman, had put before me. I laid aside one letter; it said something about travel to Germany, and that I did not need. I had already received several "invitations" to join or even lead a people-to-people group or some agricultural tour, at my own expense. No need to look at another.

Hoffman reached out and slid the letter back before me. "I think you'll want to take a good look at this one."

She was right. It was from the German embassy in Washington. "We invite you, as a leading US citizen, to come to Germany as our guest to help celebrate the twentieth anniversary of the Marshall Plan." There was more detail; I was one of fifty Americans chosen for the two-week visit, and I would see large and small industries fostered by Marshall Plan reconstruction funds. I would travel first class on Lufthansa Airlines, but I could exchange the first class ticket for two tourist class tickets if my wife could join me.

The fifty invitees, one from each state, were arranged in five groups. Our group, including spouses, totaled twenty-three, and all (except I) had evident Democratic credentials. There were Los Angeles city councilman (later to be mayor) Tom Bradley, a Massachusetts judge, the attorney general of Montana, the chair of the Missouri democratic party, a defeated congressional candidate from Indiana, a Western Michigan University regent, and a Georgia state legislator.

How did I become a member in this group? I never really learned, but my analysis led to Senator McGovern and his agricultural aide, Ben Stong. The German embassy likely contacted the Johnson White House or the State Department, and the fifty slots were rationed out among key senators.

Regardless, it was a fantastic learning experience. We spent time in Bonn, then capital of West Germany (Federal Republic of Germany), the port city of Bremerhaven, industrial Dortmund and Essen, and then Berlin and Munich. We visited farms, small craft shops, major manufacturing facilities, chambers of commerce, government bureaus, and even the Black Forest.

Our Marshall Plan group at the Brandenburg Gate. Behind Shirley is Los Angeles city council member Tom Bradley, who later became Los Angeles mayor and a K-State Landon lecturer. The two men standing nearest the camera are, on the left, our host, an assistant minister of finance for the Federal Republic, and Montana attorney general Forrest Anderson, who later became Montana governor. "Cousin Brucie" is the man holding the camera.

Our Sunday night visit to East Berlin was brief. Only we four disembarked. (East Berliners were not allowed to go to West Berlin, so no East Berliners were "coming home" on a Sunday night.) After the passport check, we ventured out onto dark, empty streets, streets with no pedestrians or cars. Shop windows were empty of merchandise. It seemed weird. After a block, we headed back to the station.

At the station, we watched West Berliners who had spent a rarely permitted day or weekend with siblings or parents in East Berlin, no doubt wondering if there would ever be another visit. They gave their good-bye hug, walked a few steps, turned and waved, walked a few more steps, turned and waved, walked a few more, turned and waved. Finally they were down the ramp, around the corner, and out of sight.

No US media coverage had adequately conveyed the grief visited upon German families. Tonight we saw it and felt it. And it would continue twenty more years.

West Germany's reconstruction and revitalization, traceable to both Marshall Plan dollars and democracy, gave us renewed respect for the post WWII leadership of the United States, as well as Britain and France. What we saw in East Berlin added an exclamation point to values we often take for granted—democracy and free enterprise.

*****

Sociology department head Howard Sauer was mild-mannered and even-tempered, but his jaw was set when he marched into my office just before noon on the first day of fall semester classes.

Majoring in Sociology, Journalism, or Physical Education?

Sauer wasted no time on a casual greeting. "One of my students just came from her genetics class and told me the instructor introduced the course by saying it was going to be difficult, so if there were any sociology, journalism, or phys. ed. majors in the room, they just as well drop the course."

I knew the instructor, a freshly minted PhD newly hired in the zoology department. This apparent attitude in new PhDs is not uncommon. Proud of their new PhD, they set out to impress the world with the scientific rigor of the discipline they have mastered.

I called zoology department head Bob Walstrom and relayed what Sauer had told me. "Bob, I can't certify these were the words used, but I want you to find out and, if they were, cure the problem." I may have added for emphasis, "Or I will."

Within the hour, Walstrom reported back. "Sauer's information was correct. I've explained rather clearly to Professor X that his words and his attitude are totally out of line. I think the problem is cured." So it was;

student evaluations of Professor X's teaching were positive all three years he was with us.

Six years later I was on a southeastern state university campus for a teaching seminar and spotted this young man in the audience. At the seminar's close, he rushed up to greet me, asking about his former colleagues and expressing appreciation for his SDSU experience. Later I mentioned him to my host dean, who told me he was a dedicated teacher who had a good rapport with students.

Sauer's march into my office was a gift to this young man.

* * * * *

We had become convinced that remote sensing, the use of infrared photography and other sensing devices from aircraft or satellites to assess crop conditions or other phenomena on the earth surface, was a rapidly unfolding area of science, and we needed a top person to initiate a program at SDSU. Briggs and I were trying to recruit Dr. Vic Myers, then at the USDA's Agricultural Research Service station at Weslaco, Texas, and the subject of a recent *National Geographic* feature article on remote sensing.

His Suit Was Gone!

Myers would meet us in Washington, where Briggs and I were attending the annual meeting of the national association of state and land-grant universities, and he would be in town for a Department of Defense (DOD) briefing. Though a USDA employee, much of Myers's research was being funded by DOD.

I flew in on a Saturday; Briggs would arrive early Sunday afternoon and we would share a room. Myers knocked on my door at ten o'clock Sunday morning; we visited and then headed downstairs for lunch about eleven thirty. Myers, who held top security clearance, did not want to carry his bulging briefcase to the dining room but expressed concern about leaving it exposed in the room. I suggested he put it in the closet.

When we returned from lunch, Myers's coat and briefcase were gone, and so were my suitcase and my suits! Myers was alarmed; he was in no mood to continue talking about a new job.

I then recalled that I had complained to the front desk that my room was cold. I had likely been assigned a new room, and our things had been moved there. I called the desk and learned we had been moved to Room 806, a bellhop would be right up with the keys to 806. Myers relaxed.

At Room 806, the bellhop opened the door. No suits, no coat, no suitcase, and no briefcase. Myers was no longer relaxed. Though our bellhop's native language was not English, it was clear he was as frustrated as we. He had gotten no tip for moving our belongings—we had been in the dining room—and now we were at his throat. He professed no idea where our things had gone.

His hand held a batch of keys, and I grabbed for them. Among them was a key marked 608. Ah ha! I took the lead to 608. Voila! All was there!

By then it was 1:20, and I was to chair a meeting at 1:30. Myers took his briefcase and coat; I grabbed my suitcase, gathered the suits off the closet rod, and we headed back to 806. Briggs had just arrived. I introduced Myers to him, picked up my meeting file, and left.

When I returned about four thirty, Briggs told me he had a great visit with Myers and that Myers was interested in our job. "However," he said, "the strangest thing happened just a few minutes ago. A fellow came to the door looking for his suit, and it was hanging in our closet."

"That is strange," I agreed. No need to go into details! It was time for me to get downstairs to greet a representative of the Scott Seed Company, who was hosting the social hour prior to our association deans' dinner. I freshened up and hurried down to the banquet room.

Our Scott Seed host soon arrived. "Sorry I'm late," he said. "You know, the strangest thing happened to me this afternoon. I checked into my room about one o'clock, hung my suit in the closet, and went out for a walk. When I came back to my room, my suit was gone. It took me an hour to track it down. I hope you haven't been waiting long."

"No problem," I assured him. "We just appreciate you and Scott Seed hosting this social hour." No need for details here, either!

Postscript: Myers resigned his USDA civil service position in the Rio Grande Valley to cast his lot with us at South Dakota State. He did a fantastic job, organized the new institute, secured continued funding, hired able faculty, and put SDSU on the map as one of the leaders in remote sensing. The institute and Myers's work also deserve much credit in getting a new federal EROS (Earth Resources Observation Satellite) agency service center located between Brookings and Sioux Falls a few years later.

*****

Because the state constitution limited the South Dakota legislature to thirty working days one year and forty-five the next, the house and senate appropriations committees held joint hearings and then retired to make their respective judgments. Their judgments rarely differed, but if they did, they were quickly worked out in a joint conference committee. My thirty minutes before that joint committee each year was valuable time.

1936 Was a Dry Year

I had made my pitch on experiment station and extension funding (instruction funds were in a separate university budget) to the joint appropriations committee, highlighting funds we needed for new research greenhouses. I had explained that the green houses would allow two or three generations of selection per year, more rapid variety development and, so, higher crop yields that would enhance South Dakota's economy. Committee members had paid respectful attention to my presentation, but I was not sure I had clinched their support.

Fortunately, the man who followed me did. Dick Daly was a seventy-year-old, second-generation farmer from near the small village of Columbia, a few miles from the North Dakota border. Daly's son was handling much of the farm work, giving Dick time to be a leader in the South Dakota Crop Improvement Association, which allocated to selected grain farmers one or two bags of seed of new crop variety releases from our experiment station. The selected farmers would grow a few acres of the new variety to increase the seed volume for seed dealers and other farmers across the state.

Daly's comments to the joint committee were brief: "Nineteen-thirty-six was a dry year. I had a two-hundred-dollar real estate tax bill and couldn't pay it. Last year was drier. I had a two-thousand-dollar real estate tax bill. I paid it, and I also had to pay some income tax. What was the reason? It was the drought resistant varieties of alfalfa and small grains and the genetic lines of corn developed for South Dakota's short growing season and limited rainfall. They were all developed by our agricultural experiment station and their use encouraged by extension staff. *We* need those greenhouses!"

Within minutes there was joint committee action recommending that both houses include the greenhouses in their capital improvements bill.

We would break ground for those greenhouses the following summer.

For several years I served as chair of SDSU's Athletic Council and representative to the North Central Athletic Conference. During that time the legislature appropriated funds for a new physical education center, and this photo is of the center's groundbreaking, September 22, 1970. To my left is Governor Frank Farrar, Brookings Mayor Orrin Juel, and Brookings Chamber of Commerce representative John Evanoff. To my right are athletic director Stan Marshall, President Hilton Briggs, physical plant director Ken Hayter, and SDSU alumni director Art Vandall. Dave Pierson, assistant to Briggs, is at the podium.

*****

My secretary stepped in and closed the door. "Two men out here want to see you, and one is pretty angry."

He Would Throw Me out the Window

I followed her to the outer office, introduced myself, and invited them in. The leader of the two was red-faced, stiff-legged, and ready to explode. Before he sat down, he let me have it. "One of your staff threatened to throw me out the window! Isn't that a terrible way to treat a person on your campus?"

I hesitated a minute, motioned him to a chair, and he sat down. "That depends," I said, and with a smile, added, "How did you treat him? Who was it? Tell me what happened." I had noted a tape recorder under his arm.

"I went in to see your extension agronomist and tried to get him to listen to this tape. He told me he'd throw the tape recorder out the window and me with it!"

"Put your recorder on the desk," I said. "I'll listen to it." The logo on their shirts told me they represented a liquid fertilizer company, one that I knew advertised heavily on the value of foliar application, spraying the liquid form of nutrients on plant leaves during the growing season. I took the angry spokesman to be a company sales manager and his partner to be a local farmer-dealer.

He flipped on the switch and I listened. What I heard was a recording from a Watertown radio station, an interview by our SDSU extension editor with one of our extension soils specialists. The topic was the various forms of nitrogen, phosphorus, and potassium for plants. The specialist made the point that farmers should buy the form that is lowest price per pound of usable nutrients, N, P, or K (nitrogen, phosphorus, or potassium). The interviewer then asked specifically about the highly advertised, liquid forms. Were they superior? Was there a distinct advantage to foliar application? The specialist responded only by reemphasizing that farmers should calculate the cost per pound of useable nutrient.

"Are there any other guidelines?" the interviewer asked.

The specialist offered, "It's always good to buy from a reputable dealer."

The interview had been initially played by the Watertown station on public service time. A local fertilizer dealer, apparently liking the message, had then purchased station time to replay the interview. The tape I listened to was from that replay, and the dealer's sponsorship preceded and followed the interview. Immediately following the interview and before the follow-up sponsorship statement, I heard laughter.

My guest was distressed by the interview, even more distressed that a competing dealer had used a university piece on sponsored time, and downright furious at the laughter.

I understood his anger, and told him so. I also told him it was inappropriate for the station to sell time for commercial use of the university tape, and I would ensure that the practice was stopped.

What about the laughter? I suggested it could have been station personnel following completion of the SDSU interview. It had been the local dealer-sponsored replay that he had taped and that I had heard.

By that time, the spokesman had cooled down. However, he was still disturbed that our agronomy staff did not understand that foliar application of their liquid material resulted in much higher yields than when similar amounts of N, P, or K was land applied. I told him I was not an agronomist but that our extension staff based their recommendations on research. "At the same time," I said, "research outcomes are always subject to challenge. If your scientists have research data, we would be pleased to see it."

I followed up with, "If you'll bring your scientists and their data, I'll gather our staff with their data. We can all be in the same room, look at the data, and discuss it." I added only one condition, that *both* of my visitors be in the meeting. (I had been watching my second visitor, who remained quiet during the exchange. He had been listening carefully, to his partner and me, and I felt he truly wanted to see the university data.)

The meeting was held a couple of weeks later, and data were presented. Company data showed a consistently higher yield with the foliar application. University data showed variation, in some instances slightly higher, in some slightly lower. In no case did the university data show a financial advantage to the foliar application, based on product cost and harvested crop value.

There were two positive outcomes: (a) company staff was exposed to the university data and research methodology and may have become more cautious in their product benefit claims; and (b) our staff had been reminded that their research is always subject to challenge, and that they should always be ready to meet and openly discuss their data with those who may challenge it.

Postscript: More than forty years has elapsed since this event. Genetic change for insect, drought, and disease resistance have brought crops closer to their yield potential, and small differences can be more precisely measured. An additive effect of foliar fertilizer applications has been clearly demonstrated in a number of circumstances. As always, it is incumbent for both researchers and producers to calculate cost/benefit.

* * * * *

Shirley and I were just finishing dinner at Brooking's Town Club steak house with our guest, a Mrs. King from Montana.

Why Would Anyone Want to Be a University President?

I had spotted and greeted a FarmHouse fraternity brother, Owen Newlin, a vice president of Pioneer Hybrids, and several of his South Dakota-based Pioneer staff as we had come in to the dining room. As his group broke up,

Newlin stepped over to our table for a brief visit, and I introduced him to Mrs. King. I did not mention that she was a member of the Montana board of regents, and that she had come to SDSU to meet Shirley and me and to quietly "check me out" with some of my colleagues. I was on a short list of persons being considered for the presidency of Montana State University.

What made Newlin both a productive scientist and effective administrator was his tendency to get quickly to an issue, which he did in this case. After a couple of questions about SDSU, he asked, "Acker, when are you going to become a university president?"

Shirley had to suppress a laugh, and Mrs. King was clearly wondering how I would respond.

"Why on earth would anyone want to be a university president?" I responded.

With student demonstrations over the Vietnam War, plus normal problems with athletics, faculty, and student or staff parking, current university presidents were not having much fun.

Mrs. King quickly jumped in. "There are a lot of reasons to become a university president!" She ticked off a few: impact on the next generation, the chance to lead young people, the impact one can have on a state or society as a whole.

Newlin soon moved on, but the incident had let me know that if other members of that Montana board of regents exhibited comparable enthusiasm for higher education, it would be an outstanding group with whom to work. Mrs. King had made clear that she believed in universities, especially state universities, and that a presidency is a noble calling.

More to the Story

The Montana State presidency did not come to pass, and for several reasons. A week later, at a university meeting in DC, I heard that Montana Governor Forrest Anderson, an ex-officio member of the Montana board of regents, had been quoted in media that he "was not very impressed with the list of finalists for the Montana State presidency." Anderson and his wife had been among the couples on that Marshall Plan tour of Germany (he was then Montana's attorney general) and we seemed to have much in common, so I was surprised by the quote. However, if a governor had doubts, I was not about to venture into the position.

That quote and the fact that our daughters were then in their sophomore and junior years in high school, both doing well and with many friends, led me to write a letter withdrawing my name from consideration.

Another week later, on a Saturday, I was in Sioux Falls with one of my economics faculty for a meeting of the South Dakota council on economic education, a business-university partnership focused on strengthening economics instruction in primary and secondary schools.

A fellow member of the Sioux Falls Norwest Bank board, John Griffin, pulled me aside. "Duane, I didn't think you would turn down thirty-five thousand dollars a year."

What are you getting at, John?"

"That Montana State job. It's yours if you want it." At no time had I visited with anyone except Shirley and Briggs about Montana State. How did Griffin get into the act?

Norwest (headquartered at Minneapolis and as of this writing part of Wells Fargo) had banks in South Dakota and Montana, and bank board members and presidents met periodically in Minneapolis. I would later learn that one of the Montana bank presidents was a Montana regent. Apparently he and Griffin had met, and Griffin had been asked to serve as go-between.

I confess that Griffin's statement made it tempting. Montana is a beautiful state, and Montana State is a land-grant university, comparable in both size and mission to SDSU. We would fit and, though I was but thirty-nine, I felt ready for a presidency. However, there was only one answer I could comfortably give Griffin. "John, I sent a letter withdrawing my name from consideration. I just cannot reverse that position."

I have often wondered how our family's lives would have been different had I given Griffin a different answer. What if, then, I had been given assurance that Governor Anderson's media quote pertained only to the number of quality people on the list and that I would have his full support? What if, then, we had taken Diane and LuAnn to visit the Bozeman school system, especially the quality of its debate program, to judge if they could survive and flourish in a new setting at that age?

Though we passed on Montana State, we would have many other experiences that were fully exciting and rewarding. Most important, Diane and LuAnn graduated from Brookings High, well prepared to enter strong universities and with a continuing circle of faculty and classmate friendships.

* * * * *

A major part of my job was representing (selling) our programs to the state's agricultural and political leadership at state or county events and, at the same time, getting feedback from clientele on how we could be even more useful to the state. Late this afternoon, I was in the back seat of the university's single-engine Cessna reading my mail en route to speak at the Zieback County Soil Conservation banquet at Dupree.

The Best Way to Dupree?

Pilot Ralph Lindsay took off his headphones and turned to me. "There's a big front between here and Dupree that we don't want to go through."

"How close can we get?" Bad weather had prevented me from attending the previous year, and I sure didn't want to miss a second time.

"We can get into Pierre; the front is still on the far side of Lake Oahe."

"Pierre it is," I said. "We'll rent a car."

Dupree is about one hundred miles north and west of Pierre, in the Mountain time zone. We would miss the meal, but with no South Dakota speed limit, we could likely get to the event in time for a short talk.

While Lindsay parked the plane, I rushed in to the terminal's Hertz counter. As the clerk handed me the rental agreement and keys, I asked, "What's the best way to Dupree?" It was a rhetorical question; there was only one way.

A fellow at the counter beside me injected, "When are you going?"

"Right now."

"That's kind of stupid; there's a bad storm coming in!" He followed up, "If you have car trouble, you could be twenty miles from a ranch house, or only five hundred feet and not know it. You could freeze to death!"

He had my attention. I remembered my friend who had frozen to death in a snow-buried car in eastern Nebraska just a few years earlier.

My new friend was persistent. "Do you have a blanket or survival kit?"

"I hadn't thought about it."

"Now is the time to think about it. Come with me." He led me out to the parking lot, opened his car trunk, and handed me two blankets, a candle, and some matches. "Take these with you," he ordered, "and before you leave town, you stop and buy a bunch of candy bars."

"How can I get these back to you?" I asked. "We'll come back to Pierre yet tonight."

"When you get back—if you get back—just leave them here at the Hertz counter. I'll pick them up tomorrow." He was a typical South Dakotan—candid, thoughtful, generous, and trusting.

By then, Lindsay had joined me. We bought the candy bars and headed west on US 14. By the time we reached the Highway 63 intersection thirty-five miles west of Pierre and headed north, the front had passed through; the moon was out and stars were shining. We walked into the Dupree community hall just as they were clearing the tables.

Back on campus the next day, I instructed our college vehicle pool manager to fit every vehicle with a survival kit, including blankets, candle, matches, and candy bars.

*****

The first time the population of Pierre, South Dakota, exceeded eleven thousand was likely the week in 1970 when carloads of SDSU students arrived in the capital to protest a board of regents' decision to close SDSU's College of Engineering and pressure the legislature to void that decision. This is the story.

A Land-Grant University without Engineering?

An earlier legislature had created the position of commissioner of higher education and charged the commissioner and the board of regents to develop a higher education master plan. Dr. Richard Gibb was hired as commissioner and, in time, he recommended converting the South Dakota School of Mines at Rapid City from primarily an engineering college to become the main campus of a western South Dakota liberal arts university that would also include Black Hills State Teachers College at Spearfish.

Loud protests came from School of Mines alumni, mostly engineers, and Rapid City residents close to the engineering programs. There were equally loud protests from Teachers College staff and alumni, as well as Spearfish leadership. They did not want their institution subservient to one in Rapid City.

The regents quickly rejected Gibb's recommendation, and moved to leave both the School of Mines and Black Hills unchanged. Instead, they decided to close SDSU's College of Engineering.

The publicly stated rationale was that, with Mines being an engineering school, closing SDSU's college of engineering would eliminate program duplication. However, this would also make SDSU only the second land-grant university in the country without a college of engineering. SDSU faculty, students, alumni, and friends saw the regents' move as foolish and indefensible.

The board had stipulated that agricultural engineering would remain at SDSU, which blew holes in the "eliminating duplication" rationale; basic engineering courses would still be needed at SDSU for the agricultural engineers. To SDSU and its friends, the regents' action amounted to a "declaration of war." Alumni, community leaders, and the local legislative delegation went into action.

Briggs reported to the board, so he had to be cautious, but he was by no means silent; he publicly decried the regent action, even characterized it with a bit of barnyard language (animal husbandry was his college major). He certainly saw to it that the SDSU supporters had the data and information that would make their arguments effective. Informational letters went out by the hundreds from Brookings to SDSU alumni and friends. I called a Sunday afternoon meeting of my department heads to be briefed by Dave Pierson, Briggs's assistant, and I pressed them to "exert their all" with their contacts throughout the state. Shirley and I, along with others, were stuffing envelopes that afternoon and into the evening.

Gibb also became a target of the SDSU family. Though he had originally recommended the changes at Mines and Black Hills Teachers, leaving SDSU's college of engineering untouched, he was now defending the board's action. That was his job.

Fortunately, the South Dakota legislature was in session and SDSU had many friends there. Some of those friends were even USD graduates. As I had worked with legislators, several with USD loyalties had told me they more often sought and obtained help from SDSU; our research and extension staff and statewide service philosophy were appreciated.

Several bills were introduced to void the regents' action. In time, supporters settled on a single bill, one that simply required a college of engineering at SDSU. The vote on the bill was close but, with the student presence in Pierre well timed, we had won; a full college of engineering would remain at SDSU.

A few days later, we were not so sure SDSU would still have a college of engineering. After the legislature had adjourned and departed Pierre, it was discovered that Governor Richard Kneip, whose staff had received copies of all introduced bills, had signed the wrong bill, not the one passed. Would that mean a pocket veto of the legislatively passed bill? Or, could the legislators be called back to Pierre?

It was time for another attorney general ruling. This time the AG was Gordon Mydland, a Brookings attorney and former state senator. Mydland ruled that the governor signing the wrong bill was inconsequential; it had resulted from a staff error. The unsigned bill was now law.

Postscript: Though Briggs survived this sequence of events, there were repercussions. Stress between Briggs and Gibb and some board members remained and the board later wrote a new policy that limited presidents to ten years in the job. The action included the stipulation that Briggs, who had already served more than ten, should retire at age sixty-two.

* * * * *

I was working at home on a speech when a call came from Governor Kneip. "Duane, we need to visit. I'm headed to Sioux Falls for a banquet. Would you meet me at the Brookings airport at four o'clock?"

The Governor and a Second Job

I was on-hand at the charter terminal when Kneip's plane arrived, and I greeted him and his wife, Pat, as they entered the lobby. "Pat, you wait here in the lobby," Kneip said. "Duane, let's get in the car and take a ride."

As we left for a short trip around a couple sections of farmland southwest of Brookings, Kneip got right to the point. "I need a new secretary of agriculture; we need to take some big steps ahead."

His words made me uncomfortable; his agriculture secretary was a good friend who a few years earlier had given me his candid assessment about the leadership of one of my college departments. His statement, "Prof is a wonderful person but is the type who would ride a train facing the rear so he can see where he has been," had told me that I should proceed with a change in that department's leadership.

Now, as head of a cabinet office, was my friend in the same situation as that university department head had been? It was clear Kneip was not satisfied.

I just drove and listened as Kneip continued. "People have a lot of respect for South Dakota State, especially the college of agriculture, the experiment station, and extension. Would you be willing to take on a second job, also be my secretary of agriculture?"

In sparsely populated and limited-budget South Dakota, many people do double duty. I had earlier played a staff role for Kneip, at a recent midwest governor's conference in Sioux City, Iowa, that he had co-hosted with Iowa's governor. I had also accompanied Kneip's predecessor, Frank Farrar, to the national governor's conference, including a breakfast session with USDA Secretary Cliff Hardin and a governors' committee that Farrar headed.

Our university entomologists, water specialists, and others were often called upon by state agencies to draft or review proposed regulations; they knew the technology and what would be considered reasonable and enforceable. They were glad to do that work, but stayed in the background.

What Kneip was proposing, however, did not seem to me to be workable. If I were responsible for state regulations (inspections, approvals, and enforcements) affecting farmers, agricultural businesses, or veterinarians, there could be situations that would rupture or at least seem in conflict with the university's education and research role.

Second, I already had a full-time job. Though I had a great management team, there were daily "pulls and tugs" in the system. Among strong and capable associates, things can get off-course; I had to be available to them and my department heads.

My response to Kneip was cautious. "Governor, I want to help where I can, but I'm worried about the regulatory role of the secretary position." I told him why, and then followed up with, "I'm guessing, Governor, that there are some good options."

Kneip had been a successful salesman of dairy equipment and had developed business and political friends across the state. Once he was elected governor, he wanted things to move, and when they did not, he started looking for options. I had also observed that when he found an item he could not move, he would back off and turn his attention to other pressing issues. I also knew that his secretary was well respected across the state.

As we finished our drive and arrived back at the airport, I wondered if political reality would let him change his agriculture department leadership, or if he would need to back off. In the end, it was the latter.

As dean I served on the board of directors of the F. O. Butler Foundation, which owned a large ranch in the southern Black Hills, the proceeds of which came to the college for scholarships. The board included, seated, from left, SDSU President Hilton Briggs, Irv Evans, and Carl Hamm, both western South Dakota ranchers. Standing, to my left, is animal science professor Richard Wahlstrom and to my right, associate dean Burt Brage, political science professor Phil Henrickson, and assistant to the president, David Pierson.

* * * * *

This next encounter was early in President Richard Nixon's second term, following his reelection over George McGovern, South Dakota's senior senator. Though questions had been raised regarding a break-in at the Democratic party's Watergate headquarters during the campaign, Nixon was still riding high, basking in his landslide victory.

Dinner at the White House

Our last name beginning with A, Shirley and I were among the first in the line to be welcomed by President and Mrs. Nixon in the East Room of the White House. From there we would be led into the state dining room. But why would the Ackers be in the White House for dinner?

Agricultural interests had been prominent Nixon supporters during his campaign, and Nixon was hosting a Salute to Agriculture Day. Leaders of farm organizations, such as Farm Bureau, Farmers Union, Farm Broadcasters, and National Cattlemen had been invited to Washington along with their spouses. As chair of the division of agriculture of the association of state and land-grant universities, my name was on the invitation list.

The day included briefings by USDA Secretary Cliff Hardin, former chancellor of the University of Nebraska, Attorney General Edwin Meese, and Presidential Assistant Alexander Haig. I especially enjoyed visits with several of my long-time friends among the USDA scientists hosting crop and livestock exhibits on the White House south lawn. A White House reception and dinner hosted by the Nixons climaxed the day.

For entry to the White House itself, we needed to present the printed invitation, and during the day's activities, I worried if Shirley and I would be admitted for the dinner. The night before at the hotel, I discovered I had failed to pack the formal invitation. I called home and asked our daughters to fold the invitation in a house coat, pack it in a small suitcase, and take the case to the Brookings airport. "Tell the agent we forgot this suitcase; ask him to check it through to Washington and our hotel." Would the bag have arrived?

With good friends at the Brookings airport, I need not have worried. The bag was on our bed when we returned in late afternoon to our hotel room.

On arrival at the East Room, we had each been handed a card with our dining room table number. In the dining room, Shirley was directed by a steward to her table near the west side; my table was along the east wall. I quickly circled my table to learn from place cards whom my dinner partners would be. They included a woman from Montana, a farm-management company vice president that I knew, and a 4-H member from Mississippi. The last card, at the setting to my left, read "Mrs. Nixon." Wow!

I stopped a steward who was checking some last-minute items, "Give me some help. I'm to the right of Mrs. Nixon. Is there any protocol of which I should be aware?"

He was most reassuring. "Not at all. Mrs. Nixon is a gracious hostess. Just enjoy the conversation."

As Shirley conversed with her table partners, including Secretary Hardin, Mrs. Bob Dole, and Iowa's Senator Jack Miller, I was asking Mrs. Nixon about the good and bad of life in the White House. Among the good, she cited the chance to meet so many interesting people from all over the world (such as a dean from South Dakota, of course). The bad was largely the isolation and confinement, with so little freedom to enjoy the outdoors and activities of a normal life. She mentioned specifically that the president loved to swim. A previous administration had covered over the swimming pool to make room for media personnel, and he had the area restored to its original use.

As our conversation continued, an idea flashed into my mind, inspired by the University of Minnesota's recent announcement that former Vice President Hubert Humphrey had become a visiting professor. Mrs. Nixon's college major was political science, and she said she looked forward to a time when they might return to a normal life. That gave me an opening. "I invite you to consider, when you leave the White House, a visiting professorship at South Dakota State."

Political science at SDSU was not in my college. However, should an acceptance to that invitation come to pass, I could find the money in our experiment station or extension budget. Furthermore, both economics and sociology were in my college. A visiting professorship in either of those departments would certainly be appropriate.

The evening included entertainment by Glen Campbell in the East Room, then coffee and liquors, plus lively conversations with Dole and others of the Senate and House agriculture committees and other guests. Then there was dancing.

Shirley and I had first danced, as teenagers, to records at a little community hall south of Atlantic. Though the dinner visit with Mrs. Nixon was an obvious highlight, it did not outshine my dancing with Shirley in the White House foyer.

* * * * *

Having worked in three states that border Nebraska, and having good relationships with the University of Nebraska agricultural leadership, I had watched with interest the changes in that university's structure. After Omaha's municipal university was made a part of the University of Nebraska in the early 1960s, the campuses at Lincoln and Omaha, as well as the university's medical center in Omaha, each became a "campus" of the university, with each campus head reporting to the university chancellor, then Cliff Hardin. (By this time, however, the title for Hardin's successor had been changed to president and the chancellor term was used for campus heads, a more common arrangement in multiple-campus universities.)

A Call from Nebraska

Nebraska's agricultural leaders became concerned that in this "two-tiered" structure, the university's agricultural programs were not receiving the attention from the regents and top administration that they deserved. They urged the 1973 session of Nebraska's single house legislature, the unicameral, to make the agricultural programs "a separate campus" to be headed by its own chancellor. (One other land-grant university, Louisiana State University, has that arrangement.) To those of us watching, there ensued what appeared to be a rather stressful political battle. Negotiations eventually resulted in a compromise that became law. It called for an institute of agriculture and natural resources (IANR) at the Lincoln campus, to be headed by a vice chancellor who would "report to the chancellor of the Lincoln campus and the president of the university on all issues related to agriculture." In addition to the college of agriculture (instruction), agricultural experiment station, cooperative extension service, and water resources research institute (all headquartered on the Lincoln's east campus), and a two-year school of technical agriculture at Curtis, Nebraska, IANR would include the conservation and survey division, a formerly independent unit located on Lincoln's downtown campus. That division is akin to the geological survey agency in most states, responsible for monitoring the state's gas, oil, and water resources and their utilization.

The university sought nominations and applications for the vice chancellor position. (Nebraska's dean of agriculture was near retirement and was headed to an overseas assignment so was not a candidate for the position.) Several Nebraska staff and alums suggested I submit my resume, but I demurred. I was totally comfortable at SDSU and did not want to get involved in the results of Nebraska's battle. Instead, I suggested others for the position. Eventually, SDSU professor Richard Wahlstrom, a Nebraska alum, told me that, regardless of my reservations, he had sent my resume to the Nebraska search committee.

A short time later, early November, I was in Minneapolis to speak to a Norwest National Bank conference of their system's bank presidents and branch managers. In the front row, and especially attentive, was Kermit Hansen, president of US National Bank in Omaha, a unit of Norwest, and who I also knew was chairman of the Nebraska board of regents. At the close of my talk, a meeting break, I noticed he rushed out to a phone booth; later in the day we had a brief, innocuous conversation.

A few weeks later, on a Sunday night, came a phone call from Lincoln campus chancellor, Jim Zumberge. He got right to the point. "I'd like to fly up to Brookings to have a visit."

My response was probably more presumptuous and less courteous than it should have been. "Chancellor, the only reason I can think of that you would want to come to Brookings would be to talk about the vice chancellor position at the university. I'd be misleading you to engage in such a conversation."

He persisted. "I'd still like to visit. It would help me learn about the agriculture programs in a neighboring state." That seemed reasonable, and I should at least be hospitable to a university chancellor. He made plans to fly up to Brookings the following Saturday morning.

I met his plane, we drove around our campus and farms, and then went out to our home where Shirley was waiting with coffee and cookies. Zumberge, a geologist, had arrived as chancellor of the Lincoln campus in the middle of the recent hassle over the agriculture programs. He described the compromise that had been negotiated and codified. (I would learn later that, as a new person on the stage, he had suggested the compromise.) His main message to me was that "the issue is settled; the administration, faculty, agriculture leaders, and regents are all on board and want to make it work. What we need is a leader."

I was impressed with the message, and even more with him. But I was still reticent; there is always some residue from a political battle, on campus or off. On the other hand, I was completing my eighth year at SDSU and was ready for a new experience.

I offered, "You no doubt have a short list of people you are considering. You proceed with those, and if those names don't work out, for them or the university, I'd be willing to talk."

Zumberge responded quickly, "We've gone through that; that is why I'm talking to you."

At that point, I could only say I would talk to Shirley, and if she agreed, we would come down to Lincoln to visit.

On January 3, we drove to Lincoln. My first hour was with the search committee, comprised of faculty, industry leaders, and student leaders. It was clear they felt their work was done; the discussion centered exclusively on the things they wanted to see happen in the months ahead. The balance of the day was with department heads, directors, other vice chancellors, and faculty leaders, and Shirley and I joined the president, chancellor, and regents for dinner.

I was sold, and so, apparently, were the Nebraskans. All that remained was formal board action at their January public board meeting, with a starting date for me of April 1.

Positive and Lasting Impact?

We left SDSU and Brookings in late March with some regret at leaving, but most important, we had satisfactions from our experiences and a belief that our time there had left some positive marks.

Our daughters, both now in college, had been fortunate to spend their maturing junior and senior high school years in such a supportive and friendly environment, a town large enough to provide needed services and small enough that one could not walk a block without meeting people you knew.

Shirley had contributed so much, not only to her family and to my work, but to the university and the Brookings community. At least three times in those eight years, she had prepared for and hosted a series of evening receptions for college faculty and spouses. She had prepared for and hosted dozens of other groups, everything from spring graduates to county extension staff to scholarship donors to the South Dakota Wheat Commission. There were also many evenings in our home for department faculty and spouses to visit with department head candidates.

With the help of Mary Helen Hopponen, wife of the pharmacy dean, she had organized The Dames Club, a student wives' group, and hosted members in our campus home. Her experience with comparable groups at Iowa State had told her it was a need to be filled.

She had also taken the lead in organizing Friends of the Brookings Library and was its first president. She co-chaired Brookings' United Way, after having served on the committee in earlier years. In the Methodist Church, she was a dedicated member of the Care Group, which met briefly each week at the church and then scattered to visit shut-ins.

For most of our daughters' time in high school, Shirley and I served as advisers to Methodist Youth Fellowship, and Shirley served a week as a camp counselor.

My professional satisfactions as dean must be shared with others, especially President Briggs, a solid boss with much common sense. His central office colleagues, Assistant to the President Dave Pearson, Dean of Academic Affairs Harold Bailey, Budget Director Wes Bugg, and Physical Plant Director Ken Hayter were appreciated colleagues and good friends.

Most credit has to go to my management team, initially Assistant Dean Burt Brage, Al Musson (I changed both their titles from "assistant" to "associate" after the first year or so working together), and John Stone. This team had been put together by my predecessor, Orville Bentley, but their loyalties had shifted to me without a hitch. My job quickly became that of pointer and coordinator. With input from staff and from across the state, I would point the direction we needed to go and then ensure coordination and seek administrative and public support to get there.

When Stone left to head a project in southeastern Asia in 1971 and Musson retired in 1972, Orville Young and Ray Moore, men I had earlier chosen as dairy and plant science department heads, joined my dean's office team. These changes also went off without a hitch.

Some of my professional satisfactions are mentioned or alluded to in the previous pages, and some are described elsewhere (for example, in my 2006 book *Can State Universities Be Managed? A Primer for Presidents and Management Teams*). However, I'll mention a few here.

Our animal disease and diagnostic laboratory was the first in the United States to achieve accreditation by a newly organized accreditation organization. We closed two research stations that had served their purposes and established a crops research unit in the Whetstone Valley, corn and soybean country in South Dakota's northeast corner. We combined the departments of agronomy and plant pathology into a single department of plant science and, to make more effective use of our top quality faculty in poultry, moved that faculty into the Animal Science department.

We formed three agricultural research and extension centers, at the Redfield irrigation farm, in a new building at the Southeast experiment farm, and a "West River" center in Rapid City. Four decades later, on a visit to South Dakota's Black Hills, Shirley and I visited the West River Center and were thrilled to see a new building constructed by efforts of the SDSU Foundation and a wide array of programs. What had begun in rented space at the Rapid City fair grounds for three livestock and range management faculty was by then a dozen faculty, plus support staff and graduate students, handling agriculture and natural resources research and education efforts for western South Dakota.

We removed from the university's course catalog a number of courses rarely taught for lack of enrollment and, in several disciplines, decreased (or increased) the number of courses in accord with enrollment. This total effort saved much course-preparation time for faculty, and every course promised by catalog listing would be taught.

Appropriations were gained for a new animal science building, greenhouses, and remodeling of Scobey Hall for Economics. We set out ten goals for the agricultural experiment station, a key to increased state appropriations, and a few years later got legislative funding for six senior scientist support teams.

We established a central vehicle pool for the college to ensure up-to-date and safe vehicles, as well as twice-weekly university plane flights to and from Pierre and Rapid City for research and extension staff. We also made the plane available for supervisors of practice teachers and others across campus. We created an institute of biological sciences, assigned a staff member to seek federal research funds in that area, and helped form the remote sensing institute.

It would be difficult to name any of the state's sixty-five counties that I had missed visiting, for a soil conservation or other banquet, to visit university research plots, to meet with extension advisory boards, or even to speak as a substitute for a US Senator who had to remain in Washington for a crucial vote.

One of my most fascinating roles was to serve as a member of the state's commission on executive reorganization. Though it required a number of long Saturdays, driving the two hundred miles to and from Pierre for all-day meetings, I learned much about the totality of state government. The commission's output was a recommended consolidation of 166 state entities, boards, commissions and other units, into twenty or fewer executive branch departments, this to be achieved by a series of ballot initiatives. Our SDSU extension staff, with help of political science faculty, played a valuable education role over the next several years, so that voters could be more informed as to likely consequences of individual consolidation proposals when they entered the voting booth.

An activity I would have sorely missed had there been time to think about it was work with students. There were two reasons for less work with students: The first was that Associate Dean Brage, department heads, academic advisers, and student club advisers were so effective that there were no significant student problems that required my involvement. Second, there always seemed to be another physical, financial, personnel, political, or cross-campus issue in the college, experiment station, or extension service that demanded a dean's attention and, often, my presence.

By virtue of my position, I was a member of the South Dakota Wheat Commission, which collected check-off funds at the wheat marketing point and helped finance three different station projects, the Weather Control Commission, the State 4-H Foundation Board and, after Stone's departure, the state USDA Committee, which included all state administrators of USDA agencies. It coordinated USDA-financed programs and served as a disaster action committee in case of a major flood, drought, or other disaster.

With Stone's departure, I had assumed the director title for extension and brought in Young with the title of associate director. My reason was to complete the integration of extension staff and programs with research and extension. There had been no schism between extension and the balance of the college, but there was a differentiation that I felt unnecessary. For example, whereas teaching and research faculty rank titles were instructor through professor, extension faculty carried such titles as Extension Rank I or Extension Rank II. I felt that inappropriate. If a new PhD in research and teaching was given the rank of assistant professor, so should a new PhD hired for an extension assignment.

We had only one extension specialist involved in research and jointly employed by the experiment station. Such joint research-extension appointments should be common. Those in extension education are more credible if also doing research. The reverse is also true; one's research is more on point if the research leader also does extension education with clientele.

Though extension specialists were housed in departments and Stone looked to department heads to provide "extension leadership," department head salaries had been paid solely by station and instruction funds. I changed the salary budgets to reflect their full responsibility. These may seem minor details, but each sends a message and can influence key people's behavior. The land-grant university is based on integration of teaching, research, and extension education. It should be thus at all levels.

*****

It seems Shirley and I rarely do things in a simple way, and our relocation to Lincoln was no exception. I left Brookings at eight in the morning March 19 in my 1929 Model A Ford, packed with potted plants, to attend my last Norwest Bank board meeting in Sioux Falls. I would meet Shirley and LuAnn, home from college for spring break, at a Sioux Falls auto dealership at noon. Because we would need two cars in Lincoln, we had traded our two-door Buick for a four-door Skylark and a small Honda, and both cars would be ready. We would then head to Lincoln in three cars, with Shirley in the new Skylark, LuAnn in the new Honda, and me "pedaling" the Model A. We would be in Lincoln by evening to greet the moving van with our furniture.

A Postscript: In a Sioux Falls Courtroom

Though I had left SDSU more than six years earlier, I was back in Sioux Falls, helping defend SDSU in court. Associate Professor of Economics Russell Berry had sued the university for back pay, claiming salary discrimination.

Berry was a good person, quiet and affable. However, he was neither a productive research worker nor an effective teacher. He had been hired as an associate professor with tenure after completing his doctorate at Ohio State, long before my time at SDSU. His doctorate thesis topic had been flexible cash rent for farmland.

Glover and Musson had briefed me on the Berry case soon after my arrival as dean. Berry had failed to focus his research on South Dakota priorities; instead, he kept reworking flexible cash rent options and issues. Student evaluations made it clear he was of little value in the classroom. Further, he seemed to have involved himself in controversial issues, usually on the negative side.

I initially considered that Berry might have been put down unduly and, with his salary unchanged several years, had become discouraged. I proposed a modest salary increase; perhaps that would bring change. Reluctantly, Briggs concurred.

Unfortunately, I had been wrong; there was no change in Berry's research focus and no change in productivity, research papers, or bulletins. He also continued to spend work time opposing any item that was mainstream or popular. Though there was political and public pressure for more irrigation in the state, especially for federal funds to move Missouri River water to irrigate the James River Valley, Berry devoted time to calculations that showed it did not make economic sense. At congressional committee hearings on the project in Redfield, Huron, or Aberdeen, Briggs or I would appear to express support. Berry would show up and ask for time to testify that it was not economically viable. (Berry's calculations were likely correct, but it was in South Dakota's interest to have such funds spent in that state to advance irrigation.)

We held his salary with little or no change. Promotion to full professor was never considered, and I was sure Berry would eventually bring his case to a faculty grievance committee or the court. (Briggs and I had been careful to make no effort to prevent Berry from testifying at those Congressional committee hearings, to interfere with his "academic freedom.")

When Berry complained to me about his salary, I was cautious in my response. After every conversation I would dictate the conversation details, and then sign and date the typed transcription for the files. Some day, I felt, those transcripts would be needed.

The afternoon before the jury trial was scheduled, I met with my successor, Dean Del Dearborn, in the Sioux Falls office of the university's attorney, and he handed me the file containing those transcripts. It was all the preparation I needed.

In the courtroom, there was first Berry's testimony, and then the university witnesses, all yet available who had been involved in Berry's supervision. When it was my turn, I described my conversations with Berry and my actions pertaining to him.

Berry's attorney then cross-examined me. She displayed a chart showing the continued increases in salary for associate professors at SDSU during my time as dean and Berry's salary, which had changed little. "Are you responsible for this disparity?" she demanded.

My response surprised her. "I'm not only responsible, I'm proud of it!" Before she could phrase the next question, I added, facing the jury, "I was determined to reward the top-quality faculty, the good teachers and productive research workers. During my eight years as dean, we not only increased the average salary of associate professors by 35 percent, we increased the standard deviation, the differences between the high and the low, by 85 percent. We aggressively rewarded the good ones!" Facial expressions and body language told me the jury liked what I said.

By no means was my testimony the determining factor, but I think it helped. SDSU won the case.

I left the courtroom satisfied with the outcome, but with lingering thoughts. Berry was still a good person; during breaks in the trial I had pleasant conversations with him and his wife. It was too late in Berry's life to be of constructive help. It was simply unfortunate that he had been improperly cast in life as a college professor.

This case reinforced my belief that university department heads and deans must be candid with young instructors and assistant professors who are less than effective or less than productive. They must see that they either get help to make them productive and effective, or else see that they move on to other occupations or settings. To let them continue in their job, or to recommend them to another university, is a disservice to the university, to the university's students and clientele, and, especially, to the person.

Chapter IX

Vice Chancellor, University of Nebraska

My time at the University of Nebraska would be the busiest of my professional life, and with more support from other administrators, faculty, regents, and industry than any university administrator should expect to have. It would turn out to be, though brief, a fully rewarding and productive experience.

My Nebraska Team

I knew most of my new leadership team. Through the great plains agricultural council and meetings of the north central experiment station and extension directors, I knew well the experiment station and extension directors, Howard Ottoson and Jack Adams. I had also met the associate dean for instruction, Ted Hartung (his title would change to dean of the college), when SDSU hosted the poultry science association the previous summer. However, I had not known Warren Viesman, director of the water resources institute, located in the agricultural engineering building, nor Vince Dreeszen, director of the conservation and survey division on the downtown campus. Since Dreeszen, a geologist, had reported directly to the campus chancellor, he may have had some misgivings about reporting to a vice chancellor, especially one less familiar with the disciplines of his unit. I had made an earlier one-day trip to Lincoln to spend some time in his shop, and that had been worthwhile. Two others located near my office in agricultural hall on the university's east campus and who would report directly to me were Dave McGill, assistant to the vice chancellor, and Charles Koopman, finance officer for IANR.

Though the college of home economics was separate from IANR, research and extension in home economics were part of the experiment station and extension service, so the dean and department heads had IANR leadership roles. That helps account for the large number of people in the accompanying photo.

Directors, associate directors, department heads in the Institute of Agriculture and Natural Resources, University of Nebraska-Lincoln, in front of the east campus library in the spring of 1975. At my right shoulder is Agnes Arthaud, interim director of extension, and from my left shoulder, Ted Hartung, dean of the college of agriculture, Howard Ottoson and Bob Kleis, director and associate director of the agricultural experiment station, and Charles Koopman, finance officer for the institute. Behind Kleis and Koopman is Dave McGill, assistant to the vice chancellor.

I would occupy the east campus office of the former dean of agriculture, but Zumberge had said I should also have an office in his suite on the downtown campus. I had some reservations; 90 percent of my staff were on the east campus. From Brookings, I had called academic vice chancellor Virginia Trotter, whom I knew well, for advice.

"Duane," she said, "you've got to have an office in this administration building. As vice chancellor you have to be considered one of *us*, not one of *them*."

So wise was that advice. Were I to truly function as a vice chancellor, an adviser to the campus chancellor, I had to be perceived by the chancellor and the other vice chancellors as "one of us." An office in the chancellor's suite and my regular presence there would provide both the perception and the reality.

I would spend part of most days in the chancellor's suite. Trotter was in an adjacent office and across the hall from my office was Ken Bader, student affairs, former assistant dean of agriculture at Ohio State and a long time acquaintance. Just down the hall was Miles Tameraasen, vice chancellor for finance, a new acquaintance I took to immediately; he considered it his job to help me and others get our job done in a financially sound way.

Dick Fleming, director of information, was a K-State graduate and would become one of my closest and most appreciated colleagues. Zumberge had charged him with helping me get acquainted with people and organizations across the state.

* * * * *

Our move from South Dakota allowed for a few days of vacation between jobs. After a day arranging furniture in our new home, we had our suitcases packed for a midday flight to New Orleans with daughters Diane and LuAnn. Fleming stopped by about nine o'clock with a list of Nebraska travel destinations he had arranged for early April.

As I escorted him to the door, he remarked, "One more thing. The association of county extension home economists has just filed suit against the university, alleging salary discrimination. Have a good trip!"

* * * * *

My first day on the job, April 1, would be considered routine for a newly arrived administrator. First was a breakfast with some state agency and city leaders plus local media people, an opportunity to make some comments for good media quotes. Next was a session with the chancellor's administrative council and, in the afternoon, an east campus meeting of all IANR faculty (with field staff linked by TV) for Zumberge to formally introduce me and express his support and enthusiasm for the institute.

My second day would not be routine.

A Faculty Pay Raise

It was about nine o'clock my second morning; I had just arrived at my office in the chancellor's suite after an hour with key staff at my east campus office.

Zumberge followed me in, waving a letter. "What do you know about this?" It was a faxed copy of a letter to Senator Richard Marvel, chair of the unicameral appropriations committee, from representatives of the agricultural industry, virtually demanding a special salary increase for IANR faculty, beyond university salary increase funds already agreed to, and suggesting political reprisal on the senator if such were not forthcoming.

"I don't know a thing," I said, "but I think I can find out." In the preceding three months I had learned considerable about the workings of IANR and its industry supporters. In addition to creating IANR in 1973, the unicameral had provided a salary boost to its faculty, a percentage increase higher than for the balance of the university faculty. The state's agricultural leadership, with obvious input from faculty, had convinced the unicameral that agriculture faculty had been grossly underpaid.

Some background: Most university faculty are employed on a nine-month academic year appointment and are paid for nine months. Most agriculture faculty, however, with year-long research and or extension responsibilities, have twelve-month appointments, with a prescribed month of vacation time (twenty-two workdays). Equity would suggest agriculture faculty salaries should therefore average 11/9 of the average salaries of nine-month faculty. Agriculture faculty had averaged much less than 11/9.

The 1973 unicameral action had only partially "leveled the playing field" for IANR faculty. An ad hoc faculty committee had continued to study comparative salary data. I knew the leader of the effort, a professor of agronomy, and I placed a call to him.

"You didn't get a copy of the letter? I'll bring one right down." Among faculty/industry leadership, there had evidently been consensus that my arrival was the time to strike for another special salary increase.

Political power of the state's agricultural leadership had been clearly demonstrated in the previous legislative session, so the letter had Marvel's attention. It also had Varner's and Zumberge's, but they could be in a box. They would want to demonstrate continued support for the IANR faculty and correct any remaining salary inequity, but they also had to be sensitive to other parts of the university. Faculty in other colleges were asking, "Why should agriculture get such special treatment from the legislature?"

By noon, a box lunch meeting was arranged by Marvel and Varner in the downtown law office of the university's general counsel. All the key players were there, including Marvel, Varner, Zumberge, the university lobbyist, several members and staff of Marvel's committee, and me. The discussion quickly centered not on "whether or not" there would be another IANR pay raise but "how much." Varner and Zumberge expressed full support; they realized that another special increase for IANR would not only make IANR faculty and their supporters happy, it could be used the following year to get more salary money for the total university. Engineering, business, or arts and sciences faculty might be envious in the short run, but they would benefit in the long run.

The unicameral lacks the "check and balance" feature of two houses. In other states, one house initiates appropriation bills, the other concurs or takes independent action and negotiation of any differences follows. The unicameral handles the "check and balance" by having any appropriations bill read and voted on three times. The bill may be amended each time but, in the end, it has to be passed three times to become law.

This particular matter did not take long. By three o'clock, a special IANR salary increase bill, drafted in the noon meeting, had been read and passed three times. At four o'clock we had another institute meeting on the east campus to announce an extra July 1 salary increase for IANR faculty.

* * * * *

About three weeks later, Varner and Zumberge stepped into my office midmorning.

"Just thought we'd stop in," Zumberge said, "to ask how everything is going for you."

Current issues gave me a ready answer. "Except for the salary suit by the county home economists, a bubbling disagreement between our corn geneticists and a major seed company, the need to be at several out-state industry meetings this week, [extension director] Jack Adam's health problem, Earl Raun's [Adam's associate director] resignation, and faculty stress in plant pathology, just fine."

Varner laughed. "We didn't promise you a rose garden!"

We talked briefly about each of the items, and they gave me some background on most. Their visit was helpful, a reminder that I had their full support as I worked to resolve those and other issues.

*****

Whereas in most states, university regents are nominated by the governor and confirmed by the state senate, Nebraska's are elected by geographic district. As with unicameral senators, regent elections are nonpartisan; political party is not mentioned in campaigns. However, candidates do need and seek exposure, especially in newspapers and radio/TV reports.

Strong Regents and Hard Candy

As I sat through my third or fourth meeting of the Nebraska board of regents, I gave thought to them as individuals and also how they worked as a group. Their support to me and my work had been, in these few months, as generous as that of Varner and Zumberge. The members were outstanding individuals, and I would emphasize the word, individuals. One should expect that in regents, strong personalities, intelligent, interested in higher education, and eager enough for membership on this prestigious board to spend time and money campaigning for election. Here is my brief rundown on the seven members:

Kermit Hansen. Board chairman and CEO of US National bank in Omaha. A former radio personality. Unlimited enthusiasm. Always available to administrators, faculty, and students, and excited about opportunities.

Rob Raun. A well-respected farmer from Minden, and a steady hand. Two younger brothers, Ned and Art, had been animal nutrition graduate students at Iowa State during my faculty years there. I could count on Raun for credible and supportive elaboration to fellow board members on any IANR issue, and to ask a question at most every board meeting about our musk thistle research. Musk thistles were a major problem in his electoral district, and his question would guarantee positive coverage in farm media.

Bob Koefoot. An MD from Broken Bow. If one could combine the educated confidence of a capable surgeon with the spirit of a frontier cowboy on a Saturday night, you would have Koefoot. Board meetings and football bowl games were releases from his demanding profession. Never bashful in his comments, he would board the Sugar Bowl-bound bus in New Orleans with a mint julep in each hand while his arm would be around my shoulder as he commented, "Great job you're doing."

Bob Prokop. He had earned both a PhD and an MD but had never practiced medicine. His career seemed be that of an expert witness for court cases and a volunteer assistant football coach for Nebraska's football team. Though Prokop had not been bestowed such a title by Coach Tom Osborne, he would be roaming the sidelines at every home game. Bright, thoughtful, and interested in every aspect of the university.

Ed Schwartzkop. He grew up in what was called the "Russian bottoms" of west Lincoln and worked his way through the university, where he was on the 1941 Nebraska Rose Bowl team. A junior high teacher and counselor in the Lincoln school system, he was a vocal defender of the university's right to ask for religious preference on student registration forms (guaranteed to get coverage in the *Lincoln Star*). If other board members' attention flagged, they would get a piece of hard candy tossed by Schwartzkop, the aim likely perfected in his junior high classes. In a short time, Shirley and I would count Schwartzkop and his wife, also named Shirley, among our good friends in Lincoln.

David Boylan. Newly elected and still feeling his way. Quiet and cautious. In the Omaha real estate business, with family roots in Guthrie County, Iowa.

Kermit Wagner. A Kansas State graduate and owner and operator of a large feed and grain business at Norfolk, as well as farming interests in the area. Quiet and steady, with little to say in meetings. Solid and strong supporter of IANR.

* * * * *

Here is what had caused the stress in plant pathology, its resolution, and the person who most appreciated the resolution.

The Problem of Naming a Corn Disease

Late summer we were in Professor Max Schuster's plant pathology laboratory to settle a problem, one that had festered long enough. Those present, in addition to Schuster, were Mike Boosalis, Schuster's department head, Joe Young, head of horticulture, Ottoson, Hartung, and me. A disagreement over the naming of a corn disease identified and characterized by Schuster had escalated into personal animosity. The disease was a bacterial infection of the corn plant that caused the plant leaves to blight (lose some of the green color, reducing photosynthesis) and wilt.

Naming a new disease may not seem like a big issue, but to a plant pathologist, the name is critical. The name should not only differentiate a disease from others, it should also become standard lexicon among all who advise in the field on disease identification and control, ensuring that all are talking about the same thing. A name may be chosen to show where in the spectrum of diseases the newly identified disease seems to fit, or it may be chosen to give credit to a laboratory or a scientist. In the Nebraska experiment station, the key scientist may recommend a name, but it and perhaps others are considered by a faculty committee, which then makes a recommendation to Director Ottoson.

In this case, the committee had recommended a different name than Schuster has proposed. Ottoson had taken the time to hear out Schuster's concern and, in due time, approved the committee's recommendation, Goss's Wilt and Blight. Goss had been a highly respected plant pathologist and dean of the university's graduate school.

Schuster had not accepted the decision well and felt maligned by his colleagues. Spillover had extended to faculty relationships on many issues and animosity between him and his department head, Boosalis, had become intense.

I had been briefed on the issue by Ottoson, Boosalis, and Schuster. Ottoson had tried to mediate and find a solution, but Schuster remained inflexible. As in most disagreements that persist, personal pride seemed to have eclipsed the basic issue. It was not a good situation, for either productive research or worker comfort and cooperation. It was time we cured the problem.

My analysis included that Boosalis was good leader, willing and able to make good decisions; he did not need this continuing problem. Schuster, by all accounts, was a good scientist—analytical and tedious. Though this bacterial disease affected the corn plant, most of Schuster's research had related to horticultural crops. The horticulture department was housed in the same building as plant pathology, and Young, the horticulture department head, was a "steady hand" who could relate well with others. He had a small department and was eager to increase his department's research activity.

I asked Schuster to briefly describe his current circumstance as he saw it, especially his "research territory," the laboratory and the technician help he depended on.

After a bit of discussion, and with the group's consensus that the problem needed to be resolved, I made a decision. "We'll transfer Boosalis, his laboratory, technician, and research budget from the jurisdiction of the plant pathology department to horticulture, effective today." I asked Ottoson to work out the budget transfer details with the two department heads, for both the balance of the fiscal year and for the following year.

Some personal animosities would remain, but most of those could be easily bypassed in the daily campus routine.

At the chancellor's faculty reception in early September, Shirley and I were in the receiving line, and Professor Schuster and his wife were among the first to come through. Mrs. Schuster squeezed my hand and mouthed a silent but intense, "Thank you!"

Luncheon meeting with ConAgra executive staff in Omaha, UNL Chancellor Jim Zumberge to my left. It seemed that half of my time in Nebraska was on the road or in the air, on my way to conferences, alumni gatherings, industry conventions, or regents meetings anywhere in the state.

* * * * *

Seventeen years after leaving Nebraska, I was back on campus as USDA assistant secretary for science and education for briefings by USDA staff stationed there. Current Vice Chancellor Irv Omtvedt (whom I had hired as animal science department head) was bringing me up to date and mentioned that the Nebraska Statewide Arboretum, hatched in my Nebraska office eighteen years earlier, had grown to fifty sites across the state.

Why not a Statewide Arboretum?

A few days after I had been named vice chancellor, the unicameral had added $50,000 to the IANR budget, for "the new vice chancellor's discretion." Though a major university may receive millions of state funds, most of the money is virtually "locked in" to existing faculty and programs. Key members of the unicameral wanted to ensure I had some financial flexibility. To me, this $50,000 was both useful money and a gesture of unicameral support.

That summer, a group of faculty and university friends called on me to seek my support for an arboretum, presumably to be developed on the university's east campus. Trees are precious in Nebraska. Virgin prairie in this semi-arid country was virtually all grass; trees were mostly limited to the river and creek banks. To establish a windbreak or shade and fruit trees, early ranchers and farmers would carry buckets of water almost daily. Though there were many plantings on the east campus, species were rather limited.

During the discussion, I learned that there were several small arboretums in Nebraska, located on college campuses and in communities around the state, and more plantings had been made around the I-80 "borrow pits" (where dirt had been taken to build the I-80 roadbed). The pits were full of water, courtesy of the high water table from the Platte River, and adjacent communities had planted trees and developed these areas for recreation.

None of these sites appeared to the group as large enough or with fund-raising potential to warrant designation as "the" Nebraska Arboretum. Would the IANR, the state's headquarters for extension and research in horticulture and forestry, be willing to take on the task of developing a first-class arboretum for Nebraska?

It appeared to me that the existing sites were a valuable resource, already benefiting many Nebraskans. If they could be collectively promoted, and more plantings encouraged, that would be more cost effective and benefit more people than to try to establish a new collection on our campus. I offered to fund, from IANR monies (that $50,000 would help), a new position of statewide arboretum director, if that group of interested people would develop the concept and establish criteria for site membership and participation. They accepted the challenge, and I followed through with the money.

I only wish I could personally thank the members of that group who came to my office in the summer of 1974, and others who joined the effort later, for their leadership and dedication.

*****

My dad had fed calves and yearlings raised in Nebraska's sand hills, usually purchased on the Omaha terminal market. He often said he "would sure like to visit one of those ranches from which they came" but never had the opportunity to do so. Shirley and I would have that opportunity.

Ten Ways to Sit on a Horse

It was close to six, and except for two hours at lunchtime, I had been on the horse since sunrise. We were in the middle of Nebraska's sand hills. I had been on many ranches in Oklahoma, Kansas, and South Dakota, and often had driven through the sand hills, but I had never seen a sand hills operation from the inside. On this day, I was both seeing and *feeling* one.

At a Nebraska cattlemen's convention in North Platte early that summer, I had met Forrest Lee, a tall, soft-spoken, and kindly rancher whose operation was in the heart of the hills north of the town of Thedford. I mentioned my longing to visit the sand hills, as well as Shirley's interest, and he was quick to respond. "When we get ready to move our heifers back home this fall, come join us. I'll let you know when we schedule it."

Lee called in early September and set the date, a Monday in October. Shirley and I drove out from Lincoln Sunday afternoon, arriving at the ranch about five. After dinner, Lee's daughter, a Nebraska animal science graduate, and her husband, who lived on the ranch and partnered with Lee and his wife, brought over a pair of boots for me. Handing them to me, she commented, "You can't ride a horse with city shoes or those Iowa clodhoppers (work shoes I had brought along)."

The boots fit, and we talked briefly about the next day's job. We were in bed by nine thirty; the next day would be a long one.

The heifers were yearlings, born in the spring of the previous year, weaned that fall, and fed hay and some grain at ranch headquarters during the winter. They had been bred in the late spring and trucked to a leased pasture about twenty-five miles away for summer grazing. They would be trailed home cross country, through the pastures of many neighbors, to calve in March at headquarters.

Lee tapped on our door at four in the morning. I could already smell the frying bacon. While he and I ate, his daughter and husband were loading the horses. It was a cold morning, about forty-five degrees, and with dense fog; I would appreciate the coveralls Lee loaned me and the insulated coat I had brought. Lee, his daughter, son-in-law, ranch hand, and I piled into two pickups, each pulling a horse trailer.

After a forty-minute ride down empty US 83, with any ranch house lights hidden by the fog, we turned west onto a dirt road, then drove over a couple of hills and pulled up to a pasture gate. Through the thick fog I could barely see the outlines of a few trees. I knew there was some history to those trees; they were the residue of a "tree claim," a means by which early settlers established ownership of the open prairie land. The Homestead Act of 1862 granted title to a quarter section of land (160 acres) to anyone who would build a home on the land and occupy it for three years, but 160 acres in this arid country would not produce enough to support a family. So the act was later amended to state that by planting and maintaining an acre of trees on a second quarter of land for three years, a settler could get title to a full half-section (320 acres).

I had seen evidence of tree claims in western South Dakota, each a small square of trees off in the distance, an anomaly in a sea of short grass. In that country, with an even shorter growing season than in Nebraska or Kansas to the south, 320 acres was still not enough to support a family, and a good bit of that homesteaded land had been abandoned, or let go back to the federal government ownership. (Much of the grazing land managed by the Department of Interior's Bureau of Land Management is such "go back" land.)

There was less "go-back" land in Nebraska; the longer growing season and the water absorbing capacity of the sand hills made the land sufficiently more productive so that when early homesteaders chose to leave, a neighboring rancher likely purchased the tract. That is one reason sand hills ranches are so large.

Back to the heifers: Lee's ranch hand opened the gate, and we pulled in and unloaded the horses. All but Lee climbed on a mount. We each carried water, and Lee's daughter had a thermos of coffee to fend off the morning chill. Somewhere out in that eighty acres of fog were twenty-five heifers.

By the time I got settled in the saddle and in control of my horse's reins, my partners were out of sight; I was alone in the fog. I pulled up on the reins and listened. Eventually, I heard a few heifers bawling, followed the sound, and soon caught the faint outline of some white faces on red bodies coming my way. I reined my horse aside and joined my partners following this small herd toward the gate.

Lee had moved the pickups and trailers back to the road and turned toward the highway. We moved the heifers through the open gate, Lee headed them west, and they trotted down what was, from there on, an abandoned roadway.

About a mile down the roadway, the ranch hand slipped his horse past the herd in order to open another pasture gate. We were to find our way through more than twenty pastures before we arrived at the home ranch that night. We moved the herd slowly, letting them grab mouthfuls of grass along the way.

Meanwhile, Lee drove his pickup and trailer back to the ranch to load the trailer with hay and pick up Shirley. They would meet us midway with lunch.

With a horse and rider on each side of the herd and two behind, we moved the heifers up and down over grass-covered sand dunes. Every twenty minutes or so, we would come to a pasture gate, usually in the corner of a section or quarter section. One rider moved ahead to open the gate, the heifers would amble through, and the last rider would close the gate behind us.

At one of the gates, Lee's son-in-law took time to show me a brass plate fixed in a buried square of concrete, a permanent geographic marker put there before the land was homesteaded. George Washington surveyed and marked ownership boundaries early in his career, but most of his work was on irregularly shaped pieces already settled in what is now Virginia and West Virginia. From central Ohio west, surveying preceded the settlers, for the most part, and the land was laid out in squares. Using a compass and a chain of prescribed length, a surveyor would walk due west, driving a stake every 320 rods, thus marking one mile. Those stakes, a mile apart north and south as well, were soon replaced with brass plates imbedded in a square of cement, like the one now before us. Imprinted on the plate was a cross, the center of the cross being the corners of four sections, and in each of the quadrants formed by the cross was the number of the section (square mile).

The earth's curvature required that the surveyors make periodic adjustments in their line of travel and the 320-rod interval; because of that curvature, the westernmost sections of a township get smaller as one goes from south to north. In most cases, an adjustment was made every six miles, the west edge of what would be a township. I had learned this early in my life, when I asked why our rectangular home farm had an odd number of acres, 130. The legal description of the farm, on the west edge of Benton Township, is "the NW fractional ¼ and the N ½ of the SW fractional ¼ of Section 30." Had each of the quarters been a full 160 acres, our farm would have been 240 acres. Such corrections or adjustments are evident as one views the rural landscape from the air. In my many trips across South Dakota in the university's single-engine planes, I would see a sudden S-curve in a stretch of highway, or a north-south row of fence-outlined "quarter sections" that were not as wide as adjacent sections.

Back with the heifers and the landscape: The fog had lifted by nine o'clock, the sun let us remove our outer coats, and I could more appreciate the sharply undulating landscape of wind-shifted sand covered for centuries with lush grass. The grass's roots go down perhaps twelve or more feet, where they reach water that has percolated in from the periodic but limited rain, and the grass and roots keep the sand in place. When the heifers were moving along peacefully, I could turn my attention to the vegetation, not only the grasses, but also the many small herbs and forbs growing among the grass. From time to time, I would spot a few tiny pink, blue, or yellow blossoms. More important than the beauty of the blossoms, perhaps, was that these herbs and forbs are leguminous plants; with root bacterial help, they fix nitrogen from the atmosphere, nitrogen that the grasses need for growth.

We had moved through perhaps a dozen pastures when we spotted Lee's pickup ahead, with Shirley also in the cab. Most important, they had brought lunch; it had been a long time since breakfast. We were also ready for a rest, the heifers as well as the other riders and me. We eased down off the saddles, tied the horses to the pickup rack, and loosened the cinch that held each saddle tightly. The horses relaxed and the heifers grazed. Rarely had sandwiches, fruit, and brownies tasted so good. However, we did not tarry long; there were miles yet to cover.

When Lee asked how I was doing, I answered, "Great," but I quickly accepted his offer to take over my horse. Shirley and I would follow along in the pickup. About two o'clock I was back in the saddle; Lee and Shirley drove on ahead to "hay the bridge" over a small creek. The bridge would be new to the animals and they might get "spooked." Lee spread out some hay at the bridge approach, as well as on the bridge itself. The hungry heifers would eat their way across.

With only modest coaxing we got the first animals up to the hay. From then on it was easy. The lead animals felt the light rumble of the bridge planks, but the hay ahead and the push of their herd mates, wanting to get at the hay themselves, encouraged the total herd across the bridge.

An hour later we crossed a wider creek on a longer bridge, the heifers now comfortable with the hay on the plank floor. However, we were now in a creek bottom, and on the far side of that second bridge was a recently harvested alfalfa field, the bales still in the field. The heifers were tired and hungry and each snitched a mouthful of leafy alfalfa from the first bale they could get to. In minutes, most of the bales were surrounded, and we had work to do. Not only did we need to keep the herd moving, the alfalfa belonged to a neighbor. As we would route a heifer from one bale, she would snitch hay from the next and stop at the third. It took us a good half-hour to get the herd through the next gate and to more dry, end-of-season native grass.

It was nearly six o'clock when we trailed the herd through the last large pasture, this a part of the Lee ranch, and moved the tired heifers up the ranch road. A lad of perhaps sixteen was beside Lee, and as I came along, Lee suggested, "How about letting this young man take your horse and follow the herd the rest of the way?" The heifers would spend the night and the weeks ahead in a small pasture next to the ranch headquarters.

I could hardly move; I barely managed to swing my right leg behind the saddle and slip to the ground. My seat was not sore; I had found a lot of angles from which to contact that saddle and, with my feet in the stirrups, had been able to stand upright part of the time. It was the calves of my legs that were sore, chafed from the boots. And I was stiff. I hobbled into the house, where Mrs. Lee poured me a glass of red wine and suggested a hot bath. It was a good prescription; there was no enduring soreness. By eight thirty, after a generous supper, we were in bed.

If only Dad could have been with us that day.

*****

Varner's 1975–76 budget proposals to be considered by the board of regents included some new program funds for IANR. If the board approved, the proposals would be considered by Governor Exon and the 1975 unicameral.

Would the regents endorse these proposals, as well as increased salaries for faculty?

Regents Action Delayed

My second month in the job, I had convened about 120 leaders of agricultural and natural resources organizations from across the state to recommend IANR priorities, what it should focus on in the years ahead. I had invited leaders of Farm Bureau, Farmers Union, Grange, and NFO, the livestock, poultry, and crop groups, a cooperative council, wildlife and fisheries organizations, and leaders of the state's natural resources conservation districts.

We divided the participants into three groups: agriculture, natural resources, and human resources, and named a chair for each group. My department heads and directors, who had helped identify the participants, would play a staff role. I emphasized they should make no proposals and not lobby for individual programs. They should respond to questions, but their task was primarily to listen and record ideas that were generated.

It was a productive day, with some reinforcement of current research and extension programs, but mostly refinements in existing programs and several proposed new programs. We would attack some of these new priorities that summer, but my major purpose was to build a base of industry advice and support for an expanded IANR program I would propose to Zumberge and Varner, and to the regents at their December meeting.

Varner had asked me on several occasions leading up to the regents' meeting, "Acker, do you have the industry groups lined up to be at the regents' meeting to support your request?" After the session in May, the participants had stayed very much involved, especially those of an "Ag 40" group who had taken the political lead in formation of IANR, as we put together the details of our budget request. In essence, this would be "their budget"; they would be at the regents' budget meeting, as well as legislative committee meetings once the unicameral was in session.

Early in the week of the regents' meeting, Varner asked me yet again, "Will the ag groups be there?" Though I had made no specific arrangement, no reminding phone calls to Omaha, Scottsbluff, Auburn, Chadron, or elsewhere, I told him, with confidence, "They'll be there."

We were in Regents Hall, across Holdrege Street from the east campus, in a room that might hold fifty. The normal attendance was seven board members, Varner, the three chancellors, and their staff, plus a few student leaders. But today, the room was packed. I counted twelve who had been involved in our May 20 meeting and in the weeks since. They were not just a random twelve; they were among the state's more politically powerful.

When the agenda got to the IANR budget proposal, Chairman Hansen, noting the presence of the IANR supporters, invited their comments. After three of the leaders spoke, making clear it was also "their proposal," there was little for me to say, and I expected a rather quick regent vote to approve.

But the action got delayed by at least twenty minutes. Every board member wanted time to say a word in support of agriculture and natural resources. They wanted those industry people to know of their support, and their quotes would likely be in the media that evening and the next day. The vote was then unanimous.

Unicameral consideration and action a couple of months later was virtually a repeat.

* * * * *

Late winter I had a difficult job to do. But if one is not willing to do the difficult jobs, one does not deserve to be in a leadership role.

A Difficult Job

I had just finished a visit with the chair of our state-wide extension advisory council regarding the continued and serious health problem of my extension director, Jack Adams, and he had concurred with my assessment that Adams could no longer give extension the aggressive leadership it needed.

Adams had been extension poultry specialist, then poultry department head before being named director of extension. He had done an excellent job as director and had taken a lot of heat. With extension staff in every county and every state senator's district, one would be naïve to believe there had not been a good bit of staff lobbying for that "separate campus for agriculture" (culminating in IANR). Adams had been accused by some of organizing such lobbying. He had certainly supported the change and made no secret of it, but others told me he had been careful to not cross the line into inappropriate lobbying and had withstood the criticism well.

I had known Adams since moving to South Dakota State as dean and had sensed a problem the day I had interviewed a year earlier. In an hour session with Adams, Ottoson, and Hartung, I had noticed a change from the Adams

I had known. It was difficult to describe, but he had shown a discomfort and sensitivity, something different from the steady and deliberate Adams with whom I was familiar. In fact, as Ottoson and I had walked side by side out of the meeting, I quietly asked him, "What's wrong with Jack?"

Working daily alongside Adams, Ottoson had not noticed the change and appeared surprised by my question. But there was clearly a change from the person I had seen several months earlier.

Soon after I arrived in Lincoln, I noticed Adams rarely sat; he carried a donut pillow to meetings. As time went by, he had his desk elevated on blocks, and would stand at the desk or in meetings. We began to notice a rash or reddish blemishes on his arms and face, and Adams confided to me he had an undiagnosed rash problem.

By January Adams was in the medical center in Omaha. His was a most perplexing problem, one that evaded diagnosis and for which no treatment seemed to have any effect.

Looking back today on the symptoms and the progression of Adams's malady, and based on our experience with our grandson, Clay, I surmise that Adams may have had a rare and very aggressive form of leukemia/lymphoma caused by a specific virus, LTVH1. In the 1990s, medical scientists and virologists in Japan and the United States focused on this rare form of cancer. Biopsies of the skin rash disclosed cell deformities that put it in the leukemia/lymphoma category, and the causative agent, the virus, was identified. LTVH1 is most prevalent in Japan, islands of the South Pacific, and the Caribbean, but rare even there. A significant number of undiagnosed cases of such described skin rash had been found among US military personnel who served in the South Pacific during World War II. Adams had served in the US Navy in the South Pacific.

The rash appears first and to a greater extent in skin not exposed to the sun or atmosphere. Symptoms may never appear in a person carrying the virus, or they may appear only after many years have lapsed. Unfortunately, classifying the malady and identifying the causative agent was too far in the future for Adams to benefit.

Back to Adams and his role as director. Adams had been released from the medical center hospital and returned home, but was in no condition to spend much time in the office. Other staff were handling the day-to-day issues, but we needed to set a course for the future and, sadly, the odds were against Adams resuming his strong leadership. In visits with Zumberge and Varner, as well as with some key staff, it became apparent we had delayed, while we hoped for Adams's recovery, long enough; we needed to move forward and identify a new leader.

After my visit with the chair of the advisory council, I called Adams and said I would like to stop by after lunch for a visit.

I had no doubt Adams knew the purpose of my visit. The visit was brief and focused on inquiry and concern regarding his condition, the effect of associate director Raun's departure, the tasks ahead, and his limitations. I told him that my judgment, concurred by those with whom I had consulted, was that it was best that he transfer to a faculty position in poultry science. Adams quickly agreed; he made my difficult job easier.

Adams would make some recovery, and I was able to visit with him a couple of times before I departed Nebraska at the end of June for Kansas State. I have been told that in the few years he had remaining, he made valuable contributions to his native discipline, including recording a history of the Nebraska poultry industry and of extension in Nebraska.

* * * * *

As I would walk behind some of our Nebraska faculty guests into the Manhattan, Kansas, country club after K-State's cattle feeders day, nearly two years after I had departed Nebraska, I would hear one guest comment, "We sure miss the Acker days." I would edge closer to the speaker; I wanted to hear more. But what I heard was not about my leadership; it was about vacation days.

The "Acker Days"

The two special salary increases for IANR faculty by the unicameral had not stilled the waters. Average IANR salaries had gotten to 11/9 of the balance of the Lincoln campus, but a faculty committee and our biometrician had done further salary analyses late winter of 1975, based on another issue.

Twelve-month faculty work a full eleven months, get only legal holidays off in addition to their recorded twenty-two working days of vacation. However, nine-month faculty do not work a full nine months. They are off when the students are off, spring break, a week or more between fall and spring semesters, and even the Friday after Thanksgiving. Calculations showed that *per working day*, IANR faculty were still underpaid. The data were solid; the biometrician's methodology unquestionable.

The unicameral had adjourned, and that, no doubt, was fortunate. It had provided two special salary increases for IANR and would likely balk at a third. As important, neither Varner nor Zumberge could support another differential increase and still remain in good stead with the balance of the university. The IANR committee understood, but felt they had been treated poorly for years and there was still a need to "make it right."

Zumberge and I discussed the issue at length. The data were irrefutable. He was frustrated, and asked, "What do you think we ought to do?"

One of my responsibilities as a vice chancellor was to protect the chancellor, to find solutions he could accept. I suggested, "Jim, let's just give the IANR faculty the extra vacation days." I then added, "They'll probably never use them." With yearlong demands from clientele, heavy field plot work in the summer, and animals and laboratory work that needed daily supervision, most IANR faculty did not even use the twenty-two vacation days to which they were entitled.

Zumberge's response reflected both his frustration and relief. "Hell, let's do it. Go write me a letter with that recommendation, outline how it would be implemented, and I'll approve it." By noon he had my letter, including the number of extra days that could be requested, that any accumulated vacation time had to be used first, a specified reason for each request, and approval by both the department head and the vice chancellor.

For the faculty, it was a victory. The administration had listened, respected their data, and provided a solution. After all, it was not really the money that was the core of concern; it was fairness. They felt the solution was fair.

Having left Nebraska for Kansas State soon after that episode, I had not learned that those extra vacation days had been dubbed by the faculty as "Acker Days." When a faculty member needed vacation time above the standard twenty-two and could justify it, he or she applied for their "Acker days."

However, sometime after my departure, Nebraska's attorney general had learned of the arrangement and declared it illegal. That was what was behind our guest's comment, "We sure miss the Acker days."

Another First Year?

Though I had never set a goal of being a university president, the comfort Shirley and I seemed to have in the duties and relationships that came with a series of jobs had made us consider the possibility. Perhaps as important, we had learned early, on the evening playing Hearts with the Oklahoma A&M's President and Mrs. Willham, for example, that a university president and spouse can be ordinary people; they are not preordained by some unique characteristics. Also, a few colleagues and friends had raised the possibility.

Iowa State's extension swine specialist, Ralph Durham, had told me after an animal husbandry department meeting on some curriculum changes I was pushing that I would likely be a president by the time I was thirty-five. His comment shocked me and I dismissed it.

A few days after my appointment as dean at South Dakota State had been announced, I was in K-State journalism head Ralph Lashbrook's office, and it happened to be President Jim McCain's sixty-first birthday. Lashbrook noted the birthday and my departure and said, "When McCain retires, you would be about ready to come back as president."

This time, I did not dismiss the comment; Lashbrook was a person all respected. He was always positive but never "spread it on too thick." Yet I shoved that comment to the back of my mind; I had a new job to go to.

I had also had the experience of being on a short list at Montana State.

McCain would retire at age seventy, and my move from South Dakota State to Nebraska, another then "Big 8" university, and with a vice chancellor title, had perhaps put me in a position to more likely be considered for that presidency. I think it was in January 1975 that I received an invitation from Kansas State's presidential search and screening committee, comprised of faculty, students, and alumni, to submit my resume for consideration.

I first declined the invitation, telling Shirley, "I don't think I want to go through another first year right now." I had never been busier, with more travel and more issues to handle, and I certainly could not expect the first year in a presidency to be any easier.

There was another concern. Would my time and efforts in Nebraska have a positive and lasting impact? I had no worries about that when I moved from Kansas State after nearly four years, or on leaving SDSU after eight. But could there be positive and lasting impact from only fifteen months as vice chancellor for Nebraska's IANR?

In time, Shirley and I began to reconsider. I could point to several impacts. Any political residue of IANR's formation had disappeared. My colleagues and I had good IANR relationships with other deans and the new structure within the university seemed to be "institutionalized," accepted by the campus as a whole. I had established that the IANR department heads reported to me as vice chancellor, with the dean and directors each carrying "program coordination" responsibilities. (Of the five land-grant universities on the great plains that "upgraded" the dean of agriculture position to vice president or vice chancellor in the 1970s or before, only the Nebraska title and structure remain at this writing. The other four, for a variety of reasons, have moved back to the dean of agriculture title and structure.)

I had promoted finance officer Charles Koopman to be assistant to the vice chancellor for all IANR finances. In addition, the forty plus leaders of the state's agricultural and natural resources organizations had established themselves as a "continuing support group" for the IANR, clearly including the geological survey unit on the downtown campus. Perhaps as important, IANR faculty believed they were now being treated fairly; the salary issue had been put to bed

At age forty-four, I should be as ready for a presidency as I could ever be. Both Shirley and I were in good health and young enough to handle the rigors we might both encounter. Kansas State was a university for which I had developed affection and loyalty, and it was only 240 miles from our Troublesome Creek farm. We decided to "go for it," and I submitted my resume.

After a Saturday-evening interview with the K-State committee at a Kansas City airport motel in late March, Shirley and I were called a few weeks later for an evening visit with the Kansas board of regents at the same motel. In that visit, I think the board was more impressed with Shirley than with me.

After two more weeks, I received a call from the regents' executive officer saying that his board would like another visit and, "If the board offers you the K-State presidency, will you accept?" He explained the board wanted another visit, but only if I answered yes. In our previous visit with the board, there had been no discussion of terms of employment or what the board expected a new president to achieve. It was clear, though, that the board did not want to risk offering the job, being turned down, and that fact becoming public.

My response was, "If the terms are satisfactory, yes." A week later, the board and I agreed that Shirley and I should be moving back to K-State, my appointment effective July 1, 1975.

We had better get ready for another first year.

*****

Editor's note: Anecdotes and experiences from Acker's eleven years in the Kansas State University presidency were published under the title *Two at a Time: Reflections and Revelations of a Kansas State University Presidency and the Years That Followed* (iUniverse 2010). A third book, describing Acker's later experiences in Washington, DC plus his work in Eastern Europe, Africa, Southeast Asia, and South America, and back on his Iowa farm, is yet to come. It may be titled *Back to Troublesome Creek, by Way of DC and a Dozen Foreign Countries.*